AF231680

MARX'S NIGHTMARE

Denis Collin

MARX'S NIGHTMARE

Is Capitalism a Never-Ending Tale?

To Bernadette, my first reader.

Official thinkers are busy hammering the last nails into Karl Marx's coffin. He's been buried for so long, he must be quite dead. Yet it seems that the corpse is still moving. The hatred with which he is still pursued would be enough to attest to this. Or the attempts to forget it. When employers, through their organization MEDEF, want to remove the teaching of Marx as an economist from high-school curricula, they are unwittingly paying tribute to a thought that has always been subversive.

The Death of Marxism?

But despite a recent, timid reappearance during the financial crisis that began in the summer of 2007 with the American *subprime mortgage* crisis—a crisis whose cause is attributed to the extravagance of a few perverted financiers—Marx's thought as a system for explaining our societies is out of favour. The fact remains: institutionally, Marxism is not doing very well. States that once claimed to be Marxist have either collapsed or been converted to the benefits of capitalism—such as North Korea, whose official doctrine is no longer Marxism, but the thinking of Kim Il-Sung, as espoused by his son Kim Jong-Il, China, Vietnam and a few other countries that have converted to the "primitive accumulation" version of capitalism. Parties claiming to be Marxist have been reduced to nothing, as in the case of the Communist parties in

France, Spain, etc., or have renounced any reference to Marxism, as in the case of the Social Democratic parties. In terms of academic institutions, things are not much better, and Marxism survives only in a few ecological niches for which there is not even a protection agency, such as for the coastline or wetlands…

Marxists seem condemned to denial. The Stalinists of the former "people's democracies" have been converted into social democrats and liberals. The Italian PCI leaders—D'Alema, Fassini, Veltroni and others—have become "left-wing democrats", then democrats and perhaps soon right-wing democrats, if they continue to dance the waltz and tango with *Cavaliere* Berlusconi. When questioned, Veltroni even pretends not to remember that the party he joined and helped destroy was called the "Italian Communist Party". Others retain Marxism only in extremely bastardized forms: the PCF, for example, has gone from being the party of the working class to the party of the people. Marxists and academic Marxism survive only on condition that they bury Marx under tons of philosophical references, either "sexier", with Foucault, Derrida, etc., i.e., the philosophy of "sixties fans", or more "honorable", less compromising for the academic career, even if it means subjecting them to all sorts of abuse. Even Marxists outside the *main stream* are not spared. Trotskyists, faithful among the faithful, often brilliant practitioners of a Talmudic Marxism, renounce being Trotskyists. Some disguise themselves as a "workers' party" with the slightly radical-socialist republican ideology of the heyday (such is the case of the "independent workers' party" launched by the so-called "Lambertist" Trotskyists), others become Guevarists (Guevara replaces Trotsky in the gallery of great ancestors of Olivier Besancenot, spokesman for the "new anti-capitalist party" launched by the LCR). A few tiny groups survive in the impotent repetition of sacramental formulas from a decomposed past. But none of that matters any more.

In short, to parody Michel Foucault's last sentence in *Les Mots et les Choses*, Marx could well disappear "like a face of sand at the edge of the sea".

... and yet Marx was Right!

This situation is, however, highly paradoxical. If Marx, the tutelary figure of Marxism, has disappeared, it's high time we realized that there is hardly a thinker in the social and historical sciences who has drawn with greater insight the outlines of a future that is our present. If the criterion of science is the experimental verification of predictions deduced from theory, Marx passes the test with flying colors. Marx's theory of the capitalist mode of production is without doubt the most scientific social-historical theory ever produced. Contrary to what is repeated by those who claim to refute Marx without having read him, the predictions deduced from the analyses in *Capital have* essentially been validated. The world Marx drew is our reality, or is in the process of becoming one before our very eyes.

Dreams often turn into nightmares. Marx believed that the capitalist mode of production, through its spontaneous tendencies, produced its own demise, paving the way for the expropriation of the expropriators and a new society based on the association of producers, called communism. Before going into detail, let's say that the essential tendencies of the capitalist mode of production have manifested themselves powerfully over the last century, but far from leading to communism, they have nourished a new revolution in the capitalist mode of production. The growing socialization of production, in contradiction with capitalist private appropriation, has not produced revolution, but has instead proved an effective means of rolling back any inclination to challenge the existing social order. Relocation and the massive expansion of world trade, expressions of the growing integration of national economies and the development of the global division of labor, have done little to develop international workers' solidarity.

Marx saw joint-stock companies and the increasing involvement of banks in company capital as proof that the capitalist mode of production must go beyond the narrow confines of private ownership of the means of production. Since then, the "socialization" of capitalism has continued to advance, without taking us one step closer to communism.

Marx rejected utopia and didn't want to cook in the pots of the future; consequently, communism, to have any value, had to be nothing other than the "real movement", unfolding before our very eyes, by which capitalism itself prepares its own subversion. This is what guides Marx's entire analysis: to show how, within capitalist society itself, powerful tendencies to abolish the barriers that capitalist property places in the way of the development of accumulation develop, generated by the very logic of capital accumulation.

Whichever way you look at it, both in broad outline and, more often than not, in detail, the main trends in the historical development of capitalism are in line with Marx's analysis. If we consider the fundamental socio-economic structures, this is almost self-evident. The concentration and centralization of capital, the constitution of a world market and a global division of labor, and even the centrality of trade between the two shores of the Pacific with the emergence of Chinese power, are all in Marx. Those theorists of "globalization" (happy or unhappy) who see it as a radically new phenomenon peculiar to the end of the twentieth century are only demonstrating their ignorance.

Joint-stock companies, investment funds, *hedge funds*, the development of speculation not on actual profits, but on expectations of future profits, *junk bonds*—in short, all the attempts by capital to overcome the barriers inherent in the capitalist relationship—are all set out in some detail in Book III of *Capital.*

The separation of capitalist ownership from the functions of managing the economic process: we're right in the middle of it, and have been for many decades, in different and sometimes contradictory forms. Between the managerial capitalism of the "thirty glorious years" and the "governance" capitalism of pension funds and other mutual funds, the same process is at work. And that's why attempts to oppose the healthy productive capital of yesteryear to the evil financial capitalism that is only greedy for excess profits are so futile.

But all this, it will be objected, has not led to communism with the "necessity that presides over the metamorphoses of nature", to use Marx's expression announcing the inevitable "expropriation of the expropriators". On the contrary, instead of a radically new society in which man would be his own end, and where the reign of necessity would give way to the reign of freedom, we have capitalism at its most extreme. More than ever, men are subject to the blind power of their exchanges, and this is because the very trends in which Marx saw communist society taking shape have asserted themselves with extraordinary force. Where this man, still a man of the Enlightenment, inhabited by the optimistic philosophies of history, from Herder to Hegel, saw the realization of all human potential, it is the most total alienation of human essence that is being accomplished.

The state and politics as separate spheres of social life are withering away, but freedom is withering away at the same time: the government of men does give way to the administration of things (in Saint-Simon's phrase, which Marx made his own), but this is because men are transformed into things, reduced to the state of human resources or brains that can be manipulated by media propaganda. Where Marx predicted a transparent society, breaking down the separation between private and public life, we have the spectacle of a political life reduced to a choice between stars who make the front pages of the tabloid press, and, at the same time, we are witnessing the end of private life (or rather, intimate life) subjected to the control of a state machine from which nothing can escape.

Even technical mastery turns against humanity. Marx saw in the development of science and its application to production the process of humanizing nature, and the realization of man's nature as a "generic being". But it is today's "future of human nature" (to use Habermas's expression) that we are led to question with anguish.

Marx was right, for the worse. Could it have been otherwise? At this point, we need to return to the decisive factor in his theory, namely the constitution of a "revolutionary class" capable of driving the historical process. It is this subjective factor that has been missing. Historical Marxism, the dominant ideology of the workers' movement, was a doctrine invented at the end of the nineteenth and beginning of the twentieth centuries by Engels and Kautsky (for the most part), and which presents itself much more as a plebeian, often statist egalitarianism, than as that philosophy of emancipation, that veritable metaphysics of freedom, which forms the most constant background to Marx's thought. Of course, it's impossible to rewrite history in the future tense, but we can look for explanations for the catastrophe of communism having historically existed.

Yet this catastrophe in no way invalidates Marx's thought, even if we must reassess it and hold it for what it is: a fundamentally unfinished work. We have not reached the end of history. No one can resign themselves to an existence of stuffed hamsters turning the wheels of the economy, or to a life of workaholics. The disgusting mediocrity and vulgarity of the dominant classes, culture and politics are not an unsurpassable horizon. The mole continues to dig. By subjecting the entire planet to its rule, by turning billions of Indians, Chinese and Africans into proletarians, by exploiting every possible field of accumulation, capitalism is preparing the moment when, once again, "circumstances themselves cry out: *Hic Rhodus, hic salta!* C'est ici qu'est la rose, c'est ici qu'il faut danser!" (Marx, *Le 18 Brumaire de Louis Bonaparte*). But nothing will ever guarantee that this leap will be made.

Postscript

For the most part, this book was written before September 2008, i.e. before the large-scale onset of the financial crisis, before the "nationalization" of a considerable proportion of the financial system, before the phase change in capitalism that we had foreseen. We didn't see any need to rework this work, given that the facts vindicated the analyses developed in it more quickly than editorial deadlines would allow. We have confined ourselves to a few notes to bring the text up to date. Experience confirms the scientific relevance of a century-and-a-half-old theory of the capitalist mode of production, but, contrary to Marx's catastrophist interpretations, we have confirmation that capitalism will never disappear from the stage of history unless there are forces powerful enough to topple it.

PART ONE

Capitalism as it Really is

There is no alternative: this was the slogan of Mrs Thatcher, the British Prime Minister of sinister memory. So often repeated that it has become an abbreviation: TINA[1]! You criticize capitalism? TINA! Do you find it abnormal that the number of poor people is growing at the same rate as global wealth? TINA! The morning columnists on public radio stations, the economic editorialists of a major evening paper, the professors of the most highly-rated faculties, the MEDEF, the PS and the UMP, all respond in chorus: TINA! German socialists and Chinese leaders, ex-PCI leaders and representatives of Algeria's military-bureaucratic regime all drink from the same cup: TINA! There's a "Coué method" aspect to all this: the powerful want to persuade themselves and others that we've reached the end of history and that capitalism is eternal.

The Turning Point of the 1970s

But there's also a reality. The sixties and seventies were years of confrontation. One might have thought that there was competition and rivalry between two systems, capitalism and the state socialism

---

1. At a time when the financial and economic crises are hitting hard at a system whose domination was supposed to be total, all we can talk about is "refounding capitalism", and politicians and economists alike are repeating that there is no question of reviving "Marxism" or sinking into "anti-capitalism".

of the "communist countries", which were dragging this or that country along as circumstances dictated. Other nations, refusing to serve as stooges for one or other of the "big boys", sought an original path, a "third way", often nationalist, authoritarian and socialist, a third way that would draw in its wake the countries of the so-called "Third World". Even in 1975, the United States' crushing defeat in Vietnam seemed to give a decisive advantage to the Soviet "camp", while in Southern Europe, one pro-American dictatorship after another collapsed, sometimes paving the way for revolutionary situations such as that seen in Portugal after the "Carnation Revolution" of 1974.

By the early 1970s, capitalism was in crisis. On August 15, 1971, Nixon announced the non-convertibility of the dollar into gold. The American currency became a forced exchange rate, and the United States was able to print money. The international monetary system founded since the Bretton Woods Agreement on the principle that the dollar was *as good as gold* no longer existed. The mad race can begin. The Arab-Israeli war of October 1973 triggered the first "oil shock". All capitalist economies went into recession, and this time it was no longer a slowdown in strong growth, but a real downturn with exploding unemployment. The political weakening of imperialism as a result of national independence struggles, economic crisis, political crisis within the dominant nations themselves, almost all of which were shaken by the great wave of protest in 1968. The revolutionary Marxist groups with the wind in their sails are announcing the "imminence of revolution", the real, permanent revolution that will set the whole world ablaze.

In fact, the seventies were to be the decade of the great reversal. Just when it seemed ready to give in at the drop of a hat, the global capitalist system asserted its power as never before.

1) The economic crisis provides an opportunity to undertake a global restructuring of the economic and social relations that have dominated until now. Statist interventionism in the service of an income policy guaranteeing "social peace" and agreement

with the unions was no longer the order of the day. From the late 1970s onwards, the "deregulation" and "deregulation" of which Thatcher and Reagan were to be the heroes were put in place. Fordism" (mass production and high wages to keep production flowing) was doomed. Social Keynesianism, the product of revolutionary liberation movements and post-war compromises, was dead;

2) The Soviet Union is proving to be a colossus with feet of clay. Forced into a costly arms race with the United States, it entered a recessionary spiral whose demographic statistics, so judiciously analyzed by Emmanuel Todd, foretell its downfall[2]. By invading Afghanistan in 1980, Soviet leaders fell into the trap set for them by the United States. Afghanistan was, it was said, the USSR's Vietnam. It was much worse than that. The United States recovered from defeat in Saigon in 1975. The USSR will never recover from the Afghan quagmire;

3) Just as the student and youth protests of 1968 seemed to put an end to all the old bourgeois values, the 1970s saw a major effort to recuperate these protests. The labor movement—which had played the leading role in France in May and in Italy in the autumn of 1968—was sidelined in favor of "societal" struggles, and not only Stalinism, but soon Marxism and the progressive tradition born of the Enlightenment were systematically called into question… The time of the so-called "new philosophers" had come. By the time the united left won in France in 1981, it was already too late. A victory of circumstance for a left that was largely disoriented, 1981 would ultimately precipitate its internal crisis: the collapse of the Communist Party, the rallying of socialism to "market values" and the "France that wins[3]".

---

2. See Emmanuel Todd, *La Chute finale*, Robert Laffont, 1976.
3. For more on this period, see Denis Collin & Jacques Cotta, *L'Illusion plurielle. Pourquoi la gauche n'est plus la gauche*, JC Lattès, 2001.

The 1980s: Capitalism on the Offence

While the 1970s saw the emergence of new trends in the capitalist mode of production, the following twenty years saw the irresistible advance of finance capital under the leadership of American imperialism, with a correlative retreat of "anti-systemic" forces[4] that took on the appearance of a rout. The countries of the "Soviet bloc" rallied almost without resistance to "liberal" capitalism. The Soviet Union disappeared in 1991, following a coup d'état fomented by old Stalinists, more or less manipulated. The United States intervened almost openly in Russia, imposing its dictates and its men to implement the economic "reforms" that would allow the country to be plundered. In the 1997 Russian elections, for example, a gigantic electoral fraud operation ensured victory for Washington's candidate, Boris Yeltsin, who was now a mere shadow of his former self[5]. China had long since entered the American game. After the official recognition of Maoist China by the Nixon administration, wisely advised by his Secretary of State Henry Kissinger, a veritable strategic alliance was forged between Beijing and Washington in Southeast Asian affairs. The Khmer Rouge thus became the weapon of war against Vietnamese (and Russian) influence in the region, and the White House supported Pol Pot's government to the bitter end, even though the latter was forced to abandon Phnom Penhet as the appalling extent of the crimes against humanity committed by these "friends" of the American and Chinese governments became apparent. China's further evolution and transformation into a factory for global capitalism had already been written into the policies of the 1970s, when Mao was still the "great helmsman", obsessed as he was with the confrontation with the Soviet Union as

---

4. We take this term from Immanuel Wallerstein. It refers to something much broader than traditional revolutionary movements. See, in particular, *Le Capitalisme historique*, La Découverte, 1996.

5. Yeltsin wasn't always the booze-soaked wreck the televisions complacently portrayed him to be. As a young apparatchik, he fought to reform the system, and his pitiful fate was not written in advance.

the principal contradiction, the contradiction with US imperialism becoming secondary, according to the sophistry of the "philosophical" manual for apprentice Red Guards, *On Contradiction.*

In the advanced capitalist countries, the downward trend is equally marked. All the social protection systems put in place after the Second World War, in a semi-insurrectionary situation and in response to the "communist threat", are being dismantled one after the other. The decisive step here was the defeat of the British miners, crushed by Mrs Thatcher after eighteen months on strike. But in "socialist" France, the situation was hardly any better. A government led first by Pierre Mauroy and then by Laurent Fabius organized the liquidation of the Lorraine steel industry. "We had to do the dirty work", apologized Laurent Fabius...[6]

The Decline of Socialism

Obviously, the collapse of "really existing socialism" and the capitulation in open country of "French-style socialism", i.e. Mitterrandism, are not really surprising events. Socialism in one country" had long been a new class society[7] and the almost absolute atony of the workers during the years 1989-1991 should have raised questions for those who considered that the USSR remained a "workers' state", despite its monstrous deformations and even its bureaucratic degeneration.

For social democracy, even revitalized by Mitterrand, there were no great illusions to be had. Prompted by its impeccably socialist

---

6. To understand the next thirty years and the political instrumentalization of immigration in the French debate, it's also worth recalling a few facts. Speaking about a strike by Renault-Flins workers, Gaston Defferre, then Minister of the Interior, declared that they were "*Shi'ites*", "strangers to the social realities of France" (January 26, 1983). Pierre Mauroy was not to be outdone: a few weeks later, when workers at Talbot (Peugeot-Citroën) in Poissy went on strike over their demands, he pointed the finger of blame at the "ayatollahs".

7. We'll come back to this question a little later.

speeches on Sundays and public holidays, social democracy had been, at least since 1914, "the loyal manager of capitalism", as Léon Blum happily put it before his judges at the Riom trial. Voting for war credits in 1914 and wallowing in the sacred union, with a few exceptions, European socialists gave their invaluable support to this gigantic massacre. In the trenches and under the gas, men were being trained and the conditions created for what was to blossom, dare we say it, into the Second World War. At a time when the Kaiser's Germany had collapsed, German Social Democracy, this time in liaison with envoys from the United States, took part in Max von Baden's government. SPD leader Ebert even offered to organize the rescue of the monarchy. A few weeks later, with the blessing of "socialist" leaders Ebert, Noske and Scheidemann, the Spartakist uprising was brutally suppressed. Rosa Luxemburget and Karl Liebknecht were murdered by the "Corps Francs", groups who were the direct originators of Nazism, and who were never bothered by Noske. The Nazis never forgot the services Noske had rendered them. In 1933, Göring asked Noske, president of the Hanover region, to remain in his post...

In France, the SFIO, which came to power without really having wanted to in 1936[8], hastened to declare a "pause" and let the Spanish Republic be strangled by a military coup supported by Nazi Germany and Fascist Italy. Non-intervention, dictated by British diplomacy, was thus the policy of the SFIO. The logical outcome was a massive vote for Pétain's full powers in 1940 (170 MPs against 36) and, after the war, the SFIO was to be involved in all the colonial adventures of Indochina, Suez, the Algerian War... Scandinavian socialism, which had long been a model, was no exception to this trend. Sweden not only remained neutral during the Second World War, but also signed a pact with Nazi Germany in 1940, allowing German military trains to pass

---

8. The leading role in the Popular Front government was to fall to the Radicals. But the general strike upset the calculations, and instead of Herriot or Daladier, the ruling class asked Léon Blum to take charge.

through its territory. It's true that Swedes were classed as "Aryans" in Hitler's racist delirium, and that Sweden had very early made a name for itself with a far-reaching eugenics policy…

Social democracy's rallying to the capitalist order, its gradual renunciation of anything reminiscent of its working-class origins, its alliance with the American Democratic Party under the aegis of Mr. Clinton, or the transformation of the *Labour Party* into the pure and simple party of finance capital and the major press groups[9], are all the culmination of a process that began almost a century ago. In most rich countries, political life appears normalized. Radical criticism or contestation of the capitalist political and social system is now confined to small groups generally excluded from any parliamentary representation, while two major parties, in agreement on the essentials, share power, taking it in turns to occupy the highest offices according to the results of a parody of democracy that increasingly resembles TV talk shows: in the USA, Democrats and Republicans; in Great Britain, *New Labour* and Conservatives; in Germany CDU and SPD; in Italy "center-right" and "center-left"; in France UMP and PS, and so on. In former "socialist" countries, voters have a choice between right and right-wing, between an ultraliberal right and a conservative, nationalist right steeped in bigotry… or no choice at all: Putin and Medvedev's Russia resembles a one-party regime serving a clan of billionaires, with a few "democratic" stooges lacking any real clout, a regime that nonetheless holds together with undeniable popular support.

Triumph all round. The European Left's alternative to capitalism is still capitalism. Decidedly, TINA! The triumph of capitalism does not only concern the "political superstructure". After all, the bureaucratization of the top echelons of workers' organizations, their rallying to the ruling classes, is an old story. Lenin denounced

---

9. From the outset, the Murdoch group supported Mr Blair's conquest of *Labour*. However, Robert Murdoch is clearly part of the most conservative right, and his newspapers and TV channels unreservedly supported the "Moral Majority" and George Bush's policies.

this "workers' aristocracy", nourished by the excess profits of colonialism, which had ended up in league with its own bourgeoisie. The sociologist Robert Michels, in a seminal work on *political parties*[10], also pointed out the fundamentally conservative nature of these new elites emerging from the socialist parties and trade unions. But today, the processes are much more profound, as they seem to have affected the hard core of resistance to capitalism, the traditional working class. Nicolas Sarkozy's election in the 2007 French presidential election would have been impossible without the rallying of significant sectors of the working class (notably those who had deserted the PCF for abstention or, in some cases, the FN vote). Berlusconi's victory in the 2008 Italian parliamentary elections was the result of a surge by the crypto-fascist *Lega Nord* party, led by Umberto Bossi, which boasts of having become the leading workers' party, following its breakthroughs in traditional ex-PCI and CGIL strongholds such as the industrial city of Brescia, breakthroughs which are now beginning to reach Emilia Romagna, i.e., the "red" Italy of almost all time. The infernal pairing of "immigration and insecurity" is in full effect in the old egalitarian and anti-establishment regions. We'll try to explain all this and show that, paradoxically, this "turn to the right" by part of the working class testifies to the stubborn persistence of the "class vote", albeit in totally unrecognizable forms. In the meantime, let's acknowledge the depth of the evil.

Social Atomization

The effects can be measured. First of all, the disintegration of old solidarities. When you consider that stress at work can lead several employees in the same company to commit suicide without any significant reaction, even though these are large companies with

---

10. Reissued in the "Champs" paperback collection by Flammarion (translated from the German by Samuel Jankélévitch).

a long-standing union tradition, such as PSA, Renault or France Télécom, this is one of the clearest symptoms of the depth of the mental pulverization to which the working class has been subjected. We're all sitting on our hands, hoping that the next bad blow will spare us.

The domination of consumerist ideology. It's not a question of making some conventional critique of the "sordid materialism of the masses", but of understanding the hold that the system of domination of what Marcuse called "repressive desublimation[11]" has on people's minds. Patrimonial capitalism, as it emerged from feudal society, preached a morality of work and savings. Puritanism was indeed the "ethic of capitalism", but this ethic corresponded to a period of birth and affirmation of the capitalist mode of production in societies largely dominated by feudal relations on the one hand, and small-scale merchant production on the other. All this has been swept away by contemporary capitalism. The pursuit of capital accumulation demands that individuals be transformed into insatiable consumers. Advertising - in other words, the dominant ideology in its clearest and most sophisticated form - repeats: we must give in to our desires, i.e. possess the object of our desire. It's a possession that is always frustrating, and revives desire as soon as the object is touched. Desublimation, because now we go straight to the thing itself. The break with Puritanism is total. The vulgarity of sexual matters is on display without the slightest modesty - think of the President of the French Republic going to the Vatican accompanied by Bigard, and we understand what a change of era we've lived through. At the same time, it's a new system of repression, because the apparent freedom of morals is entirely determined by the principle of profitability—desire must

---

11. For Freud, the repression of sexual impulses is sublimated in creative artistic activity, which presupposes a distancing from reality. Hebert Marcuse, on the other hand, shows that contemporary capitalism makes direct use of sex as a new means of social control. "Sexuality is becoming the standard theme of the best-sellers of oppression. (*L'Homme unidimensionnel*, éditions de Minuit, 1968, Seuil, 1970, "Points" collection, p. 111).

pay!—and from this point of view, industrial pornography is highly revealing of the "freedom" won by the so-called "sexual revolution".

Advertising ideology revolves around this question of repressive desublimation. For advertising is not (or not only) a somewhat futile and ultimately parasitic activity in relation to the hard core of the capitalist mode of production, the production of what has to be sold. Advertising is apparently in a secondary position: it can help to sell, but is never more than a means to an end. However, according to the processes of inversion of the real, specific to the capitalist mode of production, this is not the case. Advertising is a central part of the machinery that holds capitalist society together and shapes people's minds so that they can be integrated into the machinery of accumulation. The transformation of advertising into a "work of art" completes the process. Advertising was advertising and nothing else. It didn't look for alibis, and presented itself openly for what it was—a technically more elaborate form of sales pitch. Advertising, on the other hand, doesn't sell perfumes or toilet cleaning products; it sells ideology, and ideology wrapped up in the shimmering finery of talented designers.

All in all, modern capitalist society is made up of atomized individuals who increasingly lead separate lives, in line with the vision of man conveyed by dominant thought and ideology for nearly four centuries. Hobbes had captured the essence of this, painting the state of nature as one in which isolated individuals are condemned to confront each other in a war that is impossible to avoid or end. A fierce critic of Hobbes, Rousseau shared with him the idea that man is naturally an isolated being who takes no particular pleasure in the company of other men. That this vision of human reality is debatable, if not downright unrealistic, is pretty much self-evident. Human individuals exist only in their relations with others, quite simply because their lives depend on them. However, the theoretical, even moral, justifications of capitalism demand that the Hobbesian vision of man reconducted under the species of *Homo œconomicus* be "true". And indeed, what McPherson called "possessive individualism" has become the dominant ideology, embracing not only those who profit from capitalism, but also its victims, the dominant as well as the dominated. Which is what ideology is all about.

Here again, TINA! Not only has capitalism won, it no longer even needs a name. Capitalism is the natural economy, the natural reality of human life, the completion of history. When MEDEF bosses demand that we stop criticizing business and the market economy, particularly in the "economic and social sciences" syllabus at high school, they add that "the market economy" (an elegant pseudonym for "capitalism") is no more debatable than democracy. These kings of ROI ("*Return On Investment*"), these aces of finance, stock options and golden pensions, don't even realize the incongruity of the idea that "democracy cannot be discussed"… But never mind. Their demand is clear: to proclaim, once and for all, what seems to them a truth as certain as mathematical theorems, the truth of the eternity of capitalism and the splendors of the "free market[12]".

Societal versus Social Issues

Early capitalism could not do without religion: in other words, it could not legitimize itself through its own forces, through its own activity. It borrowed its systems of legitimization from societies of the past. Marx points out the close relationship between capitalism and Christian religion, mainly in its Protestant form. But now that capitalism is truly at home, now that it has essentially eliminated the former ruling classes and the relations of production on which their domination rested, the need for transcendent justification is

---

12. The crisis has led to some cosmetic revisions. State intervention, reviled when it came to guaranteeing the rights of the most disadvantaged, is now welcome to save the banks. There are two or three self-criticisms. But on the substance, nothing! During the crisis, capitalism continues and must continue afterwards. Boring questions won't be asked, and the mainstream media are inviting the same "experts" as yesterday.

less pressing. Founded on calculation, on economic rationality, on the tyranny of ratios and quotas, capitalism finds in modern science not only a most precious tool, but also a system of legitimization that takes the place of religion.

And there's more. In some respects, religion has become an obstacle to the development of capitalism: when religious authorities oppose the manipulation of human embryos, they are obviously hindering progress and, brazen as they are, would like to close off a potential field of capital accumulation. Lifting taboos on homosexuality has created a new market for *gay attitudes*. Lifting religious taboos on human life and the incompressible need to face up to the question of death will also open up a new market, a new field of capital accumulation. Modern science, founded on a radical indifference to values, is ideally suited to justifying, in the name of efficiency and yield, the very values of efficiency and yield as the only ones that can reasonably guide modern society. Hence the upside-down battles that break down the traditional lines between the "party of order" and the "party of movement", the right and the left. As a result, religion can become a point of resistance to capitalism. An illusory point of resistance, but illusions are also material forces. Thus, the Islamist upsurge often appears as a reaction to the extension of capitalism's way of life and values. But at the same time, it's a totally illusory reaction, since Islam, the religion of the abstract universal, is just as capable as Protestant Christianity of providing a spiritual equivalent to the world of the commodity.

The result is utterly contradictory. Capitalism, at last "at home", seeks to rid humanity of anything that might elevate it above production and consumption, and thus develops the most vulgar economistic materialism. At the same time, it nurtures the most backward forms of religiosity, between Wahhabi Islamism with its home in Saudi Arabia and the return to traditionalist Catholicism of a Ratzinger. At the same time, the stage is set: there is only room for societal debate, between those who are concerned solely with earthly well-being and want embryo research, gay marriage and euthanasia, and those who defend the rights of God, proclaim that human life exists as soon as the sperm meets the egg, condemn homosexuality as unnatural and denounce euthanasia as a crime against divine law. Not to mention master sophists in the art of overcoming contradictions, such as the mayor of Paris, Bertrand Delanoë, an avowed homosexual and champion of societal liberalism, who has named a square in his city after John Paul II… A trompe-l'œil debate into which all post-Sixties leftism has rushed, providing the ruling classes with the alibis they needed. A case in point? Of course, prolonging the suffering of the dying is inhuman. Certainly, the desire to end one's life when it has become a bed of torture is perfectly legitimate. Admittedly, religious condemnations of suicide are somewhat unseemly, and the argument of applying "thou shalt not kill" to oneself is highly sophomoric. Nevertheless, the proposal to legalize euthanasia comes at a time when people are complaining about the costly social consequences of prolonging life, and when more and more voices are calling for cost-benefit calculations to be carried out when deciding whether or not to undertake major therapies. A singular gesture whose sole justification is love, euthanasia could thus become a legalized means of regulating death-dealing capitalism.

The substitution of the societal for the social thus plays a decisive role in stifling any radical critique of capitalism. It's worth pointing out the particular role played by a certain "1968" leftism, which has made the "new struggles" its preferred terrain: as the domination of capital over labor has finally become secondary—since the working class is "gentrifying"—leftism considers that the terrain of struggle is now the family—the struggle against patriarchy and male domination—or questions of "recognition". While May 1st workers' parades now gather little more than a few militant processions, the big spring demonstration is now *gay pride*! What characterizes these societal movements is that they erase class conflicts and substitute other conflicts: gay bourgeois and lesbian workers are united in their status as victims of homophobic prejudice. In the 1970s, many revolutionary "Marxist" groups, or those claiming to be such, believed that Victorian morality and conservative familialism were intrinsic features of the capitalist mode of production. What followed was to prove them wrong. And on the same day, a Minister of Education from the most right-wing government France has had in a long time can simultaneously announce an anti-strike law, the elimination of 20,000 teaching posts and a major campaign against homophobia in schools. In other words, "leftism", which purported to be a radical critique of existing society, has made a major contribution to spreading the idea that there is no global alternative to capitalism, and that resolving the "social question" ultimately boils down to resolving the societal question for each individual, in his or her "difference".

The Immigrant instead of the Proletarian

The latest of the great battles in which part of the far left has taken refuge, the battle to defend immigrants, has exactly the same characteristics. Immigrants emerged in the 1970s as the new representatives of the revolutionary proletariat against the gentrified European proletariat. Maoism was the main force behind this vision. Immigration then became the focus of new societal struggles on the left. In response to the social demands of a fraction of immigrants—second-generation immigrants—as expressed during the 1983 "March of the Beurs", the Left came up with the slogan of integration and the slogan "Let's enrich ourselves with our differences" and, sometimes, the slogan said in a lower voice: "Immigrants, enrich yourselves by becoming capitalist buddies like the others". Non-discrimination has replaced all social content. Immigrants have emerged from the proletariat to become a special category of victims. To caricature (barely), left-wing do-gooders have rallied around the claim that immigrants should have the same right to become capitalists as everyone else[13].

---

13. All studies show that the children of immigrants from working-class backgrounds are no better or worse off in the great race for diplomas and good "jobs" than children

What makes things more difficult to grasp in the latter case is the ambivalent attitude or, more accurately, the formidable duplicity adopted by the ruling classes. On the one hand, following traditional recipes, they use the denunciation of immigrants as a diversion from social demands. If there's unemployment, it's because immigrants are taking jobs away from the French. If social security is in deficit, it's because immigrants have too many children. The transformation of "illegal immigration" into the target of repeated campaigns and legislation is, it seems, an electorally profitable business. At the same time as adopting a truly villainous directive on immigrants (June 2008), the European Union (and France is no exception) is making extensive use of new "migratory flows" and, in many sectors, capitalists are calling for greater recourse to immigration. We even saw the owner of a chic restaurant in Neuilly, frequented by French President Sarkozy and others, call for the regularization of his "illegal immigrants", who were so few in fact that they were declared to the social security and tax authorities.

In other words, however justified it may be, defending immigrants is in no way an anti-capitalist struggle, and is in fact directly in line with the strategic aims of certain fractions of the ruling class.

A Word to the Wise

This global structuring of the field of political struggles in France, Italy and, more generally, in the advanced capitalist countries has not made class divisions and conflicts disappear—far from it—but it has blurred and camouflaged them behind the creation of a vast "centrist" gathering, a conglomerate of beautiful souls, like the Italian *centro sinistra*, or the as yet unformalized coalition between

---

from French working-class families who have been in the job market for several generations. Academic failure and the "breakdown of the social elevator" are first and foremost a question of class. The support SOS Racisme has received from the enlightened bourgeoisie is therefore easy to explain: media anti-racism makes its own contribution to the suppression of the social question.

Bayrou and the PS in France—in short, all the formulas of the old dream of Giscard d'Estaing, who wanted to bring together "two Frenchmen out of three". All these people share a fundamental principle with their so-called "right-wing" opponents: "capitalism is the limit of our historical horizon". Our world is not perfect, the spokesmen and penholders of the ruling class sometimes concede. But it is the best possible; all attempts, however well-intentioned, to build a better world are doomed to failure and will produce a tyranny that would make our abysmal social injustices desirable.

As we can see, the real difficulty today is to seriously implement the alterglobalists' slogan, "Another world is possible". Another world is possible? Without a doubt. Even an infinite number of other worlds are possible. The problem is to determine whether a world better than this one is possible. In short, to know whether it is really, and not abstractly, possible to break free from the reign of capital. And this requires an understanding of the reality of this world, and the reasons for the seemingly invincible power of the capitalist mode of production.

CHAPTER II. THE WORLD IS A COMMODITY

"The world is not a commodity! This motto of the anti-globalists (*no global*) who have become, significantly, "alter-globalists" sounds curious, a cry of despair or a bad joke? The world really is a commodity. For capitalism, only commodities have value or, as a reciprocal proposition, everything of value is a commodity. And a commodity necessarily belongs to someone: a commodity available to all or no one is not a commodity. And this is why appropriating what belongs to no one is not theft, since no one is robbed. So, if you fence off communal pastures and disperse *manu militari* the peasants who stubbornly refuse to understand the natural Lockean right of ownership, you're not robbing anyone[14]. And for the misery-draggers thus expelled from their homes, they can always take over the Indians' hunting grounds, and here again no one is robbed, since the land is nobody's property. From the expulsion of peasants to colonization: the genesis of European capitalism has come full circle.

---

14. See J. LOCKE, *Treatise on Civil Government*. Locke was a supporter of *enclosures*, the enclosure of common land by landlords for sheep farming, from the sixteenth century onwards. Large numbers of peasants depended on the *commons* for their livelihood, and *enclosures* threw hundreds of thousands of wretched people onto the roads. This episode in English history is recounted and analyzed by Marx in Book I of *Capital*, section VIII, "Primitive Accumulation".

Infinite Extension of the Commodity Realm

Capitalism presents this conception as "natural". Natural law in its modern version (in Hobbes or Locke) is nothing other than the right of the capitalist owner who, in the absence of law or sovereign power to which he has given his word, has the right over everyone and everything. When Monsanto patents the plants used by Latin America's aboriginal populations for pharmacopoeia, it is simply following in this footsteps. These tribes don't know what to do with their recipes; they didn't have the idea of selling them or registering a patent. The idea of patenting belongs to Monsanto, so it can be exploited commercially.

And here's something that's hardly science fiction. Let's suppose that tomorrow a biotech firm, let's call it HGM-SA, a company specializing in genetically modified Humans, proposes a modification of the human genome that protects the individual against cancer. The company sells its patent, which is implemented in a hospital. The genetically modified human is now protected against all cancers. This human, in turn, very naturally produces a child. The child inherits his anti-cancer gene. From the point of view of "natural" capitalist property law, HGM-SA has a right to the child, who not only inherits genes that naturally belong to him—in fact, his parents' genes—but also genes patented by HGM-SA. Francis Crick, co-discoverer with James Watson of the structure of DNA, declared: "No newborn child should be recognized as human until it has passed a certain number of tests on its genetic endowment. If it does not pass these tests, it loses its right to life". This gentleman's crypto-Nazi eugenics could find industrial outlets[15].

---

15. In 2007, Crick repeated his claim that blacks are less intelligent than whites. His colleague Watson was not to be outdone. In 1997, he asserted that homosexuality is certainly genetic and that women should be able to have abortions if this gene were detected in the foetus they were carrying. Such statements could be treated with contempt. Watson and Crick obviously carry a gene predisposing them to the development of a virulent form of cretinism. The fact remains that these statements are not isolated, far from it, and that we can grasp how Nazi barbarism was not a form of turning back the

Hidden Production

Commodification is not simply an extensive process that progressively affects all aspects of human life—right down to the sale of blood, organs or oocytes[16] and the provision of one's womb. As far as these latter aspects are concerned, all the traditional forms of slavery had already demonstrated the formidable propensity of human societies to treat human beings as things, to "reify" them, as the philosophers might say. Commodification is also an intensive process. The market relationship invades areas that had remained those of direct cooperation or coordination by command (mutual aid, family life). It gradually deconstructs all stable reality, leaving only the perpetual motion of market exchange. In a traditional company, to put it simply, market relations existed in only three forms—and the third, to which we'll return later, is quite specific: (1) the company buys on the market the constant capital it is going to devote to the production process (raw materials, machinery); (2) the company sells on the market its production, which, having emerged from the furnace of production, has taken on the form of a commodity; (3) the company buys labor power from its workers. In reality, this simplistic schema is less and less valid. Exchanges take place within the company: the methods of management accounting and quality control have largely contributed to formalizing all this. When a technical assistance team comes in to repair a machine, it can be likened to an outside company offering a service. In this way, we can set up an accounting analysis system that considers each company unit as a micro-business exchanging services and goods with the other micro-businesses that make up the overall organization. In this way, the company's productive process takes on the extraordinary appearance of a pseudo-market

---

clock, but an ultramodern barbarism whose links with scientism run very deep.

16. Ukraine, Greece and Spain are leading the way in this business, which enables *in vitro* fertilization with embryo transfer to be carried out on women who have reached menopause.

circulation process in the hands of the manager. When neoclassical economics focuses on exchanges (the buying and selling of factors), eliminating production and rendering the production of surplus value unthinkable, it merely provides the theoretical expression of the very way in which companies are managed, as soon as we abandon the "archaic" point of view of the engineer or production manager to adopt that of management control and, behind it, of the shareholders who are going to shear their coupons.

This process is accelerated by two closely related phenomena: concentration and the creation of transnational firms, on the one hand, and outsourcing, on the other. Capitalist concentration does not necessarily mean the organic fusion of all parts of a large firm into a single productive entity. On the contrary, within a firm, the most frequent case is where a real market exists, with genuine financial flows between various subsidiaries of the same firm (a process that differs, oh so much, from the simple pseudo-market of accounting analysis). This fragmentation of firms into formally autonomous entities that meet only on the market offers many tactical and strategic advantages (division of personnel, possibility of organizing transfers of financial flows according to the needs and interests of the moment, etc.), and is obviously accelerating with globalization[17]. According to various calculations, more than a third of world trade is intra-firm trade. In 2008, France's automotive trade balance deteriorated sharply, not because of the massive penetration of foreign brands, but because the major national automakers are increasingly outsourcing their production: Renault with the Romanian Dacia, PSA with the Slovak 107/C1…

The former CEO of Alcatel-Lucent, Serge Tchuruk[18], had imagined a company without a factory, one that would simply have

---

17. Tax havens" are therefore not parasitic outgrowths of the capitalist system, but fundamental cogs in the global division of labor. That's why all our promises to make these offshore platforms "transparent" are just empty words.

18. This man's story deserves to be told. He had taken over the management of a nationalized high-tech company, one of the flagships of French state industrial policy. Between 2000 and 2008, under his leadership, the company divested itself of its pre-

others manufacture the products it would sell. For Tchuruk, the ideal capitalism is one that does away with production, leaving it as a mere agent in the marketplace. It's market capitalism in its purest form. Of course, it's a joke: Tchuruk and his staff, perhaps intoxicated by their own ideology, have ended up taking a thriving *high-tech* company into an extremely difficult situation. If Alcatel can subcontract the manufacture of a telephone exchange to another company, pretty soon that company should decide to sell its products directly and on its own account. It would have no reason to allow a purely parasitic intermediary[19] a share of the surplus value produced. The only hypothesis that would allow "Tchuruk-style capitalism" to work is one in which the subcontractor has no means of accessing the market alone, which is only possible if the ordering firm has some kind of privileged access to the market—for example, through public orders or some kind of operating monopoly granted by a state or region. In other words, pure market "Churukian" capitalism presupposes state monopolies in the background, and quasi-feudal relations between the big firms and an army of subcontractors... The representation made by economists (orthodox[20]) and the main players (bosses, managers, politicians) is not pure fantasy: if we consider only the exoteric economy, the sphere of circulation, this representation is "true" to a certain extent. At the same time, it constitutes an ideological

---

cious jewels, merging with lame ducks like Lucent in the USA. During this period, Alcatel's share price fell from 100 euros to 4 euros. At the age of 70, Tchuruk retires with a golden parachute worth over 6 million euros. And a massive lay-off plan in the company's factories and design offices. According to liberal theorists, the high incomes of company directors are the price of their performance, unlike "irresponsible" civil servants. This example shows just how far removed from reality the discourse of official economists (who are often paid handsomely for their work) is.

19. This model of parasitic capitalism dominated the privatization of telecommunications. In France, the new operators buy telephone communications from the "incumbent operator" (France Télécom) and resell them to individuals.

20. Not all economists subscribe to the religion of market capitalism. There are quite a few heterodox economists who try to challenge the dogma. But they are in the minority, and their voices have little chance of being heard, with the exception of former orthodoxists who have converted to (moderate) critical thinking, such as Joseph Stiglitz.

travesty in the sense Marx gives to this term in *Capital*, an inverted representation of reality, perceived as if in a *camera oscura*.

The Job Market

As for the third type of market relationship—the wage relationship—here too, long-term developments are worth highlighting. If the enterprise as a productive unit (the factory, the plant) disappears in favor of the firm, at the same time the capital-labor relationship undergoes decisive changes. In old-style capitalism, despite their status as "free workers", workers remained the workers of a specific boss, who could say "my workers", in a relationship where the wage form (a buyer and a seller of labor power meet on a market) remained largely covered by the old relationships of personal dependence, such as those between the manant and his lord, or the journeyman and his master. The boss, direct owner of the means of production, boss of the same company for life, instituted with "his" workers every possible type of personal relationship, from the most brutal slave-like behavior to social and even semi-socialist paternalism[21]. Those days are gone, as are the Fordist and Keynesian phases, when capital-labour conflict was controlled by the labour-management agreement that guaranteed social peace, in return for guaranteed employment and stable prospects of wage progression. The major trend is to replace the notions of job, qualification, workstation and working conditions with the notion of mission. The company no longer hires an employee, but enters into an agreement with a kind of service provider for an assignment. Temporary employment agencies were the forerunners

---

21. We could give numerous examples of this "progressive" patronage, from Robert Owen's attempts to create communist industrial communities in the United States to the Menier chocolate factory in Noisiel, not forgetting the "familistère" in Guise founded by Godin, the maker of the famous stove, the "little Godin". These examples are not far removed from the Christian paternalistic patronage that rallied the Gaullist "participation".

of the new "flexible" hiring possibilities that have gradually taken hold in all advanced capitalist countries. Everyone becomes their own entrepreneur! Many large companies have "outsourced" part of their workforce. FIAT, for example, made massive cuts in its workforce after the failure of the last major strike at its Turin-area plants in 1979. It encouraged its workers to set up on their own and become small bosses who went to work… for FIAT. Thus, after more than ten years of labor unrest, the big Italian firm took the lead in a counter-revolution aimed at breaking the back of the working class, a counter-revolution that paved the way for the destruction of the post-war social pact and the triumph of Berlusconi and, correlatively, the outright disappearance of the Italian Left.

Here again, we live in an empire of lies. The old wage relationships are legally renamed to perfect the illusion of the disappearance of work and production in favor of market exchange. But the real relationship between those who own the means of production and those who simply have to go to the market and sell their skin remains one of domination. It's just that, dare we say it, we've gradually done away with anything that might evoke collective rules and guarantees. To complete the picture, we might add that the main trade union organizations, such as the French CGT, have already rallied behind this new form of wage relations under the label of "flexicurity" or "securing career paths".

Individually, the bourgeois may be a spendthrift, even risking almost his entire fortune on games of chance[22], but the bourgeois class has always been acutely aware of its own interests, and its legal and political doctrines stick as closely as possible to what the rate of profit demands. The bourgeoisie as a class is close to its pennies, and the fact that it is obliged to pay workers already seems to it an intolerable constraint—indeed, it calls it "wage charges". Therefore, in this so-called labor market, in this so-called contractual relationship that is the wage relationship, we need to ensure as

____

22. Two well-known examples: André Citroën, the famous carmaker, and Baron Empain, heir to a dynasty of Belgian industrialists.

much supremacy as possible for the buyer over the seller. The buyer possesses the concentrated power of capital. The seller could possess the power of numbers, and it is this power that must be reduced, or better still, prevented from coagulating in the first place. In 1791, Le Chapelier's law not only dissolved the old medieval guilds. It prohibited in advance all workers' coalitions that were obstacles to free competition. From a capitalist point of view, an innocent mutual aid society is already an obstacle to free competition. No longer under the direct threat of death, the rescued employee can increase his demands in wage negotiations. So let's not talk about those horrible unions who claim to overturn the natural law of competition by agreeing on the selling price of the commodity labor power!

Thanks to the European Union, legal and political thinking has been enriched by a new article of faith, "free and undistorted competition[23]", which replaces the principles of popular sovereignty. By their very nature, trade unions and collective bargaining agreements are an intolerable obstacle to this "free and undistorted competition" in the labor market. For there to be a genuine labor market, labor power must become, or revert to becoming, a commodity like any other. In condemning the Swedish trade unions for protesting against the hiring in Sweden of Latvian workers paid at the Latvian tariff, the European Court of Justice has made it clear that agreements establishing a "tariff" for wages are, in essence, contrary to the principles of the European Union, even if we temporarily continue to tolerate the social legislation of the various European nations, although, in the strong words of Denis Kessler, one of the qualified representatives of French employers, it is necessary to undo everything that has been done since 1944[24]. Indeed, if the

---

23. A "constitutional principle" in the treaty rejected by the French and Dutch in 2005, the principle of "free and undistorted competition" is taken up again in the so-called "Lisbon Treaty" - which is in rather poor shape at the time of writing, following the no vote of the Irish, the only Europeans allowed to have their say.
24. Incidentally, the possibility of using workers from low-wage countries in countries with the highest wages was at the heart of the "Bolkestein Directive" and its famous

case law of the European Court of Justice is extended, nothing will prevent a French construction company, for example, from setting up a Bulgarian subsidiary and having its Bulgarian employees work in France at Bulgarian rates. Offshoring has led to some progress: Dacia's Romanian workers cost much less than Renault's French workers, and are now beginning to compete directly with the latter. But while it's possible to relocate the production of cars or socks, it's difficult to relocate bricklayers, plumbers or hairdressers. Fortunately, the ECJ ruling remedies this deplorable state of affairs by allowing services to be relocated on site! In the short term, therefore, wage agreements are under threat, as it will be easy for any company manager to argue to his employees that they have no other option for keeping their jobs than to align themselves with the lowest wage, in terms of both pay and working hours.

If everyone becomes their own entrepreneur, there's no room for cooperation. As self-entrepreneurs, employees are in competition with each other. We have already mentioned the political use of the issue of immigration. During the years of economic expansion under the "Fordist" regime of accumulation, clashes between national and immigrant workers remained relatively limited. The power of the trade unions enabled workers of all nationalities to be integrated into a "class organization". As soon as "the class" no longer exists as such, i.e., workers no longer represent themselves through their organizations, the wage system, i.e., the "labor market" (in fact, the market for labor power), can impose its rules, the first of which is that everyone must regard any seller of labor power not as a comrade with whom to forge bonds of class solidarity, but as a rival. A well-known paradox: in the realm of free competition, the

---

"Polish plumber", which was the highlight of the 2005 referendum campaign on the "European Constitutional Treaty". Officially, the TCE has been rejected and the Bolkestein directive consigned to the dustbin, but its contents apply, and the European Court of Justice has confirmed that the European Union is not going to let itself be hindered in its pious campaign by vulgar considerations of democracy. Unless we consider that the difference between dictatorship and democracy can be summed up in this joke: dictatorship means "shut up!" and democracy means "keep on talking!"

enemy is the competitor whom we must try to eliminate. To this end, there are a number of methods, the most commonly used of which are *numerus clausus* (as in pharmacies), regulated prices (the single price for books) or terror (mafias, rackets of all kinds). The FN surge in certain important sectors of the working class, relayed by the Sarkozy vote in the 2007 presidential election, clearly reflects this perception of immigrants as competitors to be eliminated once the prospect of uniting against employers has all but disappeared. Voting for the xenophobic right does not necessarily thrive on the ruins of trade unionism. This can be seen in Italy, where Umberto Bossi's *Lega Nord* has made significant inroads among workers, particularly in highly unionized regions such as Brescia and Reggio Emilia[25]. The Italian case is all the more interesting in that working-class "racism" is often directed not against "non-EU" immigrants, but against Italians from the South, who are accused of being the priority beneficiaries of social housing and family benefits… Just as it was directed against Italians in the South of France at the beginning of the 20th century, or against Poles among miners. So it's not a "racist" attitude in the true sense of the word, but a reaction engendered by free and undistorted competition.

Marx's analysis of the structure of social formations dominated by the capitalist mode of production concluded with the accumulation of misery at one pole of society and the accumulation of wealth at the other. This led to a "simplification" of the distribution of social classes: a (reduced) bourgeoisie facing a vast class of proletarians. As the most important class in bourgeois society, the proletarians had to become aware of their strength, develop their "class consciousness" and thus seize the levers of control to impose the law of the working majority on the whole of society, for the first time in history. It was even on the basis of this irresistible numerical growth of the proletariat that Marx had been led to envisage the

____

25. See *La Sociale* (http://la-sociale.viabloga.com), "Chroniques italiennes", April 18, 2008.

conquest of universal suffrage[26] and the parliamentary republic as the means of a peaceful transition to socialism. To some extent, Marx's prediction has come true. If we call "proletarians" those who, in order to live, have to sell their labor power (which includes the "new middle classes", employees, technicians, middle managers, etc.), then the proletariat is the ultra-majority in all advanced capitalist societies, and the accelerated growth of China, India, Brazil, etc., is producing proletarians by the hundreds of millions. But the situation of this proletariat, taken in itself, is what Marx calls "wage-labor". And yet, according to Marx, what precisely defines wage-labour is the situation of sellers of labour-power who compete with each other to sell their labour-power as effectively as possible. Marx saw in the dynamics of capitalism the forces of socialization, even though the dynamics of commodity production conceal powerful forces of social atomization. We can and must criticize the liberal anthropology that sees people as leading separate existences; in reality, in our scientific knowledge of social life, we know that it is cooperation that is the condition of life itself and that, consequently, liberal anthropology is absurd! And yet, the alienated forms that cooperation takes in the capitalist mode of production mean that individuals find themselves subjectively separated from one another, and are driven to see themselves as autonomous subjects, indifferent to others. This is often referred to as "individualism". Social (alienated) consciousness and social reality thus occupy opposing positions, and for "good reasons"— reasons that have to do not with a few illusions propagated by the media or public poisoners, but with the very organization and structural features of the capitalist mode of production.

---

26. In Marx's day, universal suffrage was almost non-existent. Even in the most democratic countries, it was still held by men, and many obstacles prevented the poor from gaining access to citizenship.

Commodity and Religion

Faced with this transformation of life itself into a commodity, faced with this generalized commodification, we can adopt an attitude of moral protest. How can we morally accept that everything is for sale, that everything is an object of commerce? How can we accept human life being transformed into a dead thing? This denunciation of "reification" is indispensable, and forms part of the theoretical arsenal of critical Marxism (that of the Frankfurt School, Adorno, Marcuse and their heirs). We must, however, try to understand the reasons for the strength of commodity rule. In our view, there are two reasons for the driving force of the capitalist market economy.

On the one hand, the market and competition in general (irrespective of their specifically capitalist form) have intrinsic advantages over centrally administered forms of economy—such as Soviet planning—and over traditional economies. It's not certain that these advantages will last forever, and perhaps we've even reached a stage where the disadvantages are beginning to outweigh the advantages… But these advantages are a fact that partly explains why people adhere to such an anxiety-provoking form of social life. We'll come back to this point later, when we consider the prospects for a possible non-capitalist society.

On the other hand, the world of the commodity is properly a religious world, and draws its strength from the same reasons that give religions their strength. Let's take a detour and read a well-known but highly illuminating passage from *Capital, the* one devoted to the fetishism of the commodity (*Capital*, I, first section, IV).

A commodity, says Marx, is "a very complex thing, full of metaphysical subtleties and theological arguments". As a use-value, dedicated to satisfying human needs, the commodity is not mysterious at all. Nor is it mysterious when considered as a product of human labor. The problem lies elsewhere. Commodities are such only because they are products of human labor, and are exchanged on a market according to the rule of equality of value: a quantity *x* of a certain commodity A is exchanged for a quantity *y* of a commodity B. This is the metamorphosis.

> "The equal character of human labor acquires the form of the value of the products of labor; the measure of individual labor by its duration acquires the form of the magnitude of the value of the products of labor; finally, the relations of producers, in which the social characters of their labor are asserted, acquire the form of a social relation of the products of labor. This is why these products are converted into commodities, i.e. into things that do and do not fall within the realm of sense, or social things."

It's worth noting that Marx generally defines "social things" as things that both "make sense and don't make sense". Insofar as they fall within the realm of sense, "social things" are akin to "physical things". But, says Marx, even physical things do not give themselves directly to us. It is the subjective excitation of the optic nerve that presents itself as the sensible form of something external to the eye. In other words, this transformation of what is subjective into a "thing" appearing as objective is the very essence of knowledge; we are condemned to conceive the subjective impression as the representation of something objective, but we cannot directly access the thing itself as it exists outside us. Marx, however, assures us that this conception, valid for "physical things", is no longer so as soon as we approach social things, for "the value-form and value-ratio of the products of labor have absolutely nothing to do with their physical form."

If "value form" has nothing to do with the physical form of commodities, then it is not a sensible thing, perceptible by the senses like anything that belongs to the world outside consciousness. It lies entirely within the activity of human consciousness, and is therefore not a "material reality[27]". The analysis of value form is therefore not the analysis of an objective process, a process as independent of us

---

27. This question is very important because it calls into question Marx's alleged materialism.

as the movement of the planets. It is the analysis of the process by which a thing that depends on us, that is a product of the combined activity of large numbers of individuals, a thing that is merely the outward manifestation of the subjective ("personal" says Marx) power of the producer, is perceived as a process as independent of us as the movement of the planets. A prototype for this kind of transformation, the externalization of the power of the human mind into an imaginary power that imposes itself on society as a whole, is found in "religious alienation". In other words, the process by which the commodity can circulate as a commodity is akin to the process by which religion imposes its rules on relations between men. This is why the commodity is a "metaphysical" thing.

From there, Marx moves on to the analysis of religious forms:

"The religious world is merely a reflection of the real world. A society in which the product of labor generally takes the form of a commodity, and in which, consequently, the most general relationship between producers consists in comparing the values of their products and, under this envelope of things, in comparing their private labors to each other as equal human labor, such a society finds in Christianity with its cult of the abstract man, and especially in its bourgeois types, Protestantism, Deism, etc., the most suitable religious complement."

The classical theory of "reflection", which makes religion an illusory reflection of material reality (the theory defended by Lenin, for example, in *Materialism and Empiriocriticism*), is quite incapable of accounting for this process by which "metaphysical" ideas are formed and can become so active as to structure the forms of social consciousness. Marx's brilliant analysis of commodity fetishism, which explains the forms of alienated consciousness, comes to a halt at the same difficulty. Marx regards religion as an endangered residue, not even worthy of attention[28].

---

28. Nothing is more foreign to Marx than the anti-religious struggle. For Marx, it's a trap used by the free-thinking bourgeoisie to divert workers from serious matters.

"In general, the religious reflection of the real world can only disappear when the conditions of work and practical life present man with transparent, rational relationships with his fellow human beings and with nature. Social life, of which material production and the relationships it implies form the basis, will only be freed of the mystical cloud that veils its appearance when the work of freely associated men, acting consciously and masters of their own social movement, becomes manifest. But this requires a set of conditions of material existence in society that require a long and painful development."

Religion thus appears as a double of social life, a disguised double, unrecognizable at first glance, but a double. This analysis broadly explains the content of religious ideas in their social conditioning, their genesis as forms of social consciousness, but is silent on their necessity and force in their own right.

Indeed, "mirror religion" seems to lack any force of its own. It exists only as a double of real life. But why do men need this double? Why do societies often cling to it, using every means at their disposal? There is a widespread functionalist explanation, of which there are two modalities.

First modality: men are only governed by superstition. This is the thesis that Spinoza vigorously supports in the preface to his *Treatise on Theology and Politics*.

"Quinte-Curce rightly remarked (Liv. IV, chap. X) that no means of governing the multitude is more effective than superstition. Under the guise of religion, they are easily induced to worship kings as gods, or to abhor and detest them as a common scourge of the human race.

"To avoid this evil, the greatest care has been taken to surround religion, whether true or false, with a cult and an apparatus capable of giving it more weight in opinion than any other motive, and of making it the object of the most scrupulous and constant respect for all souls. Nowhere have these measures had more effect than among the Turks, where even discussion is considered sacrilegious, and where so many prejudices weigh down judgment that right Reason no longer has a place in the soul, and even doubt is made impossible." (*TTP*, preface, § 5-6, trans. Ch. Appuhn)

The explanation is not purely functionalist, since in the preceding paragraphs, Spinoza showed how men are inclined, by a kind of natural movement, to sink into superstition[29]. Originally natural, superstition is "shaped" and institutionalized in religions for political ends.

Second modality: "religion is the opium of the people". Marx's famous expression is often misunderstood because it is taken out of context and needs to be restored: "*Religious* misery is, on the one hand, *the expression* of real misery, and, on the other, the *protest* against real misery. Religion is the sigh of a creature overwhelmed by misfortune, the soul of a heartless world, just as it is the spirit of a spiritless age. It is *the opium* of the people." (*Contribution to the Critique of Hegel's Philosophy of Right*) We're not talking here about religion as a social institution, but about "religious misery", the misery of man doomed to vain fears, and for Marx, this religious misery is both an expression of and a protest against real misery.

So religion works for two combined reasons: it provides an imaginary solution to the sufferings of the multitude, and at the same time it enables them to be governed. But we need to go a step further. In his analysis of "The Elementary Forms of Religious Life", Durkheim defines religion as a "social fact" and even "a total social fact". "Religious representations are collective representations which express collective realities; rites are ways of acting which originate only within assembled groups and which are intended to arouse, maintain or remake certain mental states of these groups[30]." Religion is not, then, a more or less fanciful narrative against which we should fight in the name of scientific truth. The religious existence of society enables us to understand how society really exists. Durkheim starts from the "religious nature of man". Religion must be seen as an institution, and Durkheim adds that

---

29. A concise, hard-hitting analysis of religious superstition can also be found in the appendix to the first part of the *Ethics*.

30. Émile Durkheim, *Les Formes élémentaires de la vie religieuse*, book one, introduction. Quoted from the electronic edition "Classiques des sciences sociales", UQAC.

"a human institution cannot be based on error and lies: otherwise it could not have lasted. If it had not been founded in the nature of things, it would have encountered resistance in things from which it could not have triumphed." And that's why, in their own way, "all religions are true". Not, of course, because of their fabulous content, their miracles or their recourse to the supernatural… They are "true" in the sense that they organize a classification of the world, that they organize the great division between the sacred and the profane, to use Durkheim's thesis. God, angels and the whole shebang are undoubtedly the stuff of fantasy. But religion, its social efficacy, the way it organizes social relations—these are very real things, social things indeed, that is to say, as Marx puts it, "things that fall and do not fall under sense", but real things of the kind of reality that "human affairs" have.

Marx's analysis of the fetishism of the commodity has a singular relevance when we consider what is happening around brands and the great masses of salespeople and "communicators" in capitalist firms. Legendre asserts that "management", which aims for *dominium mundi,* has taken over the methods and shaping of the world from Christianity[31]. But Marx's analyses end where the serious stuff begins, i.e., when the split between the world of the commodity on the one hand and the world of religion on the other ceases, and the commodity itself becomes the fundamental structure of a new religious relationship. Because Marx was a man of his time—the time of the rise of capitalism, not the time of its absolute flowering—he was unable to draw out to the end the consequences of what he nonetheless posits as an essential element for understanding contemporary society: the fetish character of the commodity. The commodity is a fetish, which means it is religious—a "metaphysical" thing that dances on its wooden head.

So, like all religions in all known human societies, the submission of all life to the reign of the commodity may seem to offer

---

31. See Pierre LEGENDRE, *Dominium mundi*. Text for the film by Gérald Caillat. Éditions Mille et une nuits, 2007.

a shoring-up of society. We could evoke the return to that very old thing, the cult of the golden calf. On American banknotes is written "*in God we trust*". The medium indicates where the truth of the phrase lies: God is the dollar. Marx says that the abstract God of Protestantism is the ideal complement to the capitalist triumph of the commodity. It's much more than that: the God of the United States is not a sacred complement to the profane cult of the dollar. It is the cult of the dollar that is sacred. But the dollar is not sacred in the same way as gold was to the Spaniards who sacked America. Gold is a fetish for peoples who are still at the previous historical stage, that of feudalism, in which the accumulation of wealth is the result, and can only be the result, of conquest, plunder and rapine. The dollar is not fetish gold transformed into a paper symbol. The dollar is a sublimated commodity, reduced to its simplest expression, almost completely dematerialized, a commodity of which only the metaphysical quintessence remains.

Just as the Catholic Church was able to circumvent the old pagan background by introducing the pagan polytheistic element into the very heart of Christian ritual through a multitude of subaltern cults (cults of saints, relics, the Virgin Mary, the Turin shroud, Saint Bernadette at Lourdes, etc.), so the cult of abstract merchandise, of dematerialized money that no longer stops at any geographical barrier with its networked banks and stock markets, is complemented by a cult of commodities that carry the weight of the world.Similarly, the cult of abstract merchandise, of dematerialized money that no longer stops at any geographical barrier with networked banks and stock exchanges, is complemented by a cult of symbol-bearing goods, cults staged with a mastery that could almost make the inventors of the liquefaction of blood at San Gennaro in Naples jealous. The "marks" displayed on jerseys, shirts, shoes, hairbands and so on, are just one of the manifestations of these subaltern cults.

Advertising deploys liturgies, as Pierre Legendre puts it. Omnipresent, it tends to shape minds according to the needs of the commodity reign. The former CEO of TF1, Le Lay, rightly made himself famous by saying that his job was to sell available brain time. Here, the cold realism of the businessman is far superior to the trendy chatterboxes who look to advertising as a form of culture ("culture-pub"). It says bluntly what's at stake here: in a world where individuals are at once all isolated and all linked by commercial exchange, an individual's brain is a device like any other; available brain time is quite comparable to a computer's bandwidth. And it can be traded in the same way. This available brain, being a usable technical device subject to the principle of efficiency, is not the seat of a soul, not the physical substratum of an autonomous subject; it's a machine like any other, interesting only for the programs it can run. That's what advertising is for: to download the programs the brain is going to run (buy such and such merchandise, watch such and such a TV channel, etc.). But the final effect (stimulating consumption in order to realize value and thus enable capital accumulation to continue) is less important than all the other transformations generated by advertising. The world is a commodity thanks to advertising. What is not yet strictly a commodity in the world becomes its equivalent through the miracles of advertising hype. Already, some of the great works of classical music have become inaudible without the majority of people associating with them an image of perfume, instant coffee or an insurance company. The body, erotic desire, the beauty of natural landscapes, family life, myths and religions, the great works of literature and even the watchwords of subversion, all pass through the advertising mill, transformed into so many signs of abstract merchandise. We're sometimes surprised that some ads are so sophisticated and plastically beautiful that we forget the "brand", the product being promoted. Perhaps it's because advertising, unlike the advertising of yesteryear, which focused on the use value of a commodity, is intended to arouse the desire for possession in general, the desire for the enjoyment of commercial exchange, an abstract, incorporeal enjoyment in line with Protestant morality.

Hegel said that reading the newspaper is the prayer of the citizen. The advertising spot is the prayer of the modern swinger.

The function of prayer is not to confess a faith, to enunciate a truth about a transcendent reality. It's about forging attitudes and reflexes, bending bodies and minds like ritual dances or military training. The same applies to advertising. It is only incidentally aimed at informing the future buyer of the product's properties and qualities. It disposes minds (free brains) to accept a given social order, the order of a commodity society based on unlimited consumption and production.

Flows and Networks: A Deleuzian World?

The world is a commodity: it's philosophy again that's telling us this, and not traditionalist philosophy, not grandpa's dusty metaphysics, but modern, hip, protest philosophy, the kind that came to the fore in 1968 and beyond. Hobbes' genius in conceiving society as the organization of war between individuals was to grasp exactly the nature of the capitalist society that was laying its foundations in seventeenth-century England. Deleuze's genius lies in his grasp of the full-blown capitalism of the late 20th century. In place of an ontology of stable entities and hierarchies of being, Deleuze substitutes an ontology of flows and networks. The world of commodities is exactly that: flows and networks, financial flows circulating in networks. In his lecture on *L'Anti-Œdipe*, Deleuze writes[32]: "What passes over the body of a society? It's always flows, and a person is always a break in the flow. A person is always a point of departure for the production of flows, a point of arrival for the reception of flows of any kind, or an interception of several flows. Marx wasn't saying anything different: the commodity conceals within itself the formal possibility of crisis: it's enough that the A-M conversion or the M-A conversion no longer takes place. And how could this happen? Quite simply, when the buyer or seller cuts

---

32. See *Webdeleuze:* http://www.webdeleuze.com/

off the flow, keeping the merchandise for himself until better times, or leaving it in the hands of the seller. The flow must never stop.

As flows circulate, they form networks. The network is characterized by the absence of hierarchy—like the commodity, it is democratic by construction. Before the commodity, i.e. before the law of value, all are equal, just as all men are "equal before the law" according to the 1789 Declaration of Rights. Like modernity, which has made change its law, the network is change itself: what makes the network what it is are flows, and the commodity is a continual flow, a flow that must never be interrupted or it will cause thrombosis and the death of the network. But within this flow, the commodity can only remain itself by metamorphosing with each interval of time it spends in the network.

Once again, it was Marx who perceived the world of merchandise in all its breadth and grasped its essence. In the traditional market, the medieval market, for example, the seller of goods sells to buy. The peasant sells his wheat to buy a garment. When the starving man has his wheat and the peasant no longer goes bare-assed, the cycle of exchange has come to an end. It has come to an end because it has fulfilled its purpose, which is external to commodity exchange: the satisfaction of needs. This elementary exchange of goods, common to all civilizations that have already become urbanized, is what the Greeks, and Aristotle in particular, called "economic". It is also what Braudel calls "economy", in contrast to the most elementary stratum of human survival, "material civilization".

Capital, or the World Inverted

But Marx doesn't stop there. The whole of *Capital*'s analysis lies in a reversal that is truly the essence, and it's because it's the essence that we've often only seen or wanted to see a drop of it. Marx sums up simple commodity circulation, or economics in the Aristotelian sense, with the formula M-A-M: I exchange a commodity I own but don't use for money, and with that money I buy a commodity of equivalent value that I need. In this cycle, we start with specific, concrete work—the work that produces wheat, for example—which is intended to satisfy someone else's need, and end up with the commodity that satisfies my need. We're fully in the "vital cycle", to use Michel Henry's expression. Marx sums up the transition from commodity to capital in another formula, A-M-A'. Apparently, it's the same formula as the previous one, seen from a different angle. The generalized exchange of the commodity can in fact be schematized as follows: M-A-M-A-… and so A-M-A is just one part of this generalized exchange. But this is not the case at all. In the second formula, the commodity is transformed into capital. A-M-A': this formula only makes sense if A' is greater than A, i.e. if A' = A + dA, where dA represents profit. In the M-A-M cycle, the starting and end points are the needs of human life. In the A-M-A' cycle, the starting point and end point are money. Money, which is merely the means of circulating goods, now becomes the end of economic activity, and goods, which were the means of satisfying human needs, become the means of increasing monetary wealth.

Marx explicitly relates this transformation of the commodity into capital to the Aristotelian distinction between economics and chrematistics. Economy is the art of providing for domestic needs: *oïkos is* the house, and economy is therefore the set of rules (*nomos)* to be followed in order to manage one's household properly. Chrematistics, on the other hand, is the art of acquisition and enrichment. According to Aristotle, economics is natural, since it corresponds to human needs, whereas chrematistics is "unnatural". And not only does Marx explicitly take up this distinction, he also pursues it repeatedly and from different angles. The lure of gain, the *auri sacra fames, is* what characterizes the capitalist. But more than moral, Marx's condemnation—like Aristotle's, moreover—reaches the ontological level: a man who spends his life accumulating money is engaged in an unnatural activity. He is engaged in an activity that denies his human nature. This is why, according to Marx, the capitalist is "alienated", since, his life being subject to the imperative of capital accumulation, he himself becomes a means of what he possesses. The "sacred hunger for gold" gradually transforms our capitalist into a "fanatical agent of production for production's sake". In capitalist production, the worker is transformed into a servant of the machine, becoming a stranger to himself. But from a certain point of view, there's a symmetrical process on the capitalist's side. But the difference remains decisive. The capitalist's alienation (his transformation into personified capital) is the source of his power, while the worker's alienation is at the same time his servitude.

The fact remains that the transformation of the commodity into capital, the inversion of means and ends and the reversal of the vital cycle signified by the domination of the commodity over all human activity, is a radical dehumanization. If humanity forms a community, the commodity realizes this community in a form that excludes humanity and reduces humans to insatiable exchangers, increasingly isolated from one another.

At a rally in Saint-Étienne on November 9, 2006, candidate Nicolas Sarkozy declared, carried away by his momentum: "Man is not a commodity like any other. In the midst of his "spiritualist" logorrhea, the future President of the Republic brutally reveals the truth of the economic, social, political and cultural system of which he is the herald and tireless defender: in capitalism, man is a commodity, admittedly not like any other, more devious, more difficult to handle than any other, but a commodity all the same. We're back to the crux of the matter.

Chapter III.
Capital, or Permanent Revolution

The question we need to ask ourselves, before going any further, is why this commodification of the world has worked so well in the end. That is, why capitalism has (temporarily?) won. For there is a kernel of truth in Fukuyama's cries of victory. Historically, capitalism has prevailed over all its competitors. Old civilizations such as China and India can only recover by submitting to the laws of capitalist production. Genuinely existing socialism", the kind built in the feverish early years of the October 1917 revolution, has left the stage of history. Communists, questioned about the rather hasty methods of the Soviet regime, replied that you don't make an omelette without breaking eggs. All the eggs were broken, and there was never an omelette. Even "democratic socialism" looks bad; the social reforms intended to avoid the unpleasant recourse to revolution are running out of steam. Under the pressure of international competition, we have to start cutting back on the social state. And Nordic social democracy is fading fast. The "communist" countries that have not collapsed have become authoritarian capitalist countries under the leadership of a communist party reconverted into a party of billionaires. Chinese scenario, but also Vietnamese scenario and tomorrow morning Cuban scenario.

Victory all round, then. To what does capitalism owe it? There are some almost obvious reasons, and a few less obvious ones. For the obvious reasons, we can give three.

Firstly, capitalism has shown its vitality and ability to triumph over the most serious crises, even if only in the short term and at a high human cost.

Secondly, capitalism has realized the utopia of the affluent society, or at least a passable form of it.

Finally, the commodity is identified with freedom, perhaps a reprehensible conception of freedom, perhaps a crazy freedom in the long term, but freedom nonetheless.

The Dynamics of Capital

The dynamics of capitalism have been the subject of so many studies that we won't attempt to summarize them. To begin with, we'll confine ourselves to giving ample extracts from the first pages of the *Communist Manifesto*, in which Marx and Engels deliver a vibrant apology for the revolutionary role of the bourgeoisie:

"The bourgeoisie has played an eminently revolutionary role in history.

"Wherever it has conquered power, it has trampled feudal, patriarchal and idyllic relations underfoot. All the complex and varied ties that bind feudal man to his 'natural superiors', she has broken them without pity, leaving no other bond between man and man than cold interest, the harsh demands of 'cash payment'. It has drowned the sacred thrills of religious ecstasy, chivalric enthusiasm and petty-bourgeois sentimentality in the icy waters of selfish calculation. It has turned personal dignity into a mere exchange value; it has substituted the many liberties so dearly won for the single, merciless freedom of commerce. In short, it has replaced the exploitation masked by religious and political illusions with open, shameless, direct and brutal exploitation.

"The bourgeoisie has stripped of their halo all activities that were previously considered venerable and regarded with holy respect. The doctor, the lawyer, the priest, the poet, the scientist—they've turned them into hired hands.

"The bourgeoisie has torn away the veil of sentimentality that covered family relationships, reducing them to mere relationships of money.

"The bourgeoisie revealed how the brutal manifestation of force in the Middle Ages, so admired by reaction, found its natural complement in the crassest laziness. The bourgeoisie was the first to show what human activity is capable of. It created wonders other than the Egyptian pyramids, Roman aqueducts and Gothic cathedrals; it led expeditions other than invasions and crusades.

"The bourgeoisie cannot exist without constantly revolutionizing the instruments of production, which means the relations of production, i.e. all social relations. On the contrary, the unchanged maintenance of the old mode of production was, for all previous industrial classes, the primary condition of their existence. This continual upheaval of production, this constant shaking of the whole social system, this perpetual agitation and insecurity, distinguish the bourgeois era from all previous ones. All social relations, frozen and covered in rust, with their procession of ancient and venerable conceptions and ideas, dissolve; those that replace them age before they can ossify. All that had solidity and permanence goes up in smoke, all that was sacred is profaned, and men are finally forced to view their conditions of existence and their mutual relationships with disillusioned eyes.

"Driven by the need for ever-new outlets, the bourgeoisie is invading the entire globe. It has to establish itself everywhere, exploit everywhere, build relationships everywhere.

"By exploiting the world market, the bourgeoisie has given a cosmopolitan character to production and consumption in all countries. To the despair of reactionaries, it has stripped industry of its national base. Old national industries have been destroyed, and are still being destroyed every day. They are being supplanted by new industries, the adoption of which is becoming a matter of life and death for all civilized nations, industries which no longer employ indigenous raw materials, but raw materials from the most distant regions, and whose products are consumed not only in the country itself, but in all parts of the globe. In place of old needs, satisfied by national products, new needs are emerging, requiring products from the most distant lands and climates for their satisfaction. In place of the old isolation of self-sufficient provinces and nations, universal relations are developing, a universal interdependence of nations. And what is true of material production is no less true of intellectual production. The intellectual works of one nation become the common property of all. National narrowness and exclusivism become more and more impossible, and a universal literature is born from the multiplicity of national and local literatures.

"Through the rapid perfection of production tools and the infinite improvement of means of communication, the bourgeoisie is drawing even the most barbaric nations into the stream of civilization. The cheapness of its products is the heavy artillery that breaches all the walls of China, forcing the most stubbornly anti-foreign barbarians to surrender. On pain of death, it forces all nations to adopt the bourgeois mode of production; it forces them to introduce so-called civilization, i.e. to become bourgeois. In a word, it shapes the world in its own image.

"The bourgeoisie has subjugated the countryside to the city. It has created enormous cities; it has prodigiously increased the population of the cities in relation to that of the countryside, and in so doing, it has torn a large part of the population from the stultifying life of the fields. In the same way that it has subjugated the countryside to the city, barbaric or semi-barbaric countries to civilized ones, it has subordinated peasant peoples to bourgeois peoples, the East to the West.

"The bourgeoisie is increasingly eliminating the fragmentation of the means of production, property and population. It has agglomerated the population, centralized the means of production and concentrated ownership in a small number of hands. The total consequence of these changes was political centralization. Independent provinces, barely federated among themselves, with different interests, laws, governments and customs tariffs, were united into a single nation, with a single government, a single law, a single national class interest, behind a single customs cordon.

"The bourgeoisie, in the course of its barely secular class domination, has created more numerous and colossal productive forces than all past generations put together. The domestication of the forces of nature, machines, the application of chemistry to industry and agriculture, steam navigation, railroads, electric telegraphs, the clearing of entire continents, the regulation of rivers, whole populations springing from the soil - what previous century would have suspected that such productive forces lay dormant in the bosom of social labor?

"The means of production and exchange, on which the bourgeoisie was built, were created within feudal society. At a certain stage in the development of these means of production and exchange, the conditions under which feudal society produced and exchanged, the feudal organization of agriculture and manufacturing, in a word the feudal property regime, ceased to correspond to the developing productive forces. They hindered production rather than advancing it. They became so many chains. They had to be broken. And they were. In its place arose free competition, with an appropriate social and political constitution, with the economic and political supremacy of the bourgeois class."

We'd be hard-pressed to find writers capable of such enthusiasm for capitalism. Stock-market columnists and writers on the business pages of decaying dailies, while boundlessly subservient to the powerful (political and financial), are incapable of praising capitalism with such enthusiasm. It's true that Marx, in 1848, thought that capitalism's progressive role was over, and that we should prepare to move on to something else, i.e., to apply to capitalism the methods he himself had applied to previous regimes. But we have to admit that Marx was largely mistaken, as devout Marxists (an endangered species, by the way) say, about the deadlines. He had announced too soon what was bound to happen sooner or later. Two decades later, Marx reaffirmed that the process leading to the "expropriation of the expropriators" was to be accomplished with the same necessity that presides over the metamorphoses of nature. In line with these messianic predictions, Marxists have never ceased to announce the imminence of this event—just as the first Christians announced the Last Judgment. In the debate on "revisionism" that pitted "orthodox" Marxism against Bernstein, Rosa Luxemburg took a radical stance, showing that capital accumulation could only continue if capitalism found outlets in a non-capitalist sector. She defended what came to be known as the "final crisis" thesis. A few years later, Lenin wrote *Imperialism, the Supreme Stage of Capitalism* (1916), a title that needs no further comment here. With the introduction of the war economy during the 1914-1918 conflict, Lenin saw the establishment of a new mode of capitalist state management, state monopoly capitalism, which he saw as the final stage before socialism. The Russian Revolution and the Great Depression of 1929 largely nurtured the idea that the end of capitalism was just around the corner. The last heirs to the tradition of revolutionary Marxism, the Trotskyists, who numbered only a handful in 1938, adopted a "program" of the "Fourth International" proclaiming that "the productive forces have ceased to grow" and that capitalism had entered a phase of irreversible decay. Although the course of events belied these predictions, they resurfaced at regular intervals. 1968, with the outbursts of youth and radicalized sections of the working class, from American campuses to the streets of Prague, Paris and Rome, once again heralded the imminence of revolution. "History is biting us in the neck", wrote one of the leaders of what was still called the Communist League (Daniel Bensaïd, 1972). Ernest Mandel, the great Marxist economist, wrote a vast synthesis published in French under the title *Le Troisième Âge du capitalisme (The Third Age of Capitalism)*[33]: the third age is that of old age, the prelude to senility and inevitable extinction.

While apocalyptic proclamations have often been derided, the history of the last two centuries has also given rise to phases in which apologetic proclamations prevailed: capitalism had found a way to resolve its contradictions, and it was only within this mode of production that we could hope to fight to improve the lot of the working classes. Bernstein's "revisionism" starts from the observation that there was no final crisis, and that the development of capitalism makes it possible to build a long-term reformist policy. Bernstein elaborated his theses a few years before the cataclysm of August 1914. During the Thirty Glorious Years, despite the threat of conflagration between the two "superpowers", there was no shortage of prophets announcing the (peaceful) convergence of capitalism and Soviet "communism", with the welfare state gradually resolving the social question while the democratization of the Soviet system seemed only a matter of time. The period

---

33. The original German title is *Der Spätkapitalismus*, "late capitalism", which is far less connotative. The expression *Spätkapitalismus* comes from Theodor Adorno.

from the Reagan-Thatcher era to the early 2000s was one of those times when capitalism seemed eternal, until, from the bursting of the Internet "bubble" to the *sub-prime* crisis, a new period of crisis began.

The two symmetrical discourses, apocalyptic and apologetic, dominate according to the oscillations of the capitalist mode of production. Marx defined concepts that enable us to understand how "ideal-typical" capitalism works, but real capitalism never corresponds to the ideal-type. There are more or less stable operating regimes, regimes that can only endure for a more or less limited period until the accumulation of contradictions internal to the capitalist mode of production ushers in a period of crisis that, until now, has been no more than the transition from one accumulation regime to another. These periods—typically the seventies—can be called "phase transitions", to use Gianfranco La Grassa's expression[34].

The evolutionary scheme of orthodox Marxism is based on the thesis of the increasing concentration and centralization of capital, leading in a more or less linear fashion to the reduction of the capitalist class to a handful of purely parasitic profiteers, opposed by the great mass of wage-earners who, from factory manager to laborer, are employed in productive tasks. Such a capitalism would be both increasingly statist and increasingly bureaucratic. But this scheme doesn't work. Real capitalism never becomes state capitalism (even under Nazism!), and oscillates between a regime of centralized, state organization and a regime of competition and strategic confrontation between the major blocs that make up capital. More on this later. In any case, there is no "natural" tendency for the capitalist mode of production to self-suppress. Nor is there any terminal stage or final crisis. The price of all this? More on that later.

---

34. *Il capitalismo oggi*, Petite Plaisance, 2004 and *Gli strateghi del capitale*, Manifesto-libri, 2005.

Consumer Society and Exploitation

Once we've analyzed the dynamics of capitalism, we need to examine its results. If happiness is measured by the ability to enjoy the products of human labor, capitalism has created an abundance like no other period in human history. Communism, according to Marx, was supposed to put an end to scarcity… and here we are. Admittedly, not for everyone and not at the same level. But it's enough to stroll through the shopping malls of the big cities in advanced capitalist countries to measure this abundance.

Comparisons with the 1900s and 1950s would be instructive. Basic goods (food, clothing, etc.) account for only a relatively small proportion of a worker's average wage, whose income is swallowed up in new needs. Marx had rejected the thesis (defended by Lassalle and taken up by Ricardo) of an "iron law" of wages that would lead to a kind of growing pauperization of workers. For Marx, wages are determined by the value of the commodities needed to maintain and reproduce labor power, but this amount has nothing to do with some biologically-determined "living wage", but rather with the social conditions of time and place. Poverty is usually only relative. If you don't have a car or an Internet connection, don't go on vacation and live in a house that's too small, you're poor. But seen through the eyes of a late nineteenth-century worker, he lacks little or nothing: he eats his fill, is cared for when he falls ill, has clothes that are quite often new, his home is heated, he has hot water and electricity, his children go to school and don't have to work ten hours a day from the age of seven or eight… and even if he's unemployed, he can always distract himself by watching television.

While the transition from independent worker to proletarian was experienced essentially as a decline and the irretrievable loss of freedom, and while real misery could refer to a happier past (see Marx's long pages on the destruction of the English independent peasantry in the chapter on the primitive accumulation of capital), contemporary misery is perhaps first and foremost the renunciation of a better future. In terms of the use values available to him, a worker at the beginning of the 21st century is undoubtedly "richer" than his counterpart in the 1950s, but his hopes and relative social situation are much lower, if not reduced to nothing. However, in advanced capitalist societies, for the time being, the average situation of the working class remains bearable, and it is borne by the poorest, even if it is badly borne, with much resentment—but resentment does not make revolutionary sentiment. To which it should be added that this resentment is hardly turned against the moguls of neoliberal capitalism or the billionaires of sport and showbiz, but rather against those who are just a little above (civil servants, for example) or those who are just a little below (immigrants).

While the working poor are a growing phenomenon in all advanced capitalist societies[35], this poverty remains relative and is developing against a backdrop of ever-increasing material wealth, not only in the old, wealthy strongholds of Europe and North America, but also in South-East Asia and, to some extent, Latin America. The lightning expansion of computers and cell phones demonstrates both the inventiveness of capitalism, capable of creating radically new needs and offering products that colonize all sectors of social life, and its ability to escape the death by thrombosis promised by orthodox Marxism. The old Marxian distinction between sector I (the production of the means of production) and sector II (the production of consumer goods) is taking on water on all sides: for example, the computer industry produces means of production that are also consumer goods. As a result, the structural misalignment between the two sectors (one of the fundamental elements of Marxian crisis theory) no longer plays such an important role.

We can argue about the value of this abundance of material goods, and underline the growth of what Paul Ariès calls "junkproduction[36]", but the fact remains that abundance itself appears very

---

35. See *7 millions de travailleurs pauvres* by Jacques Cotta, Fayard, 2007.
36. See Paul Ariès, *Le Mésusage*, Parangon/Vs, Lyon, 2007.

widely as a patent fact in the consciousness of billions of people, including those plunged into the deepest poverty, but who can see the Land of plenty almost live. The Internet even offers the illusion of a society where everything is free and everyone can take what they need. The issue of audiovisual piracy is interesting from this point of view: many Internet users find it abnormal to pay to record music and films, simply because the general Internet model is one of free access. Once you've paid for access to the network (and the cost of access itself is quite derisory, being the equivalent of a few packs of cigarettes or two rounds of aperitifs at the café), you can read newspapers, read books, listen to or watch lectures, chat with virtual friends anywhere in the world—and all without paying a cent. If I can read the whole of Molière or Shakespeare for free, why should I have to pay to listen to a decrepit crooner or a voiceless singer spouting her mawkish ritornellos? Admittedly, if we consider the whole of what revolves around the Internet, free is a myth. The software services offered by a famous search engine are paid for by advertising and therefore, ultimately, by the consumer, who is often also an Internet user. Free software is financed by foundations backed by powerful IT groups who use free software as a weapon to strike blows at Microsoft's quasi-monopoly. The law of value is harsh, but it's the law, and it continues to impose itself in the new "economic models" that are triumphing on the Internet—and which, incidentally, can only triumph there, due to the rather special nature of the "commodity" itself. But from the consumer's point of view, the Internet is the realm of both abundance and gratuity.

Capitalism and Freedom

Capitalism is a dynamic system, open to the future, to permanent innovation, and at least virtually provides abundance, but also, and this will be its moral justification, it is inseparable from freedom. Here again, beyond the ideological rhetoric produced in abundance by capital's propaganda specialists, there is a rational core whose scope must be clearly understood.

Marx, following Hegel, understands that modern bourgeois society produces "free" individuals, i.e. freed from personal dependence. In the family, and in all the social relations linked to it, when the unit of production is the household, individuals do not exist for themselves; together with the other members of the household, they form an organic unity. Within this unit, they exist only in relation to each other: son of, father of, wife of, maid of, etc. In what Hegel calls the "household", the individual does not exist for himself. In what Hegel calls "bourgeois civil society" (*Bürgerliche Gesellschaft*), individuals relate to each other through exchange (I satisfy my needs through my own labor, or through the labor of another, on condition that another can satisfy his needs through my own labor). And this is the first condition of freedom. Criticizing theories about the state of nature as well as nostalgia for the world of craftsmanship, Hegel defends modern capitalist society:

> "In the social state of industry, the individual is reduced to himself, and this sense of self is linked most closely to the requirement of a legal situation. This is why the sense of freedom and order developed mainly in cities. On the other hand, social state no. 1 has little to think about on its own; what it acquires is a gift of foreign provenance, a gift of nature; this feeling of dependence is in it something primary, and we can just as easily link to it that which consists in some men of tolerating everything that may well happen. This is why social state no. 1 is more inclined to servility, and social state no. 2 more inclined to freedom." (*Principles of the Philosophy of Law*, addendum to § 204).

Marx said as much (see excerpts from the *Manifesto* above). By breaking traditional ties, it transforms the worker into a seller of labor power who meets a buyer of labor power on the market, and between them a contract is established, a contract that presupposes the freedom of the contracting parties. Marx goes on to show that this contractual form is opposed to its actual content, since the seller of labor power does not sell a commodity that could be separated from him; he sells his skin, "to be tanned", as Marx puts it. The content of the contract-form is the domination of capital over labor[37]. But at the same time, this form is contradictory to this content.

The best authors, therefore, attest that capitalism has, at the very least, created the preconditions for the existence of autonomous individuals. The heteronomous individual, subject to the order of the *cosmos*, the Church or the *polis*, is succeeded by an individual who depends solely on himself. Standard economic theory assumes that individuals are rational, capable at all times of making the best choices for themselves, and therefore responsible for their own fate in all spheres, with some credibility, in the great tradition of philosophical modernity, that of Descartes (the "I" as the true foundation of all knowledge), Rousseau (freedom means obeying the law that one has prescribed for oneself) or Kant (especially the Kant of What *is Enlightenment?*). And this claim is not, or at least not entirely, usurped. Capitalism has ruthlessly broken the bonds of personal dependence—and from this point of view, the bourgeois patriarchal family, the target of the soixante-huitards' protesters, is not an essential element of the capitalist mode of production, but a survival from the most distant past. By banning guilds (e.g., the Le Chapelier law), by opening up social positions to everyone according to talent and merit, by making free choice of occupation an essential right, the triumphant bourgeoisie of the 19th century established a new regime of freedom that had not existed before. This is "negative liberty", as Isaiah Berlin calls it, which means being able to do whatever does not harm others, being free from political interference in one's private affairs and so on.

---

37. We can refer to the work of Jacques Bidet and his reconstruction of Marxist theory by seeking to unify the contractualist and Marxist traditions (see in particular his *Théorie générale*, PUF, "Actuel Marx" collection).

To understand the reasons behind the ideological victory of "neo-liberalism" over the last three decades, we obviously need to take into account capitalism's capacity to assume a certain form of claim to freedom. The implicit slogan of the eighties, the one under which the great ideological battle that is unravelling in the nineties was fought, was "All capitalists!" It was a swindle: by definition, for there to be capitalists, in the full sense of the term, there needs to be a mass of non-capitalists who have no other choice for a living than to sell their labor power to the capitalist who will agree to exploit them. But like all swindles, this one could only work because of the shimmering promises made: to break the shackles of statutes that prevent proper recognition of each individual's value, to give greater autonomy in the workplace, to allow greater mobility, and so on. The main theme of the management style introduced in the 1970s was freedom.

By invoking nostalgia for the thirty glorious years and a return to the "Keynesian" state, the "anti-liberals" are completely mistaken. Employees undoubtedly regret—for some of them—the guarantees and protections of that era. But, in truth, these guarantees and protections did not derive from statutory rights, but simply from full employment, which gave sellers of labor power a certain position of strength. But corporate discipline was (and still is) unbearably caporal, and promises of future well-being came at a high price. And it wasn't the bureaucratic organization of trade unions that could have given employees a space for freedom and individual initiative. The model of the "trente glorieuses" (thirty glorious years) broke down not only because of the change in strategy of the major capitalist groups, but also, and perhaps primarily, because of workers' revolts against the organization of work in large Taylorist/Fordist companies. May '68 in France was preceded by strikes which were genuine revolts, often violent and often led by young, unskilled workers. In February 1967, the 3,200 workers at Rhodiaceta in Besançon went on strike, and the plant was occupied by mobile guards. A few weeks later, in Le Mans, the town had to be surrounded by the CRS. In Mulhouse, the prefecture was attacked by demonstrators. In January 1968, the 4,800 workers at SAVIEM in Caen occupied the factory and confronted the CRS with batons and slingshots. After May 1968, this movement continued. Wage increases and the threat of unemployment were certainly among the main demands, but so were the fight against "infernal cadences" and the demand for freedom within the company, all of which were to be recuperated by the various varieties of self-management before ending up miserably in the "new workers' rights" recognized by the Auroux laws of 1982. The "May creep" in Italian companies, especially in the industrial north, with Turin's FIAT at its epicenter, followed the same lines of development.

In short, "neoliberalism" won because it succeeded in appearing as the only viable response to the massive rejection of factory discipline (and not just factory discipline). The reality of the wage-earning condition today shows that, as we might have supposed, this discourse of liberal freedom is really a swindle. Individual initiative means proving ever more ardently that we are capable of self-exploitation, of doing without a foreman to impose our own rhythms; the new management methods have above all had the function of breaking down any spirit of collective resistance and imposing "adherence" of employees to the "corporate spirit", not hesitating to resort to all the tricks of manipulation and brainwashing sometimes worthy of the worst sects. In short, liberal freedom has only been freedom for the owners of capital, and increased exploitation for the sellers of labour power.

As it happens, in France, the ruling Left has been the main organizer of this great swindle since 1982. From the apology of "La France qui gagne" (Laurent Fabius) to "Vive la crise" (the famous show presented by Yves Montand), from Jacques Delors to Bernard Tapie, the "French socialism" promised by the PS became one of the worst periods in the country's recent history[38]. The Socialist Party of the immediate post-May 68 era was best placed to bridge the gap

---

38. On this point, see François Cusset, *La Décennie: le grand cauchemar des années 80*, La Découverte, new edition 2008.

between "libertarian" aspirations and the neoliberal orientations of the ruling classes. Whereas in England, it was Mrs Thatcher who broke the back of the trade union movement during the great miners' strike, in France, it was the Left who undertook the "dirty work" (the expression was coined by Laurent Fabius, then Prime Minister) of liquidating the Lorraine steel industry and organizing the decline in purchasing power and mass unemployment that was to disrupt a workers' trade union movement that was already poorly established, except in a few large companies.

If the liberal discourse on freedom is indeed ideological—it is an inverted representation of reality—then it did not impose itself solely through its capacity to seduce and recuperate anti-authoritarian aspirations, but also through political battles and the ability of American and European leaders to understand that post-war conditions were on the point of exhaustion, and that a new historical phase was opening up in which capitalism would be able to free itself from the constraints imposed on it by the balance of power resulting from the collapse of Nazism. All this happened all the more easily because historical communism had become, in the eyes of the masses (and not just hysterical anti-communists), the most complete incarnation of "totalitarian" tyranny. A tyranny that had nothing to do with the "dictatorship of the proletariat", but whose revolts and subsequent repression, in Prague in 1968 or in Poland at the end of the 1970s, showed that it was rather a dictatorship over the proletariat.

Capitalism Constantly Revolutionizes its own Base

So capitalism is the sole bearer of the flag of freedom. And the battle now seems to be fought on opposite sides. For decades, the ruling classes found their most appropriate political expression in the "party of order". After the excesses of the revolution, the aim was to consolidate the new order and new property relations, but also to seal a lasting agreement with the old ruling classes.

Conversely, movements hostile to the bourgeois order were included in the "movement party" by which the left came to refer to itself. Conservatism versus progress, reaction versus reform or revolution, moral order versus freedom of morals, the haves versus the have-nots—all these figures in the history of the last two centuries have structured our perception of reality to the point of making it unrecognizable.

Yet we should have understood, as Marx invited us to do, that capitalism is revolutionary by its very nature. It can only survive, says Marx, by constantly revolutionizing its own productive base. Conservatism and capitalism don't mix. Let's see why. Anyone who has tried to read *Capital* seriously will know that Book III is fraught with serious theoretical difficulties, which explains why the work could not be completed before Marx's death. As we have done throughout this work, we will leave aside the voluminous Marxological as well as Marxist literature that deals with these difficulties[39]. According to Marx, the most important law is the law of the tendency of the rate of profit to fall. This law, which he attempts to show is indeed a structural law of the capitalist mode of production, was more or less verified in Marx's day. It overlapped, in a very different way, with another economic law that clearly serves as a model, Ricardo's law of diminishing returns.

This law has its origins in another law, that of the increase in the organic composition of capital. The idea is as follows: the process of capital accumulation tends almost naturally to increase the share of dead labor (constant capital) in relation to living labor (labor power): this ratio of dead capital to living capital is the organic composition of capital. Since profit derives from the surplus value realized on the use of labor power, the increase in the organic composition of capital leads to a fall in the rate of profit: "The capitalist process of production is by its very nature a process of accumulation. We

---

39. These difficulties relate to the very nature of what Marx describes as the laws of development of the capitalist mode of production. On this subject, see our *La Théorie de la connaissance chez Marx*, L'Harmattan, 1996.

have seen that as capitalist production progresses, the value that should simply be reproduced and conserved increases as a result of the growing productivity of labor, even though the quantity of labor employed remains constant." (*Capital*, Book III, "The Law of the Tendency of the Rate of Profit to Fall") The fact that the rate of profit falls does not mean that profit itself falls absolutely. By using a greater quantity of capital, we can obtain a constant mass of profit, but at a lower rate. And this is the first reason why capitalism is constantly expanding: it needs to find new fields of capital accumulation. It's for this reason, too, that capitalism must subject the entire planet to its rule.

But Marx soon comes up against a thorny problem: "When one compares the enormous development of the productivity of social labor, even considering only these last thirty years, with the productivity of earlier periods, when one considers in particular the enormous mass of fixed capital that social production absorbs apart from what is represented by tooling properly so called, one sees that it is no longer merely a question of solving the difficulty which has occupied economists and which consists in determining the cause of the fall in the rate of profit, but that it is far more important to explain why this fall is not greater, nor more rapid." (*Capital* III, X) If we add that the "tendential fall" is so tendential that long phases of rising rates of profit can be observed, we grasp the complexity of the enigma. Marx provides some valuable explanations by listing the factors that contradict the falling rate of profit. We'll follow the order of Marx's presentation.

First factor: increased exploitation of labor. The formula for the rate of profit ($pl/(c+v)$ with pl for surplus value, c for constant capital and v for variable capital, i.e. the value of labor power) indicates that an increase in c can be offset by an increase in the ratio pl/v, i.e. the rate of exploitation, or the ratio between free labor and paid labor. There are several classic methods for increasing labor exploitation.

The first method is to lengthen working hours (what Marx called absolute surplus value). For a very long time, economists (especially those on the left) talked about a so-called secular downward trend in working hours. This was generally true up to the 1970s, albeit with considerable variations. In France, the working day was limited to 11 hours in 1841. The working week was then limited to 6 days. Then in 1919, the day was limited to 8 hours, and the 40-hour week was snatched away in 1936 with paid vacations. This trend continued in France and Germany well into the 1980s, with the introduction of the 35-hour week in Germany and then in France, the increase in paid vacations and the lowering of the retirement age. For political reasons, however, these two countries are exceptions, and only in relative terms: in France, the 35-hour working week was very often paid for at the price of sacrificing long-standing gains (breaks, exceptional days off) and increasing hourly flexibility. Pietro Basso[40] shows that, over the past quarter century, working hours in all Western countries have tended to increase once again, as a result of a reduction in public holidays, an increase in the retirement age, and a fall in wages that forces many employees to hold down two jobs (a particularly common phenomenon in the United States and Great Britain).

The second method is to intensify work. Here again, Basso's book provides valuable insights. Intensification means, first and foremost, accelerating work rates and eliminating idle time. The Tokyoist factory principle of "just in time" is first and foremost aimed at eliminating idle time. On a traditional "Fordist" production line, the real useful time, i.e. the time during which the worker actually expends labor power on behalf of his boss, is around 45 seconds per minute. Organization according to the principles of Toyotism enables us to achieve a useful time of 55 to 57 seconds per minute[41].

---

40. See Pietro Basso, *Temps modernes, horaires antiques*, Page Deux, Collection "Cahiers libres", 2005.

41. Nevertheless, economists in power continue to regard the theory of labor-value as obsolete. That says a lot about this so-called "science of economics". But it's true that the economist who is paid handsomely to spout nonsense useful to the powerful isn't often interested in what's going on in the bunkers of the global economy.

Second factor: reducing wages below the value of labor power. If we consider that the value of labor power does not correspond to a biological minimum (see *above*), but to given social conditions, it is possible to reduce the wage paid below this value of labor power. For example, when we see that workers with a normal job no longer earn enough to pay for housing, sleeping in emergency shelters or in their car[42], this means that the wage has fallen below the value of labour power. The widespread phenomenon of *poor workers* in all advanced capitalist countries shows that this is by no means a secondary issue. The use of clandestine workers, most often immigrants, in sectors such as construction, catering or agriculture, can be linked to this factor. Offshoring is part of this process: you can find much cheaper labor a few thousand kilometers away! The process is never-ending: at the beginning of August 2008, we learned that the German company Adidas was considering relocating its production from China to Vietnam or Laos, because the wages of Chinese workers in the province of Shenzen reach 1,000 yuan, or 93 euros a month. Strictly speaking, Marx's thesis of absolute pauperization may be wrong, but it's clear that pauperizing the working class is one of the most common strategies employed to counter the falling rate of profit.

Real wages can also fall when the value of consumer goods included in the value of labor power decreases. For example, a faster increase in agricultural labor productivity than that of industry leads to a relative drop in the cost of food, which for a very long time had represented the essential part of the wage. If workers' living standards have risen significantly, the relative fall in the cost of agricultural products plays a decisive role. European (through the CAP) and North American governments have, moreover, steered the prices of agricultural products and intervened in a voluntarist and often highly dirigiste manner to accelerate the restructuring of agriculture. The spectacular rise in labor productivity in the household appliance and consumer electronics industries has also

---

42. See Jacques COTTA, *7 millions de travailleurs pauvres, op. cit.*

raised the standard of living of salaried workers, without increasing the share of wages in total production, i.e., without jeopardizing the rate of exploitation.

Third factor: the devaluation of constant capital. Increasing labor productivity in the production of the means of production lowers their value. This leads to an increase in the technical composition of capital (to put it quickly, the weight of machines in the overall labor process increases) at the same time as the value composition decreases. This hypothesis is clearly stated by Marx: "It may even happen that the mass of the elements of constant capital increases while its value remains invariable or even decreases." But what, for Marx, is merely a possibility, becomes the rule on a massive scale, for reasons he indicates: "The evolution that pushes for the increase of constant capital in relation to variable capital tends, through the increasing productivity of labor, to lower the value of the elements that constitute it, and to prevent its absolute value from increasing as rapidly as its material importance." This is precisely what is made possible, for example, by the revolution in automatic information processing, with the knock-on effects it has had throughout industrial and service production. Marx goes on to explain: "The depreciation of the material elements of capital under the action of the development of industry is also one of the factors which constantly act to counteract the fall in the rate of profit, although it can also in certain circumstances diminish the mass of profit, particularly when it has the effect of reducing the size of the capital employed. Once again, we see that the same causes both cause and hinder the fall in the rate of profit."

Fourth factor: relative overpopulation. Growth in labor productivity tends to replace workers with machines, leading to relative overpopulation. Marx distinguishes two effects. The first effect is the maintenance of a working-class population in conditions that are backward in relation to the general technical norm, a maintenance made possible by the drop in wages brought about by this overpopulation. The second effect is that the existence of this largely unoccupied overpopulation encourages the creation of new industries that can employ this workforce at low cost, thus generating juicy surplus profits. This is the great mystery that never ceases to amaze Keynesian leftists and blissful worshippers of reformism: how is it that the general crisis and mass unemployment benefit the owners of capital so much? Mass unemployment has played its role to the full over the last three decades, enabling capitalists to restore their profit rates, which were severely eroded in the early 1970s. This explains why, in France, the share of capital income in GDP rose by 10% to the detriment of labour income between the "turning point of austerity" (1982) and the end of the 1990s.

Fifth factor: international trade. Here again, it's easy enough to see why the development of international trade has been instrumental in restoring and even increasing the rate of profit. Whereas in the three decades following the Second World War, capitalist development remained largely self-centred, it was not until the early 1980s that the ratio between production and international trade reached levels comparable to those before the First World War. This growth in world trade was accompanied by accelerated globalization of investment and financial markets. This process, known as "globalization", is by no means new, nor a radical turning point in the history of capitalism, but it does mark an acceleration of long-standing trends. The massive integration of hundreds of millions of low-wage workers into the global division of labor has profoundly altered the balance of power between the different poles of the capitalist system—a "hierarchical national-global system", to quote Michel Baud's excellent characterization—and enabled the accumulation of colossal profits.

According to Marx, the final factor in combating the downward trend in the rate of profit is the development of joint-stock companies. Here again, there's no need to stress at length how impetuous this development has been in recent decades.

If we abandon the idea that the downward trend in the rate of profit heralds the final crisis and the end of times, and if we clearly understand the contradictory mechanism outlined by Marx, then we can understand why capitalism is forced to continually revolutionize its own base. It is forced to do so on pain of death, and it does so under the whip of competition and rivalry between the major capitalist groups, whether national or transnational.

Capitalism can only survive by constantly broadening its base. The transformation of largely semi-feudal agricultural countries such as China, India and the small "dragons" (South Korea, Taiwan, Thailand and Indonesia) into first-rate industrial powers has given the world capitalist system a tremendous boost. Add to this the collapse of "real socialism", and the scope for capital accumulation, still very limited in the fifties and sixties, has widened considerably, rendering Keynesian-style policies to stimulate growth through demand (wage policy and public spending) definitively obsolete. The global division of labor has reached a high level of specialization: consumer electronics and clothing, for example, now come mainly from South-East Asia—by contrast, the design and manufacture of *high-tech* fabrics or microprocessors remain largely the preserve of the old capitalist countries. The world's computer network extends this global division of labor to services—whether low-skilled, as in *call centers*, or R&D, as in the well-known case of Indian computer engineers.

This extensive development went hand in hand with intensive development. In the interstices of societies dominated by the capitalist mode of production, many pockets of non-capitalist economy remained, and still remain. Capitalism, as it has always done, pursues the ruthless destruction of the small independent producer. Grocers have gradually given way to the giants of supermarkets, Wall Mart, Carrefour and *tutti quanti*. All the trades that were once the realm of the artisan and the small businessman are gradually being integrated into transnational industrial production. No more carpenters to make windows, industry takes care of that. Gradually, building a house became an assembly job. Even artistic creation has fully entered the sphere of capitalist production. Cinema has long obeyed this industrial logic, but so has writing, a personal and intimate activity par excellence. The *Harry*

Potter series, the product of a veritable small-scale novel-writing factory, takes long-standing trends to their logical conclusion, notably through the writer-training techniques widely practiced in American universities.

Production and Destruction

At the same time, capitalism can only survive by massively destroying previous productive forces. Putting millions of skilled workers out of work in industrialized countries is apparently an unbridled and senseless waste. But it is part of the means used to restore the rate of profit. The systematic "youthism" of companies, preferring inexperienced youngsters to older workers who had managed to impose a minimal balance of power with their bosses, can be explained in this way. From this point of view, some operations seem totally crazy. But costly early-retirement schemes in large companies (see, for example, the "end-of-career leave" at France Télécom) find their rationality in the desire to forge a new wage-earning class, which implies the liquidation of the old one. Capitalism doesn't like conservative employees who want to preserve what they've already acquired. "Life, health and love are precarious, so why shouldn't work be?" proclaimed Mme Parisot, just elected head of the MEDEF (French employers' federation)[43].

The accelerated turnover of fixed capital and the extremely rapid obsolescence of means of production and consumer goods are also part of this "productive destruction" (which is also, in the longer term, a terribly destructive form of production). The example of the computer industry is emblematic, but the same phenomena could be observed in other sectors, such as the accelerated renewal of product ranges in the automotive industry. The dynamics of

---

43. On job insecurity, see Gérard FILOCHE, *La vie, la santé et l'amour sont précaires. Pourquoi le travail ne le serait-il pas,* Jean-Claude Gawsewitch, 2006.

innovation, quite clearly analyzed by Schumpeter, are undoubtedly the main driving force behind capitalism in a competitive environment, and it has to be admitted that Marxists have often paid it little attention.

The post-war decades had led us to believe that capitalism had stabilized, softened under the weight of bureaucratic centralization, with the capitalist technostructure drawing closer to, and sometimes almost merging with, state and union bureaucracies. This would be reasonable capitalism, "Rhenish capitalism" as opposed to Anglo-Saxon capitalism, according to a standard classification. But stability, peaceful reformism and "class collaboration" (e.g., through German co-management) are, in the long term, profoundly incompatible with capitalism itself. Even in its homeland, Rhenish capitalism has been profoundly transformed, and Bismarck's welfare system has been little more than chipped away. France and Italy have profoundly challenged their economic and social systems (massive privatizations, casualization of work, undermining of pensions and social protection). As for Great Britain, it has not always been as "liberal" as it is today: the immediate post-war period saw the establishment of a very extensive system of state intervention: massive nationalizations, free health care, etc., which lasted until the Thatcher years.

All in all, then, a capitalism rid of class struggle and based on the regulation of social relations by "social partners", a regulated and stabilized capitalism, is almost as impossible as a square circle! Capitalism is revolutionary, but revolution can be a turning in on itself, as the current "neoliberal" course seems in many respects to be. Revolutionary does not necessarily mean progressive.

This whole vocabulary has been undermined, and the inability of the Left (or what's left of it) to think independently of it explains its general decline. Marxist economists and radical leftists complain about the regressive social dynamics of capitalism today. Yet the dynamics of capitalism have never been socially progressive. As Marx reminds us: "capital arrives [in the world] sweating blood and mud from every pore[44]." The idea that there is a common good, and that the economy is at the service of this common good, is radically foreign to it, since it rests precisely on the idea that there is no common good, and that individuals leading separate existences are by nature rivals whose rivalry need only be contained within limits compatible with the principle of private ownership of the means of production.

---

44. We might also note the change in tone between the *Manifesto*'s apology for progress and *Capital,* which counts the destruction of the peasantry and colonization among capitalism's atrocities.

Chapter IV. *Memento Mori!*

Over the past century, capitalism has been confronted with a number of major crises. The crisis of 1929 even seemed to many analysts to be the "final crisis" that the author of *Capital* would have predicted. The regular upheavals of the international financial and monetary order stem from capitalism's need to overcome the barriers it itself poses to its own development. There is no "final crisis", because capitalism, like all social systems, will only disappear if there is a class or coalition of classes in the old society determined to bring it down and establish a new order. However, the crises of the capitalist mode of production are inescapable, and Marx gave the main explanations for them. "Crises," says Marx, "are the *memento mori* of the capitalist mode of production: remember that you must die! We're not out of it yet."

Marxian Crisis Analysis

Marx devotes an important part of his work to the analysis of cyclical crises[45]. Let's try to give an overview that will be useful later. The formula of commodity circulation conceals within itself the formal possibility of crises. The producer is never certain that

---

45. It's worth noting, however, that there's nothing definitive on the subject, and that the reconstruction of Marxian crisis theory has been one of the Marxists' favorite pastimes.

his product will find a buyer. Misalignment between production and consumption can interrupt the cycle of capital's reproduction, opening the way to a crisis that affects all sectors. But formal possibility does not yet mean real possibility, still less necessity. Marx wasn't the first to wonder about these highly paradoxical crises of the capitalist mode of production, when misery suddenly sets in, not because of scarcity, but because of abundance! Economists have all noticed these periodic crises that profoundly affect the course of business, and have sought more or less exogenous explanations for them: Jevons, for example, even linked them to cycles of solar activity. Hard-line liberal theorists usually attribute them to market "rigidities": if competition were free and undistorted—for example, by social laws hindering the free labor market—crises should disappear, as the market automatically adjusts supply and demand. Keynesians, on the other hand, advocate state intervention as an instrument of anti-crisis regulation. By stimulating demand, the business cycle should be smoothed, and state intervention should be counter-cyclical: in a recession, the public deficit should be used to stimulate the economy through demand (e.g., through public works); in a period of sustained growth, the state should pay down its debts, benefiting from the gains of economic prosperity. Marx's analysis can be summed up in two theses.

In the first place, periodic crises of overproduction are intimately linked to the laws of capital accumulation and, from this point of view, they are necessary—necessary because they follow from these laws, and necessary because they play a role in the very development of this accumulation. In other words, crises are "necessary" insofar as they derive from the structural laws of the capitalist mode of production, and from the permanent tendency towards the overproduction of constant capital. So "anti-crisis" techniques can only defer the crisis, masking its most obvious effects, but by no means eliminating them. During the "thirty glorious years" of capitalism, cyclical crises of overproduction were masked by simple growth slowdowns—except in the USA. But 1973-1974 marked the great return of the crisis.

Second key idea: these crises are not, or at least not primarily, crises of overproduction of commodities for consumption (they are not crises of underconsumption), but crises of the overproduction of capital: the crisis arises because there is too much capital to put to work at the average rate of profit of the previous period. The mass unemployment that strikes in times of crisis simply expresses capital's endemic tendency to produce an overpopulation of workers, the "industrial reserve army" we spoke of earlier in connection with the tendency of the rate of profit to fall. From this it follows that, for Marx at least, the idea of fighting recession and unemployment by boosting consumption would have been considered childish. Workers have an inalienable right to fight for higher wages, but this is no way to boost consumption and stabilize capitalism! On the contrary, we can consider that workers' resistance in the early seventies, often imposing a sort of sliding wage scale, was one of the decisive factors in the great crisis of 1973-1974, which signaled the death warrant of the capitalism of the thirty glorious years. For the reformist Keynesian left (including its variants on the "left of left"), this is an unpleasant truth to hear, but one that can hardly be escaped if we persist in believing that Marx helps us understand the world we live in.

There are at least two ways in which Marx approaches the question of crisis. The *Communist Manifesto* sees commercial crises as the "revolt of modern productive forces against modern relations of production", crises which, by their periodic return, "threaten more and more the existence of bourgeois society." In *Capital*, the first task is to explain the jerky movement of production.

"If this regime endows social capital with a sudden force of expansion, a marvelous elasticity, it's because, under the spur of favorable chances, credit makes extraordinary masses of growing social wealth flow into production, new capital whose possessors, impatient to make use of it, are constantly watching for the opportune moment ; it is, on the other hand, that the technical springs of large-scale industry make it possible both to convert suddenly into additional means of production an enormous surplus of products, and to transport goods more rapidly from one corner of the world to another. If the low price of these goods initially opens up new outlets and dilates the old ones, their overabundance gradually tightens the general market to the point where they are suddenly rejected. In this way, commercial vicissitudes combine with the alternating movements of social capital, which, in the course of its accumulation, sometimes undergoes revolutions in its composition, sometimes grows on the technical base once acquired. All these influences work together to bring about sudden expansions and contractions in the scale of production". (*Capital*, book I, chap. VII)

In fact, Marx distinguishes—though not always clearly—the historical destiny of the capitalist mode of production from the structural laws of its operation: the Marxian theory of crises is not logically linked to a theory (or philosophy) of history that makes communism the ultimate goal of the adventure of human civilization. Anyone who dislikes philosophies of history can reject the latter without denying the scientific character of the former.

In theory, the pursuit of "productivity gains" enables us to pocket a surplus profit: a firm with a technological lead, for example, can sell its products at a market price far higher than the social labor time actually used in production. But these surplus profits can only be temporary, and in the long run lead to a general fall in the value of commodities, as technical innovations become accessible to all producers. The capitalist mode of production thus paradoxically produces both an increase in the working-class population, as it gains a foothold in all the sectors abandoned by small-scale independent production and replaces the more archaic relations of production, and a relative (and sometimes absolute) overpopulation, as fewer and fewer workers are needed to put the same capital to work.

"But would the exorbitant expansion of production, which forms the starting point, be possible without a reserve army at capital's command, without a surplus of workers independent of the natural growth of the population? This is achieved by a simple process that throws workers on the streets every day: the application of methods which, by making work more productive, reduce the demand for it. The ever-renewed conversion of part of the working class into as many half-worked or completely idle hands, therefore, gives the movement of modern industry its typical form."

Note that, for Marx, crises do not have a single cause: they are the result of a combination of several factors: trade movements, credit inflows and transformations in production. But in the final analysis, they are played out at the level of relations of production. These crises arise from a necessity analogous to that of the laws of nature: "Just as celestial bodies, once launched into their orbs, describe them for an indefinite time, so social production, once thrown into this alternating movement of expansion and contraction, repeats it by mechanical necessity. Effects become causes in their turn, and peripatetic events, at first irregular and seemingly accidental, increasingly take on the form of a normal periodicity."

The crisis led to a massive devaluation of capital. Throwing millions of workers out into the street, it put pressure on wages. Eliminating the "lame ducks", it simultaneously lays the foundations for a new phase of expansion… until a new crisis arises. Crisis is therefore part of the "normal" functioning of the capitalist mode of production. It is a consequence of the development of the contradictory character of capitalist production, but, at the same time, it brings about the destruction necessary for the resumption of the cycle of capital accumulation.

No Crisis of Under-Consumption

Let's take a closer look at the vulgar "Marxist" argument that reduces the crisis of overproduction to a crisis of underconsumption, which can be overcome by boosting popular consumption. The capitalist monopolizes labor for free, but he can only do so on condition that the goods produced are sold (roughly at their value) on a market. Let's assume a society composed entirely of workers and capitalists. The workers consume part of the goods produced—the part corresponding to the total value of their wages. But who buys the goods corresponding to free labor? The goods produced in the production goods sector are bought by the capitalists themselves—to replace the constant capital used up in the production process. The consumer goods corresponding to workers' wages are bought by the workers themselves. But how is surplus value realized? Part of the surplus value is used to buy new machines and build new factories, and is reconverted into additional capital. To this must be added the consumption of the capitalists themselves, who, even if they don't follow the austere Protestant ethic, cannot consume all production. Such a system therefore produces more and more commodities (since it increases its productive capacity with each cycle) and, at the same time, produces a smaller and smaller market, since the share of wages in total capital invested tends to shrink. To realize the value of commodities, and thus pocket surplus value, capitalists must sell their products in non-capitalist sectors: this, according to Rosa Luxemburg and her followers, is the main cause of the development of colonialism. But with the development of world trade also comes the development of capitalist production, and the "final crisis" will come when capitalists can no longer find a single non-capitalist sector in which to realize the value of their goods. We could also imagine capitalists paying their workers more to enable them to buy the additional consumption, but then it would be profit that would be cut, and it's hard to see why anyone would invest in capitalist production to get nothing out of it. So, in the long run, neither workers' consumption nor that of non-capitalist sectors can realize the value produced. Hence the crisis. And even the final crisis!

However simple and effective this explanation may be, it has a number of flaws. The main one is this: this mechanism does explain crises of overproduction, but it doesn't explain phases of expansion at all! If overproduction can be explained by mass underconsumption, then, since underconsumption is permanent, the first crisis should have been the last. The same applies to theories that base crises on the growing disproportion between production in the producer goods sector and production in the consumer goods sector. While underconsumption and disproportion are the forms in which crises manifest themselves, they are not their causes. To understand crises, we need to focus on the overall dynamics of capital[46].

The Casino Economy

Let's continue. One of the most common explanations for the crises that regularly afflict capitalism today is the "casino economy". The crisis triggered by the Southeast Asian stock market crash in August 1997, the crisis triggered by the bursting of the Internet bubble in the 2nd half of 2000, and the *subprime* crisis of 2007-2008 are all said to be the result of speculation and unhealthy capitalism, as opposed to healthy capitalism, which is concerned with the production of surplus value on the basis of real activity. But this explanation, in vogue on both left and right, is no better than the previous ones.

Speculation in all its forms is closely linked to the development of the capitalist mode of production, and has been from the outset. Far-off trade" laid the first foundations on an international scale[47]. Anyone who takes the trouble to read or reread Balzac will see just how important speculation was to the idle classes of the 19th century. Coupon clippers" were legion at the end of the last century and the beginning of this one, until the October Revolution, by refusing to honor the Russian loan, organized the first mass euthanasia of rentiers.

---

46. A useful clarification of this question can be found in Paul MATTICK, "La théorie des crises chez Marx", in *Crises et théories des crises,* translated from the German by Champ libre, 1976.
47. See Fernand BRAUDEL, *Civilisation matérielle, économie, capitalisme, XVᵉ-XVIIIᵉ siècle,* Armand Colin.

J.K. Galbraith has skilfully recounted[48] how wild speculation was the direct cause of the 1929 crisis. And this story is highly instructive, as it sometimes seems to be the story of the eighties and nineties, including the denouement. The Florida land deal, which Galbraith takes as his starting point, was a good example of the purely speculative system that was to develop right up to the famous crash. Since the sun was thought to be a future value, Florida was divided up into plots of land to house future holiday homes. The land was sold with a 10% cash payment. A farmer who thought he'd made the deal of a lifetime by selling a few unhealthy plots was moping around the following week, as prices had doubled in the meantime. The land was not interesting for its own sake. Buyers had no intention of spending their old age in these non-existent towns with only vague plans for roads and amenities. In speculation, as Galbraith puts it, "the income from property or the pleasure it gives becomes an academic value [...]. What is important is that tomorrow or next week stock values will rise as they did yesterday or last week, and a profit can be made."

That's why you don't really buy land in Florida, but purchase rights, which in turn can be sold. "The worst constraint of ownership, whether of land or any other asset is the need to advance the money represented by the purchase price." The principle of options considerably reduces this burden, while maintaining the essential advantage of ownership, which is that it can be resold at a profit. This is already the massive "securitization" of debt. The same principle was at the root of the explosion of the stock markets in the 1980s; all amateur *golden boys* know how to buy shares and resell them, pocketing the profits without ever having to take a penny out of their own pockets. What Galbraith called the "margin business"—today we'd call derivatives—became just that: business. Here's another passage that applies today:

---

48. J.K. Galbraith, *The Great Depression of 1929. Anatomie d'une crise financière*, 1961, Petite Bibliothèque Payot, 1981 for the French edition.

"[The arrangements that allow these businesses to develop] are admirable only in relation to the goal they propose to achieve: to arrange the speculator and favor speculation; but this goal cannot be recognized. If Wall Street were to admit it, thousands of principled men and women could only reproach it for promoting something harmful, and call for reforms. Margin trading must be defended, not because it helps the speculator efficiently and ingeniously, but because it creates an increased volume of transactions that transforms a thin, anemic market into a strong, healthy one. At best, it's an uninteresting and dubious by-product. Wall Street in this respect is like a beautiful, accomplished woman who must wear black cotton stockings, thick wool underwear and flaunt her knowledge as a cook because, unfortunately, her supreme talent is prostitution."

The analogy between Galbraith's story and the present day can be taken quite far. All leveraged buyouts are completely in line with the methods tested with such success in the 1920s. The idea is to buy a company without paying a single cent. The purchase price is paid by dividing the company up into apartments and drawing on its profits. Of course, there are losers: the employees who are discarded as part of the "restructuring" process.

There is, however, a notable difference between Galbraith's account and today's financialized capitalism: speculative fever appeared as a sick state of the capitalist mode of production, which the crisis purged. Today, financial speculation is no longer temporary or limited to the upper stratum of capitalism, but tends to become its normal mode of operation; all production is subject to it, and now exists only as a variant of possible financial investments. As all prudential boundaries are gradually broken down, anyone can speculate. Deposit banks solicit their customers, even the most modest, to take part in the great game of speculation. Hypermarkets sell insurance and financial investments. And if you want to buy a car, it's easy to see that the salesman isn't so much in a hurry to sell you his latest shiny model as to arrange the credit that goes with it. Liberalization and globalization, which developed simultaneously and reinforced each other from the late 1970s to the present day, have been the means of this expansion and domination of the financial sphere over the entire economy.

The origins of this transformation in the functioning of the capitalist mode of production can be traced back to the late 1960s, which saw the first signs of the crisis in the International Monetary System (IMS) resulting from the Bretton Woods agreements. In August 1971, Richard Nixon ushered in a new period by declaring the dollar inconvertible into gold. Until then, the American currency had functioned as an international currency because it was supposed to be *as good as gold*: one ounce of gold was represented by 35 dollars. With the Nixon Declaration, the dollar became nothing more than a "paper currency" with a forced exchange rate. The SMI crisis paved the way for financial speculation, with the introduction of the floating exchange rate regime in the late 1970s, the demonetization of gold and the development of Eurodollar operations (dollars held by European banks, mainly British and Soviet): *Eurobank*, a subsidiary of the USSR central bank, played a central role in the development of this new market. These events led governments to change their economic policies and abandon the principles of regulation that had marked the previous period. Paul Volcker, head of the US *Federal Reserve Board*, was to drive the monetarist turnaround, which was to find its political expression in the *Reaganomics* and Mrs Thatcher's policies. Financial deregulation dominated these policies, which were implemented by the most powerful states—which, from this point of view, demonstrated the effectiveness of politics over economics. In particular, all existing barriers between the various types of banking and financial establishments were gradually removed, barriers which had been put in place after the 1929 crisis to prevent another crash.

Secondly, the instability created by the floating exchange rate system and ongoing deregulation will lead to a proliferation of derivative products, in particular those designed to hedge against future risks. Finally, in line with monetarist dogma, the only remaining regulation will be through money supply and high interest rates. Thus, whereas the previous period was marked by low and sometimes even negative interest rates, the new period will be one of high real interest rates, reaching 6% in certain periods, which has practically never been seen in the entire history of capitalism. Interest-bearing capital is bleeding the entire "real" economy dry.

This new phase in the capitalist mode of production seems to have stunned opinion and experts on the traditional left; thanks to Keynesian theory, they had found an alternative theoretical corpus to the old Marxist one. By theorizing state intervention and regulation, and organizing the redistribution of the fruits of growth, Keynesianism was the ideology best suited to the objectives and average thinking of European social democracy, in that it seemed to hold the key to that miraculous third way between "unbridled capitalism" and "bureaucratic socialism". The monetarist/deregulatory phase that began at the end of the 1970s undermined the very foundations of social-democratic politics by disrupting the operating conditions of the capitalist mode of production. The idea that the interests of workers and capitalists could be reconciled in the long term, in a mode of accumulation based on the sharing of productivity gains, was now deprived of any serious basis. To understand what's at stake, we'd have to go back to Marx's analyses, but that's the last thing on the minds of social democrats—if social democrats can still think, which remains to be proven.

Fictitious Capital

There's nothing mysterious about the creation of a unified global financial market. It corresponds to the development of "fictitious capital", of which government bonds are the most complete form. Financial capital can be divided into two categories that are usually confused, but which are nevertheless radically different in nature:

1) medium- and long-term loans to finance productive investments, where the interest earned is basically a deduction from the surplus value produced in the production process;

2) "Phantom" capital, represented by receivables exchangeable against future cash commitments, whose value is derived entirely from the capitalization of anticipated income with no direct counterpart in productive capital.

Let's follow Marx's reasoning for a moment. "The form of interest-producing capital makes all definite and regular money income appear to be the interest of capital, whether or not it comes from capital." (*Capital*, Book III, Section V) "Fictitious capital" is based on a retrospective intellectual operation, which presupposes an inversion of means and ends, an operation peculiar to the process of producing ideological representations. "Monetary income is first transformed into interest, and, from there, we also find the capital that is its source." Here, Marx simply describes the concrete workings of the capitalist mode of production. Thus, the sale price of a piece of real estate is calculated on the assumption that this property is interest-bearing capital, the latter being represented by rent. But this process has an important consequence: "any sum of value appears as capital, as soon as it is not spent as income; it appears as a principal sum by contrast with the possible or real interest it is capable of producing."

The example of government debt is particularly illuminating in terms of the consequences of this process: "Every year, the government has to pay its creditors a certain amount of interest on the capital borrowed. In this case, the creditor cannot cancel his loan, but he can sell his claim, the title that assures him of ownership. The capital itself has been consumed, spent by the State. It no longer exists. What the creditor possesses is (1) a title of ownership, (2) what follows from this, namely a right to an annual levy on the proceeds of taxes, and (3) the right to sell this title. "But in all these cases, the capital that is supposed to produce an offspring (interest), the payment from the State, is an illusory, fictitious capital. This is because the sum lent to the State not only no longer exists, but was never intended to be spent as capital." For the creditor, lending money to the State in order to obtain a share of the tax proceeds, or lending money to an industrialist in return for interest, or buying shares in order to receive dividends, are equivalent operations. "But the capital of public debt is nonetheless purely fictitious, and the day that bonds become unsaleable, that's the end of even the appearance of that capital."

But public debt is not the only form of fictitious capital. Fictitious money capital" includes all the varieties of interest-bearing money-market securities that circulate on the stock market, as well as equities. Then there are the many "new financial products", all of which, in one form or another, aim to "securitize" credit and circulate debt securities as capital. This category obviously includes "high-risk products" such as junk bonds, which are highly leveraged because they are based on bad debts. Clearly, subprime mortgages were among these "rotten" loans.

Referring to Marx's analysis, Robert Guttmann notes: "Whereas Marx's reference to credit money as fictitious capital only concerned fiat money not covered by gold reserves, today we operate exclusively with money in this form." And consequently, it is money itself that must be considered as a "form of fictitious capital".

It is the very dynamic of the capitalist mode of production, as analyzed by Marx, that tends towards this "financialization" of the economy. It is not, therefore, an accident or a bad policy on the part of capitalist managers, but a strong tendency, immanent to the social relationship that is capital. The growing parasitism of this "political economy of the rentier" and the progressive blurring of the distinction between sound and fraudulent business are the inescapable consequences of these processes, which affect the very foundations of the economy. The fact that mafias played a central role in the introduction of capitalism in Eastern Europe and the USSR, and that the mafia (in this case the *camora*) is still to be found as an intermediary between German or northern Italian industrial firms in the Naples waste crisis, is not simply a contingent trait, a result of the specific history of these countries (the mafia is far from being a Sicilian speciality!), but one of the essential dimensions of capitalism as a whole. This is demonstrated by the fabulous revenues generated by the drug trade, and more generally by all illicit businesses, which are then recycled into the "healthy" economy.

The development of the financial sphere is tending to get out of control. The following figures, drawn from the best sources, give an idea of the scale of financial transactions and the evolution of financial markets[49].

	2002	2003	2004	2005
Derivatives markets	693.1	874.3	1,152.2	1,406.9
Foreign exchange market	384.4	533.4	556.8	566.6
Financial market	39.3	33.3	42.3	51.0

The financial market concerns operations to finance corporate activity (bank loans, bond issues, etc.). The foreign exchange market concentrates speculation on currencies. Finally, the derivatives market, which has gradually submerged the entire financial sphere, is the options market that Galbraith mentions in connection with land in Florida. As we can see, transactions that concern the "real economy" account for only a small proportion of the financial markets (barely 2%): raising funds to build a new factory, pay for patents or buy new machines is clearly no longer what occupies the trendy capitalism of the third millennium. What's even more striking is the extraordinary growth of derivatives markets, especially when compared to their 1989 level of $1.7T. These markets essentially correspond to "hedging" operations: a company planning to buy a certain quantity of a raw material in three months' time can protect itself against a price rise by placing an option with an intermediary who undertakes to supply the quantity of merchandise requested at the price requested. If, on D + 3 months, the price of the raw materials has fallen, the intermediary pockets the profit; if

---

49. Sources: IMF, World Bank, FIBS. Quoted in *Le nouveau "mur de l'argent"*, by François Morin, "Nouvelles fondations" magazine, n° 7-8, December 2007. Amounts are given in teradollars (T$ = trillion dollars).

the price is as forecast, he will be satisfied with a commission; and if the raw materials have risen, he will be out of pocket. In fact, it's an insurance market for buying and selling operations on real markets or on financial transaction markets. It is curious, to say the least, that at the very moment when ideologists are extolling the virtues of risk in the name of market fluidity, this market for insurance against the hazards of capitalism is developing in a totally uncontrolled way.

These amounts obviously don't correspond to real wealth. If I spend the day exchanging 10-euro bills for their equivalent in dollars with my friend, at the end of the day we may have a fabulous cumulative amount of transactions, but nothing will have happened other than losses and gains on one side or the other. But this fictitious wealth has very real effects, even if they are only limited in time, and it gives people the power to act and to dispose of the social surplus. Of course, these derivatives markets do not create any new wealth—even their most charitable defenders may concede that they facilitate risk-taking and therefore wealth crea-tion—and they live solely from the deductions they make from global surplus value.

This general financialization of capital is not only a source of growing injustice, pushing social inequalities and inequalities between nations to a point that has probably never been reached before in history. The frenetic nature of the markets and the inability of decision-makers to calculate over the long term "seem to compromise any attempt to promote the minimum macroeco-nomic stability required for accumulation". Indeed, we can only ask the same question as François Chesnais: "Isn't there some connection between financial globalization and the pronounced sluggishness, if not stagnation, of industrial production (manufac-turing and services combined) and investment, as well as the rise in unemployment in OECD countries, including Japan?[50]

---

50. François *Chesnais, La Mondialisation financière*, Syros, 1997.

Against the Fetishism of Finance

We must not, however, fall prey to descriptions that emphasize speculation and turn today's economy into a purely parasitic one. Parasitism can only develop if there is a living body to parasitize. Speculation is only possible if the living body of the real economy allows it. Michel Husson points out that "discourses on the casino economy provide useful descriptions and operational critiques, but they don't get to the root of things. The main limitation of many approaches, even those that claim to be critical, is that they fail to break with a certain fetishism of finance[51]."

In effect, this discourse leads to the mistaking of signs of wealth for real wealth, virtual magnitudes—for example, the sum of transactions, generally electronic, carried out in a single day on all the financial markets that operate continuously, with the Western markets taking over from Hong Kong and Singapore—and real magnitudes—trade in automobiles, computers, wheat and sports shoes. This is precisely the kind of phantasmagoria into which fanatical apologists for networks, globalization, the manipulation of symbols replacing the manipulation of things, virtual reality supplanting material reality and other such nonsense frequently fall.

The changes in the workings of the global economy, summarized in the expression financial globalization, actually express a change in social relations between classes. The pattern of accumulation that the regulation school calls "Fordist" assumes that the distribution of national income between wages and capital income remains globally fixed, with productivity gains benefiting wage earners as well as capitalists. At the same time, interest rates remain low (or even negative, in the case of real interest rates), so the share of financial rents is negligible. This so-called "golden age" was the era of managers, strong economic growth and a certain type of balance

---

51. Michel Husson, "Les trois dimensions du néo-impérialisme", in *Actuel Marx* n° 18, 2nd semester 1995.

of power between social classes, in which capitalists could afford, or were forced to buy, social peace, often at a high price. The so-called "oil crisis", i.e. the first great recession, shows the exhaustion of this operating regime of the capitalist mode of production, mainly due to the fall in the rate of profit, which goes hand in hand with a crisis in productivity. With a more or less clear awareness of what needed to be done, and knowing that appetite comes with eating, the managers of the major capitalist groups moved in the second half of the seventies towards a different type of income distribution between wages, financial rent and corporate profit. Let's quote Michel Husson again: "The primary division between wages and surplus value today obeys a fairly simple trend law, according to which real wages are not increasing, so that the bulk of productivity gains are appropriated in the form of relative surplus value. Extremely high real interest rates correspond to drawing rights on this surplus value, which tend to capture a growing share of national income and therefore, at the margin, of productivity gains."

The "Fordist" regime had the advantage of ensuring solvent outlets through workers' consumption. Under the new system, the question arises as to who will buy the extra production. "This question obviously admits of only one lasting answer, and that is as follows: to ensure the realization of production, part of the surplus value must be redistributed to social strata whose consumption will provide the outlets needed to increase production.

In other words, the financialization of the economy does not constitute an increase in overall real wealth, but a gigantic transfer of wealth from wage earners, either directly in the form of lower wages, or indirectly through the unemployment of a proportion of wage earners and the worsening exploitation of those lucky enough to still have a job, to the capitalist class at large. This includes a section of the middle classes who live directly or indirectly off this financialization, through the rents it procures, which can quite quickly be substantial, or through the jobs linked to this explosion of financial markets, or through the development of parasitic activities linked to communication, advertising, etc.

Far from being the victims of financial globalization beyond their control, governments are, on the contrary, major players. Their indebtedness, which seems catastrophic to the taxpayer, is on the contrary a blessing for speculators. For it is public debt that will be one of the main levers enabling this transfer of income from the working class to financial rent. Indeed, the financialization of the world began with a spectacular boom in trading in government debt securities. Between 1980 and 1993, the daily average in the United States rose from $13.8 billion to $119.6 billion; in France, between 1986 and 1993, the daily average rose from $200 million to $13.7 billion.

In France, real long-term interest rates have risen from 2% to around 6% over the same period. High interest rates make financial investments particularly attractive, especially in government bonds, treasury bills, etc. At the same time, they increase public debt, since these interest rates mean that debt servicing accounts for a growing share of public budgets. At the same time, governments' financing needs increase, driving up interest rates. This infernal mechanism is implemented by the famous "Maastricht criteria", which seem to have been tailor-made for the needs of speculation. "The forma-tion of bond markets, the securitization of public debt and the increasingly rapid growth in the proportion of OECD countries' budgets devoted to debt servicing mean that the most important mechanism for capturing and transferring debt is now that which passes through these countries' direct and indirect taxation. Part of the growth of the financial sphere is due to flows of wealth that are first formed as wages and salaries, or as peasant or artisanal income, before being siphoned off by the State through taxes, and then transferred by it to the financial sphere as interest payments or repayment of the principal of public debt". (Chesnais, 1997)

This assertion can be corroborated by a wealth of direct and indirect evidence. An analysis of data on national debt shows that there is "a direct link between the rise of globalized and liberalized finance on the one hand, and the increase in public deficits on the other" (Dominique Plihon in Chesnais, 1997). (Dominique

Plihon in Chesnais, 1997) For a long time, liberals justified the rise in interest rates by the lack of available capital and the need to boost savings. Indirect proof that high interest rates were merely a means of transferring income from one class to another is provided by the fact that, contrary to what the dogma predicted, the savings rate kept falling while interest rates rose.

A Word to the Wise: Two Types of Crises

The analyses we have just outlined are beginning to gain ground. The enthusiasm of the turn of the millennium has cooled. Authors little known for their unbridled Marxism, such as Joseph Stiglitz[52], are proclaiming the "end of neoliberalism". After the Keynesian recipes for counter-cyclical policies, the so-called neo-liberal policies are now exhausted. We are beginning—timidly—to talk again of state regulation[53]. The WTO (formerly the GATT) is only hiccupping. Unbridled optimism has given way to concern. A global turnaround is underway. But this new phase change does not herald a radical mutation. Those who saw fit to swap anti-capitalism for anti-liberalism may well find themselves in an uncomfortable position if we move towards authoritarian capitalism with strong state intervention—if, for example, China and Russia show the future of this mode of production.

There are therefore two kinds of crisis: the "small" ones that punctuate the business cycle every few years, and the "big" ones, those that involve radical, global reorientations, overturning

---

52. "Nobel Prize" winner in economics in 2001, former vice-president of the World Bank.

53. The partial "nationalization" of the banking system, first implemented in the USA by the Paulson plan and by British Prime Minister Gordon Brown, was the first act of a general political turnaround. We even saw the very liberal President of the French Republic propose the rebirth of industrial policy through the creation of a public investment fund to rescue strategic industries in difficulty (cf. Sarkozy plan, October 2008). Such an industrial policy had been officially abandoned in 1983 by Mitterrand during his "austerity turn"...

the balance of power between capitalist groups and between the dominant and the dominated. Let's repeat that, in themselves, these crises are not fatal. Capitalism survived the 1929 crisis and many others. However, these great crises open up the possibility of capitalism's demise and its replacement by another system, whether we call it socialism or communism, it matters little. Possibility does not mean necessity: a possibility can remain a mere possibility forever. But the possibility contained in the crisis prevents us from considering capitalism as the natural state of human life. It remains a historical mode of production, and history is not over. In fact, it's a never-ending story.

Chapter V. The Future of an Illusion

Where do we stand? Even as "the end of history" was recently announced, the question of the historical future of the capitalist mode of production is once again being posed. The "spontaneous order" of the economy must once again call for massive state intervention. Competition for dwindling resources (oil, for example!) is heightening tensions, and local conflicts could well turn into major confrontations. History returns with a vengeance. Exit Fukuyama.

Indeed, capitalism's vitality and capacity to resist do not make it any more sympathetic. Of course, the ideologues and parrots of the ruling class keep repeating that capitalism is unsurpassable, that it "limits our historical horizon", as the PS congressmen said almost two decades ago[54]. But the reasons for wanting to change society, to attack capitalist social relations of production, are as strong as they were almost two centuries ago, when the first socialist and communist organizations were born. It's not enough to have reasons for opposing capitalism; the possibilities, forces and programmatic perspectives must also exist for this overthrow to take place, and these questions will be addressed in the next chapters. For now, let's confine ourselves to examining the reasons for believing that capitalism is not the natural state of human society, but a historical mode of production that could suffer the fate of all things historical.

---

54. PS congress held at the Arche de la Défense in 1991.

The Limits of Accumulation

The first question is that of the very dynamics of the capitalist mode of production. Its growth and capacity to resist stem from the possibilities for expansion opened up first by colonialism, then by the integration of hundreds of millions of previously marginalized people into the very heart of the global division of labor. They are also due to this intensive expansion, which is progressively subjecting all sectors that previously escaped it to the law of capital (cf. *above*). But sooner or later, this expansion will reach its limits. Firstly, because the planet is finite, and it's hard to see how the Moon or Mars could, within a reasonable timeframe (and for a capitalist, a reasonable timeframe is never very long), constitute new fields of capital accumulation.

As we saw above, capitalism is revolutionary in essence, and can only subsist through accumulation. At the same time, this accumulation threatens the rate of profit and the very existence of capitalism. Capitalism therefore necessarily develops in conflict. Let's assume a single capitalist—for example, competition has come to an end and there is only one firm left, the "Monde SA" firm. Let's also assume that this single capitalist (it could also be a collective capitalist, an assembly of shareholders) has sufficient means of persuasion and coercion to guard against potential competitors or the revolts of the dominated. Such a capitalist would no longer have any interest in accumulating capital, and we would no longer be in a capitalist regime, but in a kind of despotism such as may have existed in ancient societies[55]. To exist, capitalism must be broken down into competing capitals.

As long as accumulation is possible by peaceful means, i.e. by purely economic means or by the rapid subjugation of colonized peoples, competition is expressed on the market: the best win and the others, ruined, close up store. But in reality, things don't

---

55. See the discussion of "Asian despotism" and "hydraulic societies", from Montesquieu to Karl Wittfogel to Marx.

always work out this way. At the beginning of the 20th century, the great imperialist powers divided up the world. International conferences delineated spheres of influence and redrawn the maps of entire continents. Great Britain and France were primarily concerned with protecting their empires. Germany, the latest newcomer to the European concerto, complains of not having an empire commensurate with its industrial and financial power, and its demography. The United States, which has also embarked on colonialism (on its southern border and in the Pacific), is waiting patiently for its turn. We all know how that affair ended! Capitalism "carries war with it like the cloud carries the storm" said Jaurès, who understood, if only intuitively, the link between the global expansion of capitalism and the threat of war. In *Imperialism, the Supreme Stage of Capitalism*, Lenin sketches out an analysis of the economic and political underpinnings of imperialism as a particular stage in the evolution of capitalism, and not simply as a "tendency to annex", as Kautsky characterized it. Whether this is indeed the "supreme stage", or whether other stages are still possible, is a rather idle question. We could also discuss Lenin's theses on the almost irreversible tendency towards monopoly (see *above*). The fact remains that this little pamphlet captures the essential elements of a system under which we still live, and which makes conflict between capitalist groups and nations for world domination the dominant character of capitalism. At the same time, Lenin refutes two theses that are now widely shared by all varieties of "reformists". Firstly, the thesis of the peaceful development of capitalist globalization, through the simple laws of free competition, and secondly, the thesis of the constitution of a "super-imperialism" capable of imposing a re-edition of the *pax romana* on the whole world.

Let's look at the rest of the story for a moment. The First World War didn't end in 1918 or 1919, but rather in 1945—it's Éric Hobsbawm who defends this idea of a single war, 1914-1945. After the armistice between the main belligerents, the Allies committed themselves to the Russian front in support of the Whites, and thus bore a crushing responsibility (but one that has been overlooked in recent historiography) for the continuation of this merciless civil war and the atrocities that marked it. If we were to look for those responsible for the birth of the Stalinist system, we'd have to include Clemenceau[56], Churchill and a few others. The Treaty of Versailles organized the partial occupation of Germany and its partial dismemberment with the famous "Danzig corridor". As soon as Hitler took power, the resumption of the war was already on the agenda. The remilitarization of the Rhineland, German claims to the Sudetenland and the open intervention of Hitler and Mussolini's troops in Spain: as we can see, the Second World War had begun long before September 1939. If we add that Japan invaded China as early as 1931, we can see that the two decades between the open confrontation between the great powers were largely dominated by war, for, as Hobbes puts it, "the nature of war consists not in actual fighting, but in a known disposition to fight, all the time there is no assurance to the contrary." (*Leviathan*, chapter XIII)

Is the Era of Imperialist Wars Over?

And let's not forget: from 1941 onwards, the Second World War mainly pitted the Anglo-Saxon powers, temporarily allied with the USSR, against the Axis powers (essentially Germany and Japan), but we mustn't forget the "secondary contradictions". The war in the Pacific was an opportunity for the United States to finish taking the place of the British in this part of the world. The fate of France (and consequently of its colonial empire) had long been up in the air: Roosevelt sought to play the Petainism card without Pétain

---

56. Clemenceau's blindness after the victory over Germany is one of the most distressing episodes in the life of a man who had already buried his republican past by shooting workers in 1908. Clemenceau was one of the "crime-pushers" behind the Treaty of Versailles, the iniquitous treaty that served as an ingredient in Nazi propaganda.

(Giraud). Finally, right up to the last weeks of the war, major forces in both Great Britain and the USA sought to negotiate a separate peace with Germany in order to forge a new alliance, this time against the Soviet Union. In the early 1920s, Trotsky had analyzed the Europe/America antagonism as the fundamental antagonism between imperialist powers. Taking all the data into account, it cannot be said that the course of events has proved him wrong.

The "Cold War" period relegated the antagonism between the imperialist powers to the background, not least because of the inability of Europe, and its individual nations in particular, to play an independent role. Since 1945, Western Europe has been largely subjugated by the United States, which has imposed its laws (particularly trade laws) and military bases. General de Gaulle's desire for independence is of secondary importance. The instrument of this vassalization has been, and remains, the construction of Europe, intended by the United States as a bulwark against the Soviet threat and as an extension of the NATO military system under American leadership.

But the "Cold War" wasn't really cold. Not only did it almost turn into a "hot" war, particularly catastrophic at the time of the Cuban rocket affair, but "peripheral" conflicts never ceased. The dismantling of colonial empires claimed millions of victims, and was the occasion for far greater bombing raids than in the whole of the Second World War. French Indochina was the scene of a virtually uninterrupted war from 1945 to the late 1970s. The Middle East was a powder keg that exploded at regular intervals. Conflicts between China and India or between India and Pakistan continue in other forms and will resurface in the future.

When the Communist International was created, in the wake of the Russian Revolution, its founders, first and foremost Lenin and Trotsky, predicted that the coming century would be a century of wars and revolutions. A prognosis verified beyond anything we could have imagined. The difference is that revolutions have all failed, giving way to more or less stable military-bureaucratic tyrannies, more or less "totalitarian[57]", and that it is above all counter-revolutions that mark the century, or "reactionary revolutions" such as Mussolini's Fascism or Nazism. Unquestionably, since the collapse of "real socialism", we have entered a new historical phase. But we are by no means in a new peaceful era, in a democratic "new world order". If anything, the global situation is even more dangerous today. The USSR was a force for social preservation: the ruling bureaucracy feared nothing so much as uncertainty. Even the invasion of Afghanistan, that contingent event through which[58] necessity was realized, was dictated solely by the fear of challenging the existing order. As we know today, and as Brzezinsky, former advisor to President Carter, has said again and again, the United States fomented the Islamist rebellion, armed it and financed the Bin Laden group, because it thought it was time to lure the Soviet Union into the trap and, in turn, pull off "the Vietnam trick". A trap into which the ruling caste, blind, worn out, aged, plagued by palace conflicts and undermined by mafias, rushed headlong. Russia's new capitalism, led by a man with a firm grip like Vladimir Putin, may not have the same prudence…

The United States is a wealthy but declining power—think of Rome in the 2nd and 4th centuries. Their economic decline is particularly marked: foreign trade deficits, indebtedness, a shrinking share of world trade. To cut a long story short, American households are in debt, the State is in debt because, as Emmanuel Todd ironically puts it, their specialty in the global division of labor has become consumption. For the time being, the Chinese are lending the Americans the money they need to keep buying

---

57. The word "totalitarianism" is so widely used that it has lost much of its force and we hesitate to use it. Mussolini perhaps gave the best definition: "Everything in the State, nothing against the State, nothing outside the State. From this point of view, contemporary China is not at all totalitarian, and neither is Cuba. And perhaps the USSR of recent decades wasn't really.

58. Necessity: a brilliant work by a young sociologist and demographer, Emmanuel Todd, had already announced *La Chute finale* (*The Final Fall*) *in* 1976, at a time when the entire press was vying to warn public opinion against the Soviet ogre.

"made in China" products. While it's true that capital from the USA is massively invested in China, and that some of the profits are therefore repatriated to Uncle Sam, this situation can't last forever. China has become considerably richer (even if this is far from being the case for the vast majority of Chinese), and Chinese capitalism has no intention of remaining subordinate to US capital. The Chinese breakthrough in Africa gives a foretaste of the ambitions of Beijing's leaders. But what's true of China is also true, perhaps to a lesser degree, of India and Brazil[59]. These are capitalist powers that are asserting themselves and competing with the old capitalist powers of Europe and North America, and quite naturally feel that their turn has come. And it's hard to see how they can be proved wrong. India and China are also military powers, possessing nuclear weapons.

On the other hand, the United States, precisely because it is in economic decline, must maintain its military supremacy at all costs: this is the *sine qua non* if the whole world is to continue to accept dollar payments, and this is why the Pentagon has set itself the target of having a budget greater than the combined military budget of the fifteen countries that follow it in the order of military expenditure. The invasion of Iraq had no other purpose than to establish new military bases in the region, which President Bush had set out to "reshape". The aim, of course, was to control oil resources, but also to ensure a strong presence throughout Asia to counter the rising power of China. The map of US military establishments in Asia is illuminating: only Iran is missing from the "Silk Road" that encircles Russia and China. The pressure on China is only set to increase, and it's becoming clear that some North American strategists are thinking about how to break up the "Middle Kingdom". The Tibet affair on the one hand, and Uyghur

---

59. "Lula" may not have been the president his "alterglobalist" friends dreamed of, and his concern for social justice hardly went beyond helping the most disadvantaged, but he was a serious defender of the assertion of a Brazilian national bourgeoisie whose interests he steadfastly took to the international arena.

independence in Xinjiang on the other, could resonate with strategies of this type, and we would see that the former Yugoslavia was ultimately no more than a testing ground for a method of enslaving nations to Washington's *big brother*.

The installation of anti-missile bases in the Czech Republic and Poland, theoretically directed against Iran but practically aimed at Russia, is part of the same process. As is the forced march towards European integration, the most important element of which, although systematically glossed over, is the creation of a "common European defense" under the authority of NATO, which would nullify the neutralist pretensions of countries such as Sweden, Austria and Ireland.

Whereas military budgets had been relatively reduced in the years following the collapse of the countries of "real socialism", arms spending has risen sharply again, and some countries, such as Japan, have once again openly become military powers capable of taking action on foreign soil. No one can deny this reality, which has given lasting structure to our times: the "global governance" so vaunted by "experts" and economists is nothing more than the continuation of war by other means... and if these other means fail, all the protagonists are preparing to give the floor back to arms one day or another. For the time being, it's all about posturing—an art in which the Chinese are masters. There's also a lot of posturing going on around Iran, since the conflict between Washington and Teheran should not obscure their deep-seated agreement over Iraq—the government in Baghdad is friendly to Teheran and supported by the White House.

Finally, although Putin's Russia no longer has anything to do with the former USSR in ideological and economic terms, the antagonism between Russia and the United States is no less acute than it was during the Cold War. Militarily, Russia remains the USA's only real competitor, and its hydrocarbon reserves give it enormous economic clout. The persistent tensions in the former Soviet republics of the Caucasus and in Ukraine are all linked to the confrontation between Moscow and Washington—the "Orange" revolution in Ukraine did a poor job of concealing its star-spangled banner, and Georgia is obviously an American pawn in the region, which explains why the Russian government, giving the USA and the EU a run for their money in Kosovo, is supporting independence for South Ossetia.

The fact remains that at these games, a serious slip-up can never be ruled out, and we're always in that situation where there's "a known disposition to fight" and "no assurance to the contrary", to use Hobbes' phrase.

What consequences can we draw from all this? The very dynamics of capitalism, and its most salient recent developments, once again raise the question of strategic conflict between the major capitalists, and the real possibility of a major international crisis. This prospect alone, this possibility alone, would be enough to convince any sensible person that it is impossible to leave the direction of common affairs in the hands of the current "masters of the world".

Capitalism Destroys the Sources of Wealth

A second, equally distressing question is the relationship between human society and nature. Marx argued that capitalism destroys the two sources of wealth, land and labor, and conversely, he saw the way out in society's passage under the direction of "associated producers" who "rationally regulate their exchanges with nature and subject them to their common control instead of being dominated by the blind power of these exchanges; and they accomplish them with the least possible expenditure of energy, under the conditions most worthy of and most in keeping with their human nature." (*Capital*, Book III)

As a man of the 19th century, heir to the Enlightenment, Marx believed in the possibility of unlimited progress for the productive forces of mankind. This belief, because it is indeed a belief, or, to use Kant's language, a "postulate of practical reason", is in itself most reasonable. If by "productive forces" we mean the capacity of human beings to know reality, to master their own living conditions and to develop their power to act, we have no reason to renounce the goal of this development without it being possible to decide in advance where the ultimate limit, if any, lies. We know that the power of nature infinitely surpasses the power of man, and that while the solar system (and with it the Earth and the human species) has a finite duration, nature is eternal and infinite. If we keep to this level of metaphysical generality—but metaphysics is nothing to be ashamed of or pejorative about, on the contrary—Marx's theory of "productive forces" can be retained. And, to tell the truth, the vast majority of human beings, fundamentally, are driven by the same movement: overcoming disease, getting rid of the burden of backbreaking work, extending knowledge and culture, varying pleasures and needs (civilized man is man rich in needs, says Marx), only chagrined minds, animated by that masochism and death instinct of bigots, can refuse it.

But "productive forces" have often been identified by a whole tradition of dogmatic Marxism of the Second and Third Internationals, with the growth of industry, machinismo and the industrial exploitation of nature[60]. This conception of "productive forces" is exactly that of the capitalists, who identify social wealth with the accumulation of capital and the unlimited exploitation of all natural resources as soon as they can be converted into commodities. The sacred union of capitalist big industry and vulgar Marxism is a well-known fact, and its ideological underpinnings are easy to spot. Conversely, by advocating "degrowth", making "progress" their prime target and, for some of them, even proposing a return to the pastoral and convivial life of the pre-industrial era, ecologists and other varieties of environmentalists are committing exactly the same confusion, but this time with a negative sign.

---

60. On the theoretical issues raised by the concept, or rather pseudo-concept, of "productive forces" in Marx and the Marxist tradition, we can only refer you to *Comprendre Marx, op. cit.* chap. II, section "Les forces productives et le 'productivisme' de Marx".

Let's sum things up with an example: when capitalist industry ravages a landscape, pollutes the soil and thus destroys the very basis of human life on earth, the capitalist calls it "growth"—whereas it's a massive and often irreversible destruction of wealth belonging to humanity—and the ecologist calls it "degrowth". It's hard to imagine worse confusion. We'll come back to this later. However, it has to be said that by sounding the alarm, even if sometimes in a haphazard and confusing way, ecologists and environmentalists are putting their finger on a real problem: we are reaching a point where the accumulation of capital is running up against objective barriers and calling into question the very conditions of life on this good old planet. Whether it happens in a year, ten years or thirty, the oil crisis is inevitable, and it will shake the entire capitalist production system, which is largely based on the ideal of the automobile as the true materialization of modern man's freedom. The proposals for alternatives are all equally derisory. Agrofuels are bottomless pits that will devastate arable land and starve the planet, as we began to see in the food crisis of 2007-2008… so much so that many leaders are wondering whether this is really a good idea, even if it has the support of powerful lobbies in the United States and France. The electric car is a gag we've been talking about for over a century, simply because the storage of electrical energy in the form of chemical energy (in batteries) is determined by the general laws of nature, and we'll never be able to propel a car with a few LR6 batteries! But that's not all. Electricity isn't free. It also has to be produced, and if thermal power plants are shut down for lack of fuel and because of greenhouse gas emissions, we'll have to build more nuclear power plants, and then face considerable safety problems… and uranium scarcity. Wind and solar power (we once believed in tidal power) are undoubtedly useful complements, but will not be anything else in the foreseeable future. Then there's the sea serpent of "nuclear fusion", which works very well for destroying the planet (we know how to do it, and we make H-bombs), but which we'll be unable to harness for peaceful purposes for a long time to come, if not forever. That leaves hydrogen to power fuel cells. But this element, so simple and so common in the universe, is quite rare in a free form on earth, and so its production is costly in terms of energy[61]. Well, the famous Shadoks[62] had a solution: pump the fuel into the universe, thanks to the ingenious invention of the "cosmogol pump", but most episodes of this hilarious series ended with: "the Shadoks were always pumping, and the more they pumped, the more there was nothing." Basically, the only solution to the energy crisis is to spend less, to be "thrifty", and therefore to stop following the miracle recipes of growth-at-all-costs economists.

As such, the energy crisis is not fatal: reformists of all kinds are trying to convince capitalists that the production of energy-saving means is a promising sector for capital accumulation. And some capitalist groups have already jumped on the bandwagon. But in the long term, an industry based on saving energy and raw materials cannot be an attractive field for capital accumulation. For example, we could, because we technically know how, produce truly durable consumer goods: household appliances that, like old refrigerators, could last a human lifetime, economical automobiles with inexpensive, easy-to-replace parts, and so on. But with such ideas—which are truly economical and in no way call for reducing people's comfort or material wealth (quite the contrary)—the household appliance or automobile industry would be forced to produce much less, and its profit rate would quickly fall to zero. The rapid obsolescence of all manufactured products is programmed and organized to maintain the possibility of capital accumulation—which is not at all the same thing as the accumulation of use values available to all. If consumers weren't persuaded to buy the latest cell phone, which doesn't just make phone calls, but also allows them to watch TV on screens the size of postage stamps, and doesn't even make a toaster,

---

61. Hydrogen can be produced by catalyzing methane or ethanol. But you need methane or ethanol…

62. Famous in their day (1969-1973) when they let their squealing laughter be heard on (public) television, which had not yet been completely transformed into a machine for selling available brain shares.

at least half of all cell phone factories would have to close down. And so on.

Similarly, once all buildings have been insulated, all boilers replaced by efficient ones, and people educated to stop wasting energy and to prefer a good sweater to a turn of the heating dial, there will be nothing left for the energy-saving industry to do, and its rate of profit will fall to zero. The reformers of capitalism — environmentalists, social democrats, "alternatives" of all stripes— precisely because they can't or won't consider the overall movement of the capitalist mode of production, announce miraculous new solutions every morning. They hold conferences, publish magazines and produce speeches galore. But the law of capital is harsh, and the massive destruction of wealth is a condition for the continuation of accumulation. This is why the arms economy has played such a major role in the overall process of capital accumulation over the last century, and why wars are, in the end, the best means capital has found to put an end to its periodic overproduction of capital. Degrowth theorists and other mirage merchants are merely trying to sell a solution to capital overproduction compatible with the capitalist mode of production. They catch a glimpse of the problem, but ultimately fail to see what they see, because their horizons remain limited by the categories of bourgeois political economy, because their brains are permanently clouded by the excessive consumption of ideology, of which, incidentally, they are also the producers.

A thrifty, "sustainable development" production system (to use the "novlangue") would be a system centered on the production of use values, and would produce goods only because of their reasoned use and the real gain in comfort they provide. However, the capitalist system is not centered on use value, but on exchange value insofar as it is a moment in the circulation of capital. The theorists of liberal capitalism, Adam Smith for example, postulated a kind of pre-established harmony governing the social order: by producing for exchange and profit, individuals would at the same time produce for the satisfaction of human needs, and thus individual egoism is converted into social value, the individual is reconciled with society. But Marx's genius lies precisely in having understood that this was an illusion, or more precisely, an ideological representation of reality. Beneath the apparent indefinite circulation of commodities converted into money, then into commodities and so on (M-A-M-A…), Marx isolated two contradictory moments: M-A-M, the exchange of commodities for use, and A-M-A', the circulation of capital for accumulation (see *above*). The "environmental crisis", the problem of the limits of development, degrowth, sustainable development and so on all point to this fundamental contradiction between the two forms of the cycle of commodity exchange, while masking it.

If we start from this contradiction—that is, from the truly "dialectical" understanding that the form of production and exchange in societies dominated by the capitalist mode of production is a profoundly contradictory form, and an explosive contradiction at that—then we can reset our perception of reality and break out of the *camera oscura* of ideology. On the one hand, there are no supporters of science and technical progress who are in favor of GMOs, nuclear power, freeways and electric cars, and, on the other, irredeemably reactionary environmental obscurantists: false debates that amuse the gallery and even allow the so-called rationalists of the left to perform virtuoso acts in the service of multinationals. Quite simply, the question is the purpose of work and production, and therefore of the economy in its most general sense: is it to satisfy human needs, or the needs of capital accumulation? And these are two contradictory objectives. If we want to satisfy human needs, GMOs are perfectly useless and even harmful[63], but on the other hand, they are indispensable if we want to satisfy the appetite for profit and power of large corporations like Monsanto,

---

63. Not necessarily for health reasons—for the time being, we're mostly uncertain on this issue, and we can only point to a few unfortunate precedents, such as those illustrious assemblies of honorable scientists who swore up and down that asbestos was absolutely harmless… There are other agronomic reasons (and agronomy isn't just molecular biology) and reasons of agricultural economics.

Novartis and a few others. If we want to satisfy human needs, there's no need to multiply the number of nuclear power plants or to transform two-thirds of agricultural land into a means of filling the tanks of 4X4s, which are only used to climb hills as steep as the Champs-Élysées, or of powerful sedans with engines of several hundred horsepower, with the aim of doing an average of 12 km/h in the Paris region and reaching 130 km/h on freeways, which we did very well in the fifties and sixties with very ordinary vehicles… On the other hand, we could easily satisfy human needs by relocating production (which would massively reduce transport costs), by breaking down the absurd mobility imposed by "restructuring" and rethinking urban planning from top to bottom, which means that workers spend a considerable amount of time getting to work, and so on. A policy along these lines would improve everyone's life… but not that of the capitalist Moloch.

This contradiction between human needs and capital accumulation is as old as capitalism itself. In *Capital*, Marx shows how the unquenchable thirst for profit led capitalists to endanger the physical existence of the British working class—the lengthening to exhaustion of the working day, appalling working and living conditions, child labor from an early age, led to the physical degradation of workers:

"Dr. Boothroyd, a Hanley physician, states that "each new generation of potters is smaller and weaker than the previous one". Likewise another physician, Mr. Mac Bean: "During the twenty-five years that I have been practicing my profession among potters, the degeneracy of this class has been strikingly manifested by the decrease in height and weight of the body." (*Capital*, I, X)

In the same chapter, Marx again reports this testimony from a North Staffordshire doctor:

"As a class, male and female potters… represent a degenerate population both morally and physically. They are generally of stunted stature, badly made and deformed in the chest. They age quickly and live short lives; phlegmatic and anemic, they betray the weakness of their constitution by stubborn attacks of dyspepsia, disturbances of the liver and kidneys, and rheumatism. Above all, they are prone to chest disease, pneumonia, phthisis, bronchitis and asthma. Scrofulosis, which attacks glands, bones and other parts of the body, is the disease of more than two-thirds of potters. If the degeneracy of the population of this district is not much greater, it owes it exclusively to its recruitment from the neighboring countryside and its cross-breeding with healthier breeds…"

On several occasions, Marx refers to the adulteration of bread, commonplace in London. "There are two kinds of bakers in London, those who sell bread at its real value, the *full priced*, and those who sell it below that value, the *undersellers*. The latter class makes up more than three-quarters of the total number of bakers (p. XXXII in Government Commissioner H. S. Tremenheere's *Report* on the *Grievances complained of by the journeymen bakers*, etc., London, 1862). These *undersellers*, almost without exception, sell bread adulterated with mixtures of alum, soap, lime, plaster and similar ingredients, just as wholesome and nourishing. (See the Blue Book quoted above, the report of the *Comittee of 1855 on the adulteration of bread* and Dr Hassal's *Adulterations detected*, 2nd edn, London, 1862). Sir John Gordon told the 1855 Committee that "as a result of these adulterations, the poor man who lives daily on two pounds of bread, does not now obtain a quarter of the nutrients which would be necessary to him, to say nothing of the pernicious influence which such food has on his health." To explain how a large part of the working class, although perfectly aware of these adulterations, nevertheless endures them, Tremenheere gives this reason (I.c., p. XLVII) "that it is a necessity for them to take bread from the baker's or the retailer's store, as it is willingly given to them." As the workers are only paid at the end of the week, they can only pay themselves at that time for the bread consumed during that time by their families, and Tremenheere adds, based on the assertion of eyewitnesses: "It is notorious that bread prepared with these kinds of mixtures is made expressly for this kind of practice." (*It is notorious that bread composed of those mixtures is made expressly for sale in this manner.*) "In many agricultural districts in England (but much more so in Scotland) wages are paid fortnightly and even monthly. The worker is obliged to buy his goods on credit while waiting for his pay. Everything is sold to him at very high prices, and he finds himself, in effect, tied to the store that exploits him and squeezes him dry. Thus, for example, at Horningsham in Wilts, where he is only paid by the month, the same quantity of flour (8 lb.) that everywhere else he gets for 1 shilling 10 pence, costs him 2 shillings 4 pence." (*Sixth Report on Public Health by The Medical Officer of the Privy Council*, etc., 1864, p. 264) "In 1853, the printing workers of Paisley and Kilmarnoch (west of Scotland) resorted to a strike to force their bosses to pay them fortnightly instead of monthly." (*Reports of The Inspectors of Factories for 31st. Oct. 1853*, p. 34.) As an example of the exploitation that results for the worker from the credit he gives to the capitalist, we can cite again the method employed in England by a large number of coal mine operators. As they only pay the workers once a month, they make advances to them while waiting for the term, especially in goods, which the workers are obliged to buy above the current price (*Truck system*). "It is common practice among coal mine owners to pay their workers once a month, and to advance them money at the end of each intervening week. This money is given to them in the *tommy shop*, i.e. in the retail store belonging to the master, so that what they receive with one hand they give back with the other." (*Children's Employment Commission. III Report*, London, 1864, p. 38, n. 192.)" (*Capital*, I, section II, chap. IV)

Pollution, degraded living conditions, "junk food", it's all there. In July 2008, in modern Europe, subject to veterinary and health controls, we learned that: "11,000 tonnes of spoiled or out-of-date cheese were 'recycled' in Italy and Germany to be incorporated into new cheese products. Some of these rotten cheeses contained worms, mouse droppings or even packaging residues. Instead of destroying their out-of-date or spoiled products, some forty major Italian, British, German and Austrian companies shipped them to four companies, three based in Italy and one in Germany, run by a Sicilian businessman. The rotten cheeses were then "recycled" by being mixed with "fresh" cheese products, a base then used in the manufacture of mozzarellas, gorgonzola and other processed cheeses sold throughout Europe. Some of the companies that disposed of their non-consumable products also bought back the recycled paste. A total of 11,000 tons of cheese were "reworked" in this way over the last two years, and the four recycling companies reportedly generated sales of some 10 million euros. The investigation by specialized police officers lasted two years and three people were arrested." (Agency dispatch, reprinted in the press, notably *Le Monde* of July 5, 2008) We are indeed in the world of which *Le Capital* speaks.

The difference with the time when Marx wrote *Capital* is perhaps that, firstly, capitalism's capacity to cause harm has increased tenfold and now covers the entire planet and, secondly, even elements of the ruling class are beginning to be affected by the degradation imposed by the capitalist mode of production. The industrial disasters of Bhopal, Seveso and Chernobyl are only the most striking events, but no-one keeps a daily record of the victims of Chinese or Indian industrialization. Sea pollution and overexploitation are reaching terrifying levels. It's not just a question of dwindling fish stocks (one of the main sources of protein for hundreds of millions of human beings), it's not just a question of this gigantic island of waste, made up of millions of tonnes of plastic residue floating in the Pacific. It's about the destruction of coral reefs, with incalculable consequences for the ecosystems of countless islands that could simply disappear with the death of the coral. It's also about the destruction of soils and forests. It's about the explosion in the number of cancers, an explosion that the most serious studies attribute to the "background noise of modern society". Above all, for the first time in human history, we are facing a situation where human activities can profoundly and unpredictably alter the future of the planet and its (sometimes) rational inhabitants.

The "ecological crisis" is real, and we can only wonder about the reasons for the prolonged blindness of a certain number of scientists (?) like former minister Allègre, to name but one of the most caricatural. But this crisis is not the product of some mysterious human *ubris* ("excess"), nor is it the vengeance of nature, nor the ransom of "progress", it is quite simply one of the most blatant manifestations of the consequences of capitalism[64]. As there will be no "final crisis", we can carry on for a long time yet, hoping that only our neighbors will pay the price (according to the logic of a certain bourgeois NIMBY environmentalism[65]). But that's really unreasonable! "We're on the brink of the abyss, let's take a giant step forward", say the advocates of the revival of capitalism. Should we follow them?

It will be objected that this waste of resources, this unbridled consumption that threatens to engulf the human world, is in line with the wishes of individual consumers, and that it is not up to us to decide what is good and what is not for others. Our purpose is not to determine which needs should be satisfied and which should not. We have no intention of arguing that a little barley bread and fresh water is all that's needed to be happy—even if Greek ethics of fair measure should be revived. We are merely pointing out the widening gulf between human needs and what the capitalist machine produces. Many needs have only become needs as a consequence of capitalist development, a development that is guided not by the needs to be satisfied, but by the rate of profit. Evicting the poor from city centers and housing them in more or less dormitory towns (because it's not always easy to get a good night's sleep there) is not a response to the needs of the

---

64. It could be argued that the countries of "real socialism" have often outstripped capitalist countries in this respect—the drying up of the Aral Sea, Chernobyl—but this is not an objection, since these countries, engaged in "primitive accumulation" and in competition with the capitalist powers, were fundamentally subject to the same logic as that of capital accumulation in the countries of private capitalism.
65. Acronym for *Not in my backyard*. NIMBY is the environmentalist who fights for public transport, but against the railroad line that passes near his home…

poor, but to land speculation. On the other hand, this creates a need for transport, and as public transport is not profitable from a capitalist point of view, the only way to avoid being locked into your housing estate (which is sometimes beginning to resemble the black housing estates of apartheid South Africa) is to take your car to buy what you need a few kilometers away in one of those hideous shopping areas that now surround most cities. So the need for an automobile is not a false need—it's absurd to ask individuals to do without one—since it derives from the necessities of a way of life that was never produced by human need.

So it's not a question of imposing a rationing of needs in the face of an unchanged production system and organization of social life. This is exactly what a certain official ecology demands: it tells the poor to "tighten your belts to protect the planet". And in so doing, it contributes to the reduction in the value of labour power, and thus to capitalist profit. And she takes her message a little further by flying on planes that are among the biggest producers of CO_2. No, the problem is to change the mode of production and therefore to change the mode of production of needs. Faced with a system that is by nature excessive, we need to return to a sense of proportion, as indicated in Marx's text quoted above: to regulate our relationship with nature rationally—and not to follow the partial rationality of profit, which leads to global irrationality—and to produce what we need with as little energy as possible. But this implies that we are no longer dominated by the blind power of exchanges, but rather that we dominate them. None of this is possible as long as the direction of society is in the hands of the "fanatical agents of production for production's sake" who, according to Marx, are the capitalists. It's impossible to claim that we can defend the future of the planet without asking this question. And that's why Al Gore-style numbers and "Grenelle de l'environnement"—style ecology are pure and simple frauds.

The Steel Cage of Modern Capitalism

We may agree with Freud that no one will be able to transform human beings into termites, and that, consequently, the increasing submission of life to the constraints of the capitalist mode of production will meet with powerful resistance and produce its antidotes. For the development of the capitalist mode of production directly calls into question the foundations of human civilization, i.e. the idea we have had, since the origins of religious and philosophical thought, of what it is to be human.

Capitalism was born and developed on the basis of the culture it inherited. Its genius lay in its ability to harness the free productive forces of science and culture. There comes a time—the seventeenth century—when economic forces and intellectual life at its most abstract enter into a highly productive interaction. As a mathematical science, the new science of Galileo and Descartes enabled prediction and the construction of technical applications, and conversely, technical progress led to new scientific breakthroughs. Unquestionably, the economic boom and far-flung navigation were the breeding ground on which the culture of the Enlightenment and the majestic edifice of modern science were to grow. The boundless greed of the adventurers of nascent capitalism combined with the disinterested knowledge cultivated by these disinterested, austere scholars, ready to sacrifice everything from the pleasures of worldly life for the love of truth. A dialectical unity of opposites that gave capitalism its impetus. This combination worked right up to the 20th century, and was reflected in education—at least that of the ruling classes—which was both increasingly scientific and technical (think of the considerable educational achievements of the French Revolution, the Directoire and the Empire) and, at the same time, an education founded on the tradition of the classical humanities, as if we didn't want to forget that modern science was born at a time and in a movement when ancient Greco-Latin culture was restored to its full dignity, which was the hallmark of that great revolutionary era, the Renaissance.

The 20th century marks a turning point in the cultural history of Europe. The turn from the nineteenth to the twentieth century, which appeared to be extremely fertile in scientific terms (two major physical theories, general relativity and quantum mechanics, were conceived in the space of a few years), was also the moment when a whole intellectual current hostile to rationalism crystallized, giving rise to the "ideology of war" analyzed by Domenico Losurdo[66].

Until the 20th century, scientific progress, moral progress, political progress and economic development seemed to go more or less hand in hand. The twentieth century shattered this beautiful harmony: scientific and technical progress was placed at the service of the worst kind of barbarism. Far from regressing, war was unleashed as never before, hitting civilian populations hard. Modernity" and the cult of machines and science were put at the service of a new kind of tyranny: Fascism and Nazism. In 1945, the USA dropped the absolute weapon, the atomic bomb, on the populations of Hiroshima and Nagasaki, gripping humanity with horror. Scientific rationality was thus placed at the service of total madness. Capitalism directly challenges the very existence of human civilization. This, in turn, feeds a current of hostility to science, which is accused of all the sins. Descartes is to blame for all this, with his Promethean project to "make us like masters and possessors of nature" (*Discourse on Method*, VI).

Far be it from us to blame the "master thinkers" of the classical age for the madness of the tyrants of the "century of catastrophes", as Hobsbawm calls it in his *Age of Extremes*, devoted to the "short 20th century" (1914-1989). Descartes was a brilliant thinker, and he grasped the full extent of the possibilities opened up by the social and intellectual revolution that was unfolding before him. His unshakeable confidence in the powers of human reason is first and foremost confidence in man's ability to use reason well, as the very condition of happiness. This has nothing to do with any project of

---

66. See Domenico Losurdo, *Heidegger et l'idéologie de la guerre*, PUF, 1998, "Actuel Marx Confrontation" collection.

absolute mastery, of "arraisonnement", to use Heideggerian terms. From Descartes to Kant and Hegel, via Spinoza and Leibniz, science is conceived first and foremost as the source of true joy, the joy that comes from using "the best part of ourselves", the intellect, as Spinoza puts it. And it is therefore inseparable from the search for happiness that can be shared. From the 19th century onwards, a scientism began to emerge that reduced science to operative activities, and assumed that this kind of activity was sufficient to regulate all human affairs properly. Positivism played its part in this evolution, cutting science off from philosophy and metaphysics, and aiming to make human government a sort of sub-branch of engineering. This new situation reinforces anti-rationalist tendencies and develops a reactionary hatred of science, while at the same time science is progressively subjected to the technical imperatives of capitalism.

The destruction of culture by capitalism is visible in all areas. On the one hand, traditional culture is subject to the law of the market. We need only look at the transformation of the Louvre into a shopping mall to understand what modern museology is all about: the "coca-cola-ization" of masterpieces. On the other hand, a mass culture is produced that no longer bears any relation to popular culture, a mass culture based on the passivity of individual consumers, brainwashing and methodical dumbing-down, of which the major television media with their reality shows and variety shows are a particularly disgusting example.

This destruction of culture goes hand in hand with the destruction of the frameworks of communal life, and with the controlled cutting of individuals who are monitored, spied on and conditioned with the help of the "human" sciences.

Finally, capitalism can lead to the "surpassing of man" himself. Some prophets are talking increasingly loudly about the "posthuman", a posthuman that is being prepared with work on genetically modified organisms, research into the "bionic man" and experimentation with new methods of enhancing bodily performance, It's for this reason that protests against doping and demands for "clean" sport are either nonsense or an expression of the consummate art of lying that characterizes our "transparent" societies.

Capitalism up to and including the 20th century was never pure capitalism. Its development was initially hampered by the weight of the past, by the heritage of a certain conception of the values that should govern human societies; it was a capitalism marked by the society from which it emerged. It was then seriously limited, and had to come to terms with the labor movement and the fear of communism. From 1945 to 1975/1980 in France, the policies of the various governments were shaped by social demands. Right-wing governments had to disguise themselves as "social" or "social-democratic" governments: in 1974, Jacques Chirac called himself a "Laborist", while his mentor Pompidou used the Swedish social-democratic experiment as a means of warding off the Communist threat. These two obstacles to the free play of capitalist forces have been overcome. The rural world, the refuge of conservative tradition and a certain resistance to capitalism, is no more than a memory, and the European Union has programmed the extermination of the last holdouts within ten or fifteen years. Crafts and small businesses are on their last legs, and with them the very idea of trade, replaced by that of employment. The values of the past are buried. The modern bourgeoisie doesn't give a damn about the family, hates the fatherland and only likes to work for others. The revolt against the moral order has removed the last obstacles to the brutal commercialization of everything intimate, and has made pornography one of the major sectors of the "cultural industries".

Thus, the continuation of the "unlimited" development of capitalism is the order of the day, but this only makes it all the more likely that the fundamental trends we have identified will be expressed:

1) Development of confrontations between capitalist groups, with the multiplication of armed conflicts over greater or lesser areas,

and the dislocation of former state units, provoking a chaos in which the former Yugoslavia was no more than an amiable warm-up;
2) Continued and accelerated destruction of natural resources and likelihood of large-scale ecological disasters;
3) Destruction of human culture and the very idea of the individual as a free subject.

At the beginning of the 20th century, Rosa Luxemburg, against Bernstein's illusions of a continuous, painless transformation of capitalism, clearly posed the alternative: socialism or barbarism. The catastrophe of 1914 signed the death warrant of European socialism and paved the way for the barbarism of the new "Thirty Years' War", 1914-1945. We are once again faced with this alternative. *Hic Rhodus, hic salta!*

SECOND PART

Socialism and Communism in the Last Century: Deadly Illusions

Chapter VI.

The Abolition of Wage-Labor and Employers

Taken as a whole, the capitalist mode of production has developed and continues to develop along the same lines as the author of *Capital*. There is much to be said for Marxism and its fate, but Marx's analysis of the structure and operating principles of the capitalist mode of production has been largely validated by historical experience. And when Marx was wrong, it was most often when he slipped from the terrain of scientific description of reality into prophecy—for example, when he predicted that the expropriation of the expropriators would take place with the necessity that presides over the phenomena of nature.

At the same time, it's clear that not only has communism not triumphed, but nowhere has progress been made towards the expropriation of the expropriators, and the communist ideal itself seems to have foundered. We could separate Marx's objective description of the capitalist mode of production from his projections into the future of a humanity liberated from the exploitation of man by man. However, Marx has great difficulty separating the descriptive from the normative. For him, communism is not an ideal to which we should try to conform reality. Communism is "the real movement" itself, the movement that abolishes the existing order. But the "real movement" not only did not abolish the existing order, it arguably reinforced it. Historical communism and socialism, the great movements that in part dominated the historical scene of the

20th century, have all but disappeared: all that remains are labels and flags whose meaning has been lost on most citizens, especially the young. Let's try to understand what justified the Marxist optimism that ultimately produced unexpected effects.

The Expropriation of Expropriators

French revolutionary syndicalism had summed up its subversive objectives in a single formula: "abolition of the wage-earner and the boss". It was another way of proposing the disappearance of antagonistic social classes.

Marx's idea is as follows: capitalism was born of the expropriation of the individual producer, transforming peasants and craftsmen into wage-labourers, with nothing left of their own but their labour power—and that of their children—to sell to the capitalist. But the story doesn't end there. This first expropriation paved the way for another: competition between capitalists led to the concentration and centralization of capital, further reducing the ruling class to a handful of isolated owners in a largely proletarianized society.

"This expropriation is brought about by the immanent laws of capitalist production, which lead to the concentration of capital. Correlative to this centralization, to the expropriation of the large number of capitalists by the small, is the development on an ever-increasing scale of the application of science to technology, the exploitation of land methodically and together, the transformation of tools into instruments powerful only through common use, hence the economy of the means of production, the interweaving of all peoples in the network of the universal market, hence the international character imprinted on the capitalist regime. As the number of capitalist potentates usurping and monopolizing all the advantages of this period of social evolution diminishes, so does the misery, oppression, slavery, degradation and exploitation of the ever-growing and increasingly disciplined working class, united and organized by the very mechanism of capitalist production. Capital's monopoly becomes a hindrance to the mode of production that has grown and prospered with it and under its auspices. The socialization of labor and the centralization of its material resources reach a point where they can no longer fit into their capitalist envelope. That envelope is shattering. The time for capitalist ownership has come. The expropriators are in turn expropriated.

Capitalist appropriation, in line with the capitalist mode of production, constitutes the first negation of this private property, which is merely the corollary of independent, individual labor. But capitalist production itself generates its own negation with the same fatality that presides over the metamorphoses of nature. It is the negation of negation. It re-establishes not the worker's private property, but his individual property, based on the acquests of the capitalist era, on cooperation and joint possession of all the means of production, including the soil.

The transformation of private, fragmented property, the object of individual labor, into capitalist property naturally required more time, effort and trouble than the metamorphosis of capitalist property into social property, which in fact already rests on a collective mode of production. There, it was the expropriation of the mass by a few usurpers; here, it's the expropriation of a few usurpers by the mass". (*Capital*, I, section III, "The Historical Tendency of Capitalist Accumulation")

Communism will come easily and necessarily, because capitalism already has most of the work! Marx's analysis is obviously not as simplistic as the summary he gives in this penultimate chapter of Book I might lead us to believe. We must therefore focus on what constitutes the major articulation of the Marxian conception of social revolution, namely the term "producer". Marx is commonly thought of as the theorist of the historical role of the working class. But in *Capital,* the worker appears in the singular or plural only as a term antagonistic to capital. The one who carries a positive charge is the producer. *Strictly speaking,* producers are not a social class, yet it is their association that is the key formula of the coming social revolution. The notion of production is an "anhistorical" one: in any society, there are producers, and the producer is simply the one who implements the means of labor, whatever the mode of production. The producer is not only the agent who produces material goods—the worker, in the strict sense—but also all those who play a useful role in production. Thus, the work of supervision and coordination is necessary "wherever production takes the form of a socially coordinated process" (*Capital*, III, V). Of course, this is only one aspect of this work in the capitalist mode of production, where the worker is subject to factory discipline. This task of organization and supervision has traditionally fallen to the boss. But with the development of joint-stock companies and the centralization of capital, we see a separation of capitalist ownership from the functions of coordination and supervision, and when discussing this process, Marx shows that the factory manager cannot be equated with the capitalist. On the contrary, he refers to the role of the manager in a workers' cooperative: "In the production cooperative, the contradictory character of managerial work disappears, since the manager there is paid directly by the workers, instead of representing capital vis-à-vis them." (*ibid.*)

Marx envisages labor as a totality. But in the capitalist mode of production, this totality is "a combination of labors" and therefore it is a unity "whose constituent parts are alien to each other, so that collective labor as a totality is not the work of individual labor, and the work of the various workers combined constitutes a whole only insofar as they are forced to combine their efforts, powerless to be themselves the authors of this association." (*Manuscripts of 1857*) In other words, in its capitalist form, cooperation, the formation of a collective worker, is at the same time alienation, which is clearly expressed in the critique of machinismo, but it is at the same time a cooperation that carries within itself the possibility of a new social organization. Indeed, by developing machinismo, the application of science to production and the ever-increasing integration of individual labor into collective labor, capital not only develops the productive forces of humanity in general, it "works for its own dissolution." Simple labor has "become scientific labor, which subjects natural forces to the service of human needs". Immediate work—the worker's immediate activity—loses its importance in relation to the organization of production and the development of machines. Consequently, producers—all individuals integrated into this global productive process, into this "general work"—are not limited to workers, but include all those who play a role in this global process: engineers, technicians, specialists in work organization—what certain sociologists, a century after Marx, would call the "new working class". And for those who don't want to understand, Marx severely criticizes those socialists who make class differences about the amount of income[67]:

> "Grobian common sense[68]" transforms class difference into "lumpiness of the purse" and class antagonism into "unraveling of trades". The size of the purse is a purely quantitative difference, by means of which two individuals of the same class can be aroused against each other at will. It is well known that medieval guilds were pitted against each other "according to trade". But it is also well known that the modern difference between classes is in no way based on 'trade', that it is rather the division of labor within the same class that produces different modes of labor." (*Capital*, Book III)

In the final analysis, the only difference between the manager and the worker is a "purely quantitative" difference in the size of their wallets, and to set the latter against the former would be nothing other than to stir up "division within the same class", even though both, of course, have "different modes of labor". This conception is consistent with Marx's general statements on the evolution of the capitalist mode of production. The great mass of wage-earners is increasingly at odds with the small minority of capital owners, who appear more and more clearly as a parasitic class, as the socially useful function of the bosses is delegated to employees. This extreme polarization leads to social revolution, and necessarily

---

67. Just as we do today with the all-purpose, totally shapeless notion of the "middle class".
68. Rude.

so, because capital itself has already integrated producers into an overall process, rendering the capitalist superfluous.

It is this process, which Marx still calls the "increasing socialization of production", that corresponds to the natural development of capitalism, which inevitably tends to clash with the narrow character of private appropriation, which increasingly appears as external to the production process itself. In short, the abolition of wage-earners and employers, and their replacement by the collective of "associated producers", is not an external watchword, a program for cooking in the kettles of the future, but an objective reality of which communists need only be the subjective, conscious expression.

The Illusions of Communism according to Marx

The difficult problem is this: basically, things are going as Marx analyzed them in the mid-nineteenth century, but the results are not at all what Marx expected! The separation of capitalist ownership from the management of the production process by "managers" is an obvious fact, absolutely indisputable on a large scale. Ownership of capital is so dispersed that it's often hard to tell who the real boss is. Alongside a few individual "reference shareholders" who own a significant stock of shares, there is a mass of small shareholders whose voice carries very little weight, and above all the "zinzins", the institutional investors, banks, investment funds, insurance companies and pension funds. For these "zinzins", buying shares in a company is not about becoming its owner, it's about buying a drawing right on future capital gains, or simply the opportunity to make a killing on the market[69]. The second half of the

---

69. The Kerviel/Société Générale affair, where we saw that a trading room employee could commit ten times the amount of his bank's capitalization to high-risk speculative operations, showed the extent to which banks in general were involved in all these processes that make the economy look like a casino table.

20th century also saw the development of capitalist firms without capitalist ownership in the strict sense: nationalized companies. In varying degrees, but sometimes on a very large scale, Western European countries nationalized their banking sectors and large corporations. In France, nationalization is even constitutional. In Austria, 80% of industrial production was nationalized as a kind of preventive measure, to avoid the dismantling of the Austrian economy promised by Soviet troops. The colonial countries that gained independence also carried out massive nationalizations. Between the paradise of capitalist ownership (the USA, where the *New Deal* and its policy of large-scale public works was the height of "socialism") and the state-controlled, planned economy of the USSR, there was a whole range of intermediaries, companies confronted with capitalist competition, ultimately subject to the criteria of profitability.

There is capitalism, but not always capitalists, or else the definition has to be changed. All those who earn a little more than a living wage *nolens volens* enter the "capitalist" machine[70]: SICAVs, PEAs, "sustainable" savings plans, but also supplementary pension plans appear as investments for fathers of families, a kind of woolen stocking a little better protected against the wear and tear of time. But if the bank can guarantee its customers a regular income from their investments, it needs to commit itself to a slightly riskier market, that of securities or highly speculative markets such as derivatives. Only the rentier can believe that money can grow on its own!

In other words, we have this curious situation: capitalists who are no longer all capitalists, and proletarians who are beginning to be a little capitalist. Let's take things a step further: if we were to develop workers' shareholding a little more consistently than is the

---

70. Two birds with one stone. The centralization of capital goes hand in hand with a far-reaching ideological operation: workers are attached to the company's success. Anyone who avoids redundancy is likely to see their share price rise. The capital-labor association, an old Gaullist fad, is one of the elements of this corporatism, which is one of the major trends in the capitalist system.

case today, we could envisage wage-earners becoming the majority owners of companies, and socialism being achieved peacefully, by means that could hardly be more capitalist. A number of "reformist" currents have already taken up this cause.

More generally, the question of the legitimacy and durability of capitalist property is raised either directly by certain authors who do not come at all from the Marxist tradition (such as Jeremy Rifkin, who envisages a capitalism without property in *The Age of Access*), or indirectly through massive economic processes. Pension funds, which are becoming increasingly widespread even where pay-as-you-go retirement schemes still dominate, are a way of saying that capitalist ownership has had its day, and that the economy can only function if it is owned by everyone! Obviously, for those who defend these funds, it's not a question of abolishing employers and wage-earners, only of making wage-earners bear the burden of the capitalist (without having the advantages in terms of decision-making power) while maintaining them in their condition as wage-earners subjected to domination and exploitation. In short, we want to have our cake and eat it too, or, as the Italians say more picturesquely, to have a full barrel and a drunken wife! But this does not diminish the theoretical significance of the new forms of capitalist property.

Finally, modern methods of corporate leadership that seek to rely on the initiative and commitment of individuals show that it is ultimately the salaried condition itself that is the main obstacle to progress in labor productivity. Reuniting the worker with the means of production (restoring the worker's individual property on the basis of the acquests of the socialization of production, to use Marx's expression) is precisely what is at issue in all discussions on work organization and human resources management. But here again, we want the benefits without paying the price.

Dialectics" is based on the idea that every historical reality is a contradiction in act. In all aspects of the development of capitalist relations of production, this contradiction between emancipatory potential and the tendency to absolute domination is radically in evidence today. So why is communism in a state of collapse, if objective reality shows that modern society—ours, not the backward Russia of 1917—is in the throes of this transformation? The answer lies in the limited nature of the sociology Marxists use to understand social relations. By fixating on the framework of the enterprise, subject to the search for optimal relations between means and ends, we end up distinguishing only two categories: the most numerous, the productive workers (the producers) and the parasitic profiteers, a handful of individuals. It's tempting to consider that, objectively speaking, workers, executives and even managers have the same interests, and that the alliance of producers (an old watchword from Saint-Simonism[71]) will be imposed on all reasonable men. In the sixties and seventies, a theoretical elaboration of this kind underpinned the PCF's strategy. But we could have pushed utopia a little further and pointed out that if capitalists had any sense, instead of chasing the chimera of the power that money gives, they would do better to join in the common efforts to help build a fairer, happier society!

Wage-Labor is Competition between Proletarians

In reality, the process of capitalism's development has absolutely none of the linear, positive effects Marx expected.

Consideration no. 1. Let's start with what Marx knew, stated and sometimes seems to forget in *Capital:* wage-labor is not simply the situation of individuals who work for a wage, it is first and fore-

---

71. Claude-Henri de Saint-Simon is one of the founders of socialism, and his influence on Marx is often greater than has been claimed. His ideal of a harmonious industrial society calls for an alliance between producers, the producer-capitalist and the producer-worker: "Industry is one: all its members are united by the general interests of production, by the need they all have for security in their work and freedom in their exchanges. Producers of all classes, of all countries, are therefore essentially friends; nothing prevents them from uniting, and the coalition of their efforts seems to us, ... the indispensable condition for industry to obtain all the ascendancy it can and must enjoy." (*Social Physiology*)

Chapter VI. The Abolition of Wage-Labor and Employers

most the competition between sellers of labor power to sell their labor power on the labor "market". It's true that it's in the interest of workers to form cartels of labor power sellers called unions, but at the same time it's in the interest of each individual to practice the strategy of the *free rider*, or, as sociologists say, the strategy of the stowaway. If we look at the immediate objective situation, then, the proletariat is driven to union (to get the best rates) and at the same time threatened by division and selfish strategies. For workers to go beyond this, they must acquire "class consciousness", i.e. act for motives other than those dictated by their immediate situation, for ideal motives even if these ideal motives are based on a thorough scientific understanding of capitalist social reality. In other words, even if we accept the highly risky hypothesis of a radical simplification of the social structure, opposing a large mass of wage-earners and a handful of exploiters, there is nothing to indicate that this large mass of wage-earners necessarily subjectively wants to do anything other than maintain wage-earning in an improved form, i.e. a situation in which competition is perpetuated between wage-earners who combine their efforts well in production, but are not the authors of the productive unit they form, and therefore are not an association of producers.

Lenin had little more than an intuition of this problem, in *Que faire?* when he argued that the working class, by its own efforts, could not go beyond the stage of trade-unionist class consciousness. What the "Leninists" have never wanted to understand is that the whole Leninist conception of the party as a centralized party of "professional revolutionaries" stems from this terrible observation for orthodox Marxism: the working class cannot emancipate itself. Faced with the same question, Gramsci saw the party as the "new prince" that alone could give the people the strength and intelligence to wage a prolonged struggle ("the war of positions") against capitalism.

Can a Dominated Class become Dominant?

Consideration no. 2. We can generalize. No dominated class in history has ever become a dominant class. Slaves may have risen up, but they never achieved anything other than insurrection without a future. Significantly, Spartacus had no other project than to leave Italy (and not to overthrow the domination of the slave-owning and trading class). Poor peasants staged Jacqueries, which sometimes covered up to two-thirds of the French territory[72], but it was the bourgeoisie that led the 1789 revolution—or rather, the bourgeoisies, as the direction of the process passed from one fraction to another in the pendulum swing from 1789 to the Empire. The working class is no exception to this law. It can only defend its place in a "class front" involving other fractions of the dominant classes. In the end, Marx believed that the problem would resolve itself through the alliance of factory managers and unskilled workers alike. But this perspective is purely speculative.

In fact, the working class would have to be able to build islands of communism within capitalism, from which to organize the overall struggle against capitalism. Companies or communes that seriously wanted to start building elements of communist society within society would be subject to the terrible pressure of the capitalist environment and, economically speaking, would have to face up to competition on the capitalist market. Workers' cooperatives, with the best will in the world, have to produce under such conditions that their products are competitive on the markets, and therefore workers' wages and working hours are not fundamentally different from those of ordinary capitalist enterprises. What's more, worker control, the responsibilities it entails and the time it demands, are very difficult to maintain over the long term. Very quickly, it's only the best-trained, the most ambitious, the most skilled in the art of the spoken word who exercise real power on behalf of the

---

72. See Boris PORCHNEV, *Les Soulèvements populaires en France au XVIIᵉ siècle*, Flammarion, 1972.

workers' collective. What is striking, if we look at the evolution of the last three decades, is that virtually all the demands for control, management and corporate governance that, however confusedly, expressed the aspiration for new social relations of production, have disappeared.

Perhaps there's a logical contradiction in all this: a dominated class that becomes dominant is no longer dominated. This superb tautology is not as empty as it sounds: when a fraction of the working class becomes dominant, it is no longer a fraction of the working class. The permanent staff, the experts and the bureaucrats who claim to speak for the working class are no longer members of it, even if they do originate from it. Whether we're talking about the apparatuses of social-democratic (and similar) parties and trade unions, or the bureaucrats of the countries of real socialism, their social positions and powers derive from this operation of prestidigitation: disguising the workers in the name of the political power of the working class. At the same time, these bureaucracies do not even form a real ruling class, but only a substitute for one. That's why the USSR and other "socialist countries" have officially been the scene of generally non-violent social counter-revolutions. In his excellent *Underground*, filmmaker Emir Kusturica describes a group of communist resistance fighters locked in a cellar during the war; their leaders, once the war was over, made them believe that the war was still going on, and for three decades they lived an invented heroic life. According to the director, this allegory of Yugoslavia applies to socialism and communism in the 20th century as a whole.

Workers' power has never succeeded in stabilizing itself over the long term. In "hot" periods, in revolutionary phases, there are indeed forms of "workers' power", more or less developed—the Paris Commune, workers' councils, soviets, people's assemblies— but as soon as the situation returns to "normal", i.e. as soon as workers return to work, these forms disappear or are emptied of all substance.

Class Contradictions and Contradictions within the Proletariat

Consideration no. 3. Competition between capitalists produces competition between workers, and this phenomenon is absolutely inevitable. As soon as the only serious prospect to which workers can cling is bargaining for the best price for their labor power, everything that underpins the national and international unity of workers shatters. Indeed, every worker's "trade-unionist" interest is that his or her capitalist should prevail in competition with other capitalists. Renault workers have a vested interest in Renault gaining market share, which puts them in a better position to negotiate wage increases. But if Renault gains market share, it is necessarily to the detriment of other manufacturers, and therefore to the detriment of workers employed by these other manufacturers to negotiate with their own capitalists. Of course, for a long time there were a number of ideals and moral values that counterbalanced this spontaneous tendency. But here too, these ideals and moral values seem to be a thing of the past. Patriotism has long been used to combat internationalism—the patent bankruptcy of internationalism dates back to August 1914. But "corporate patriotism" has grown considerably in recent decades, aided by modern management techniques. We have even seen trade unions (including the CGT) congratulate themselves on the fact that their nationalized companies (EDF or France Télécom) are capable of buying up companies in the same sector abroad. It's easy to see why they were unable to resist privatization when it came to France.

The support of a sizeable number of wage earners for anti-immigration politicians is part of the same perspective, that of workers competing with each other. Racism is invoked. Racist prejudice undoubtedly plays a role, but it's far less important than is often claimed. It's easy for an executive not to be "racist", since he's not competing with immigrant workers. On the contrary, "national" workers are in direct competition with immigrants on the job market, but also for access to welfare benefits and housing.

That racism plays only a secondary role in these confrontations between certain sectors of the working class is easily demonstrated by the Belgian and Italian examples. In Belgium, Flemish "nationalism" is based on the protectionism of Flemish workers against Walloons. The surge in support for a party like Bossi's *Lega Nord* is based on the resentment of Italian workers in the North against Italian workers in the South, as much or more than against non-Italian immigrants. When Bossi considers a Roman to be almost a foreigner, it's easy to see that it's not just about racism. That's why the so-called "fight against racism" being waged by the socialists and liberals is sheer tartuffery. On the one hand, they claim to promote the values of equality between men, non-discrimination and even fraternity (we're all "buddies"!), while on the other they defend a way of relating between individuals based on competition, rivalry and, ultimately, the idea that the law of the strongest is always the best.

Many other factors contradict the idea that capitalism is producing its own gravedigger, by creating a proletariat that is ever more numerous and ever more unified by living conditions and the development of the division of labor. Objectively speaking, there is indeed a "proletarianization" of society as a whole. Firstly, because salaried employment is now totally hegemonic, and independent professions are in full decline. Secondly, because the conditions of salaried workers are converging. The social difference—which does not only include income—between a blue-collar worker and an engineer has narrowed considerably between the end of the 19th century and today. The "proletarianization" of intellectual workers is a fact—even if we can't draw the conclusions that Antonio Negri, for example, does. But at the same time, the life of the working class has very often become similar to that of the intellectual salaried class, albeit more meager and uncertain. It's absurd to talk about the gentrification of the working class (suffice it to say that the median wage in France is below 1,400 euros to see how obscene talk of gentrification is). Nevertheless, many working-class people have bought their own home or detached house, and live under the constraint of long-term loans that must be honored at all costs. The way of life is more individualistic, notably due to the transformation of urban planning and the distances separating the home from the workplace. Leisure activities are no longer linked to membership of the working class and its organizations. Dreams no longer lie in the collective emancipation of the working class, but in the hope of "getting by" individually. The transformation is particularly marked among the younger generations of workers, who often have a much higher level of education than their fathers, and who experience the working-class condition as a failure and almost a decline[73]. As Marx said of French peasants in the mid-nineteenth century, despite the homogeneity of their social conditions, they did not form a class: "the great mass of the French nation is constituted by a simple addition of equivalent magnitudes, in much the same way as potatoes in a sack form a sack of potatoes". He concluded that plot peasants "do not form a class. Their identical interests do not form a common interest, and they are therefore incapable of having their own political representation. The atomization of the working class today poses a similar question. If the working class is still simply an "addition of equivalent magnitudes", it's only because a number of state or semi-state institutions continue to structure a certain perception of a common interest, a class interest that transcends divisions of branch, trade or origin. These include social protection, pensions and labor law (the open-ended contract, industrial tribunals, etc.). This is obviously very important, and in France and Italy, the biggest mobilizations since 1968 have taken place precisely in defense of these institutions, the crystallization of decades of struggle. But it's also revealing: the only unity of the working class lies in the forms of organization of social relations in bourgeois society at a certain stage of its development. It bears witness to the past, but prefigures no future, other than to limit the damage and safeguard the gains as best we can. At the same

---

73. See, for example, Stéphane BEAUD and Michel PIALOUX, *Retour sur la condition ouvrière. Enquête aux usines Peugeot de Sochaux-Montbéliard*, Fayard, 1999.

Chapter VI. The Abolition of Wage-Labor and Employers

time, autonomous working-class organizations (or those that claim to be so) are in the doldrums. Workers'" parties are deserted by workers, and trade unions survive only in the public sector or among pensioners (this is the case in Italy, and is largely due to the way pension funds are managed).

The Question of the Middle Class, Again

Consideration no. 4. Capitalism's managers and senior officials are structurally bound up with capitalism, and while individuals from these classes may become socialists or communists, in general the class or social stratum itself is not at all ready to overturn the social order. More generally, the stratification of the ruling classes is highly complex, and nothing absolutely certain can be drawn from it in terms of historical perspectives.

This last point is obviously crucial. If the working class, taken in the *strict sense, is* the oppressed class par excellence, it can only hope to create a new social order by dragging along with it all strata and classes whose interests are not strictly linked to those of the capitalists. In other words, engineers, managers and financial executives must be counted among the working class's objective allies in the "associated producers" front. For Marx, this is one of the most obvious postulates: all the intermediate classes between the capitalists and the working class are bound to tip over to the side of the working class as it asserts itself autonomously on the political terrain. Against the supporters of Ferdinand Lassalle, who considered "a reactionary mass" all social strata and classes that were not part of the working class, Marx polemicized harshly in *Critique of the Program of the German Workers' Party*, recalling the words of the *Communist Manifesto*, "the middle classes… are revolutionary… in consideration of their imminent passage to the proletariat".

Marx's assumptions were not without foundation. He himself was well placed to know how the intellectual petty bourgeoisie

148

could rally to communism! Even a fraction (albeit a minority) of capitalists were not insensitive to socialist or communist ideas. Capitalist and entrepreneur Robert Owen was the first to attempt to create communist enterprises. Proudhonian and Fourierist ideas often inspired otherwise pragmatic entrepreneurs. As for Engels, he spent the most important part of his life in charge of the Manchester branch of the firm Engels & Barmen… The leaders of the nascent workers' movement were often craftsmen or journeymen, workers still close to the craft: for example, August Bebel, one of the main leaders of German Social Democracy, was a turner and, after his journeymen's apprenticeship, founded a small business. Intellectuals, teachers and schoolteachers in particular, played a key role in the creation and organization of socialist and communist parties—particularly in France, where for decades schoolteachers, who were also heavily unionized, were in the vanguard of the workers' movement, particularly in its revolutionary syndicalist variants. Agrarian communism also played an important role in certain regions of France (Allier, Limousin) and Italy (Tuscany).

But the historical reality of the last century is much more mixed, to say the least… The middle classes often played a revolutionary role in colonial countries, where they were a kind of ersatz of a very small capitalist bourgeoisie, mostly dependent on the colonial powers (the so-called "comprador bourgeoisie"). But in advanced countries, these same middle classes often played a counter-revolutionary role, notably in the rise of Fascism and Nazism. During the Russian Revolution, peasants and the intellectual petty bourgeoisie tended to support non-Bolshevik or anti-Bolshevik revolutionary parties, and the producers' association soon gave way to the use of "bourgeois specialists", whom the Bolsheviks resolved to call on at all levels of the apparatus to work with a gun to their heads.

The pendulum swing of the middle classes continues. During the thirty glorious years, the new intellectual middle classes, the "white-collar workers", tended to draw closer to the working class, to the point of forming a "new working class", to use Serge Mallet's expression. Winning over the ITCs (engineers, technicians and managers) was one of the central concerns of the CGT and the PCF in the sixties. But from the 1970s onwards, the movement began to move in the other direction. The official story, generally circulated today, is that intellectuals discovered the reality of "real socialist" countries thanks to Solzhenitsyn, and turned away from Marxism in favor of liberalism. For those who wanted to know—and one might think that the first task of an intellectual is to use his intellect, and therefore to seek to know—the truth about "real socialism" was perfectly well known, and had been since the 1930s. It was with full knowledge of the facts that Malraux, Romain Rolland, Aragon, Éluard and so many others turned a blind eye to the Moscow trials and the reality of the Gulag, which Trotskyist correspondence and the accounts of those who, like Victor Serge, had passed through the Stalinist dungeons revealed in some detail. Just as the role of Soviet agents in the murder of POUM militants during the Spanish Civil War was well known. No, the explanation that a hidden reality began to emerge in the 1970s with Solzhenitsyn's books doesn't hold water. If the upper stratum of the educated classes is turning away from communism (and not just from the Stalinism its members had often worshipped), the reason is the change in global power relations, a change in power relations within the ruling classes and a change in the way capitalism is managed, sketched out as early as the 1975s and accelerated by Reagan and Thatcher. Educated in "social-democratic" or communist schemes, or in any case more or less egalitarian, part of the middle classes began to see the good in inequality as soon as they could benefit from it. With the crisis in full swing, they will seek to consolidate their positions and protect themselves against the threats posed by the impoverishment of a growing proportion of the working class. We are witnessing what Christopher Lasch has called "the revolt of the elites[74]". This revolt of the elites is not the passage of the educated

---

74. See C. LASCH, *La Révolte des élites*, translated from English by Christian Fournier, Climats, 1996.

classes from left to right. The moral values of the Victorian era are of no interest to these trendy social classes. It's about something else. Studying the phenomenon in the United States, Lasch gives a vivid description, emphasizing that the rise of this educated upper middle class is linked to the mobility of capital and the emergence of a planetary market:

"The new elites are in rebellion against "*Middle* America" as they imagine it: a nation technologically backward, politically reactionary, repressive in its sexual morality, petty-bourgeois in its tastes, satiated and self-satisfied, boring and corny. Those who aspire to belong to the new aristocracy of brains tend to congregate on both coasts, turning their backs on the deep country and cultivating their ties to the international market through hypermobile money, luxury, haute couture and popular culture. One wonders if they still think of themselves as Americans. In any case, it's clear that patriotism doesn't rank very high on their scale of values. On the other hand, "multiculturalism" suits them perfectly, as it conjures up the image of a universal bazaar, where one can indiscriminately enjoy the exotic cuisines, styles of dress, music and tribal customs of the whole world, all without unnecessary formalities, and without the need to commit oneself seriously to any particular path. The new social elites feel at home only in transit, on their way to a high-level conference, the gala opening of a new franchise store, the opening of an international film festival, or a pristine tourist resort. Their view of the world is essentially that of a tourist—a perspective unlikely to encourage a passionate love of democracy." (p. 17-18)

A description that corresponds exactly to what in France we call the "bo-bo" (for "bohemian bourgeois"). This upper middle class, which sees itself as a "brain aristocracy", has little in common with the nationalist, racist petty bourgeoisie that formed the political basis of fascism. It is just as hostile to traditional socialist and communist demands. It is hostile to discrimination based on race or sexual choice, but considers social class distinctions to be perfectly natural. In one of his provocations, Jean-Marie Le Pen claimed to

Chapter VI. The Abolition of Wage-Labor and Employers

be politically right-wing and socially left-wing (to say that he was addressing the traditional social base of the left). The "aristocracy of brains" takes the opposite view of the FN leader: it is politically (culturally) "left-wing", but socially right-wing.

However, we must avoid overly sweeping analyses. First of all, only a fraction of the educated classes have sided with liberalism and the new "bo-bo" bourgeoisie. The relative lowering of incomes and the absolute lowering of social prestige of the teaching profession has brought them closer (at least objectively) to the working class and employees. Small and medium-sized civil servants may not be revolutionaries by nature, but they have played a significant role in resisting French-style "thatcherization"—for example, during the period of mass strikes and demonstrations against the Juppé plan in 1995. Then, on the whole, nothing is certain: the undeniable shift to the right in the center of gravity of developed capitalist societies is certainly only temporary. And when French right-wing leaders boast of having "won the ideological battle", they may be selling the bear's skin a little too quickly. We'll come back to this in the last section.

Word to the Wise:
The Real Movement is Not What we Expected

From these considerations, it follows that the "real movement unfolding before our eyes" does indeed objectively possess the fundamental characteristics analyzed in *Capital.* But the effect is not the march towards communist society, but the development of a pure capitalist society, stripped of the "socialist reveries" that were perhaps no more than a nostalgia for the world of exchange producers and lost individual freedom. From a certain point of view, the dictatorship of pension funds is the dictatorship of the proletariat, let's say of one part of the proletariat over another part of the proletariat... and sometimes over the individual proletarians of that same proletariat! The abolition of wage-earning takes the form of the abolition of the protected legal status of wage-earners, and the possibility for wage-earners to switch to non-wage-earning status as quickly as possible. In dreams, desire often takes the form of a nightmare (the ultimate trick of the vigilant superego, even in sleep). The same seems to apply to the Marxian theory of the expropriation of expropriators.

CHAPTER VII. THE DECLINE OF THE STATE

In the classical Marxian perspective, the expropriation of the expropriators and the replacement of capitalist domination by "associated producers" have a corollary: the prospect of the disappearance of the state. If, indeed, the state is the instrument of domination by one class over another, then the disappearance of class antagonisms must lead to the disappearance of the state. A gradual disappearance, since class antagonisms cannot disappear overnight. Let's leave aside the various variants of this idea and the Byzantine quarrels to which it has given rise. The Marxian perspective of the "decline of the state" takes on a special significance, because it is claimed by the gurus of the global economy, by a large number of analysts, political scientists, philosophers and even—strangely enough—political leaders. In the age of globalization, they say, the sovereign state can no longer exist. Of course, the mothballing of sovereignty (in whatever form) and its replacement by governance does not mean that we are moving towards a stateless society—on the contrary—but it does give shape to the trend analyzed by Marx towards the elimination of the opposition between civil society and the state. From NGOs to supranational organizations (EU, etc.), the forms of political power are being profoundly transformed. We speak of "governance", a neologism meaning that we are beyond government, i.e. beyond the traditional functions of the state in an in-between where states and civil societies interpenetrate and from which new forms of regulation emerge.

Fading of the State: Myths and Realities

What's the truth behind the smoke-and-mirrors rhetoric we hear on a daily basis, the essential function of which seems to be to depoliticize our societies even more than they are? Before getting to the heart of the matter, let us take another detour into Marxology. In the previous chapter, we said a few words and even a little more about the Marxian communist formula of "associated producers". It should be pointed out that this formula is not Marx's own. It comes straight from Saint-Simon. The Saint-Simonian association of producers is conceived as an alliance of proletarians and capitalist entrepreneurs (as opposed to idlers), and may seem opposed to the Marxian association, which is based on the expropriation of capitalists. But if we agree with Marx that the expropriation of capitalists takes place through the immanent laws of the capitalist mode of production, and that the functions of the capitalist are performed by a "functionary" representing capital, but also performing necessary work, under any mode of production, we see that Marx and Saint-Simon can be very close. Another of Marx's great formulas comes directly from Saint-Simon. In the *Manifesto*, Marx speaks of the "transformation of the state into a simple administration of production. Engels develops this formula in *Utopian Socialism and Scientific Socialism*, recalling that Saint-Simon had already set out the task of scientific socialism: "the transition from the political government of men to the administration of things and the direction of the operations of production". The formula was taken up by Lenin in *The State and Revolution*. It could hardly be more Marxist[75].

Now, this formula for transforming the State from a political institution governing people into a mere administrator of things

---

75. It's true that Marx never uses Saint-Simon's exact expression, taken up by Engels, but he regularly compares the functions of public authorities in communist society to the administration of production, and when he speaks of the withering away of the state, he makes this explicit by saying that the state loses its political character. So it doesn't seem possible to pit Marx against Engels on this point.

and director of production is precisely the "governance" formula defended by the officials of the major international institutions (EU, WTO, etc.). A surprising convergence. As usual, a more or less distorted expression of real processes is mixed up here, an expression whose rational core needs to be extracted, and a veritable ideological smoke-and-mirrors operation.

Let's start with the ideological underpinnings of the argument. Globalization" would mean the end of the central political role of states, integrated into larger regional groupings (NAFTA or the European Union) and subject to the transnational power of "networked" firms and major global organizations (IMF, World Bank, WTO). Several authors define globalization as the growing interdependence of economies and financial flows, whose main characteristic is to destroy the concept of state sovereignty. States are being devoured from above and below. From above, to the benefit of international organizations and the governance that is replacing government[76], and from below, through the "networked" organization of society and the opportunities that new communication technologies offer individuals to escape state control.

Admittedly, theorists of this new decline of the state concede that it retains strong symbolic attributes, and that it is only within this framework that democracy is exercised. But this concession generally goes hand in hand with an apology for the superiority of governance over "sovereignist" democracy. The main argument in support of the "decline of the state" thesis is twofold:

1) The source of law is less and less state-based and more and more supranational. It is increasingly the result of arrangements between economic players, rather than a sovereign act by the legislator;

---

76. On the concept of governance, see the vigorously polemical book by Philippe ARONDEL and Madeleine ARONDEL-ROHAUT, *Gouvernance, une démocratie sans le peuple?*, Ellipses, 2008.

2) If the state is to remain the sovereign power it claims to be, it no longer has the means to implement its policies. On the economic front, for example, Keynesian demand-led stimulus policies have become impractical in the face of globalization.

Indeed, legal rules are very largely external rules imposed by the globalization of trade, telecommunications networks and the creation of vast supranational groupings. As a result, European decisions can now be imposed against the decisions of national parliaments in a whole range of areas. Trade law standards are highly standardized, and are governed by binding agreements such as those that created the World Trade Organization, since violations of these agreements can be sanctioned by international courts. As an essential prerogative of States, the voting of their own budget is subject, for members of the European Union, to a strict framework, that of the Maastricht Treaty and the "Stability Pact" adopted in Dublin in 1996, confirmed in Amsterdam in 1997 and to some extent constitutionalized by the Nice agreements and the Lisbon Treaty. If budget deficit limits are exceeded, a Member State could be condemned to pay heavy fines.

As we can see, capitalism does indeed call into question the old forms of the state, but it does not relinquish its authority in favor of the self-organization of society, as some liberals would have us believe. On the contrary, this divestment of the national state is accompanied by a strengthening of norms (just think of the European Union's bewildering production of norms and their translation into national law) and a weakening of citizens' power to contest.

Neoliberalism and Enlargement of the State

The abolition of state regulation of the economy, the great achievement of the 1980s, in which governments of all colors collaborated (the most "deregulatory" French governments were

158

undoubtedly the last governments of François Mitterrand's second seven-year term), does not at all mean a weakening of the state. Indeed, deregulation gives capitalists more freedom to act as they please, unhampered by regulations that are always "archaic" (in neoliberal "novlangue", a regulation is always "archaic"), but at the same time, this freedom of capitalists must be protected both against social movements and against those who take a little too seriously the basic principles of liberal egoism, "may the cleverest man win"! The result is a weakening of the social protection state, but a hypertrophy of the repressive state.

The facts are well known. Let's recall them briefly.

First and foremost, the prodigious development of video surveillance: it's becoming impossible to walk around without being recorded and included on the list of potential suspects. In Beijing's Tiananmen Square, there's a camera every 20 meters, but London, home of *habeas corpus* and personal safety, is right on the heels of the "communist" dictatorship. All cities are following more or less the same course. Of course, total surveillance by human operators alone is impossible without the use of considerable resources. Video surveillance systems are therefore increasingly assisted by image analysis software programmed to detect individuals in a crowd who are not behaving like the others. There could hardly be a more striking illustration of the evolution of our so-called democratic societies: anyone who doesn't behave like everyone else is a potential criminal!

All basic individual freedoms are being torn to shreds. The freedom to come and go no longer exists in a society where identity checks are authorized without the slightest judicial control, where a policeman can ask three times a day for the papers of a young person he knows perfectly well: "Come on, Mohammed, I'll check your identity!" This absurd invitation is enough to show that we are already on the other side of the border between the rule of law and tyranny. Car searches, spying on communications—everything indicates that the idea of the private home is on the way to being abolished. Marx had already pointed out that it was the capitalist mode of production (and not the communists) that abolished private property. The whole evolution of the doctrine of public security in our societies confirms this.

Monitoring private communications using modern telecommunications. In the past, the secrecy of correspondence was one of the fundamental guarantees of freedom. Only tyrannical regimes would open letters to check for subversive messages. As part of the Cold War, the United States, in collaboration with the United Kingdom (always at the forefront of the destruction of individual liberties), developed a gigantic program to spy on all electronic communications, the Echelon program. The origins of this system date back to 1947 and the secret pact between the UK and the USA. New Zealand, Australia and Canada then joined in. But it was only in 2000 that the existence of the Echelon program became public, following the declassification of certain documents by the US National Security Agency. These long-standing spying resources were reinforced by the adoption of the *Patriot Act* following the attacks of September 11, 2001. But the Anglo-Saxons quickly followed suit. The "anti-terrorist" law adopted by France in 2005 is a (still pale) copy of the American law.

Governments have always devoted considerable effort to networks of spies, snitches and other provocateurs in the pay of the police. Technological progress, with the widespread use of the Internet and cell phones, has given a particular boost to current developments. Internet correspondence retains the formal aspects of private correspondence. The e-mail icon is a small envelope. Don't worry: writing by e-mail is just the modern form of ancient correspondence. We now entrust to the network what we once entrusted to the post office or courier. The only difference is speed! Electrons move much faster than horses. That's what the thurifers of technology would have us believe. Of course, this is not the case. Unlike sealed private correspondence, which is only exceptionally open and will only become truly public through lengthy and costly operations, e-mail is by nature a public conversation. The secrecy of correspondence has been definitively abolished, and governments are not even hiding from the fact. The latest security laws in France make this abundantly clear.

The collection, cross-referencing and centralization of personal information means that the individual is now completely transparent to the powers that be, at least potentially. *Once you're born, you can't hide anymore.* The title of Marco Tullio Giordana's film on immigration is perfectly appropriate for all citizens. With biometric identity cards, it's no longer possible to disguise oneself. With the means now available to governments and the forces of repression, Resistance would have been impossible.

The next phase is already underway. Biometrics combined with information technology and telecommunications networks enable surveillance at all times: individuals can be tracked. Iris detection, fingerprint scanning, surveillance bracelets—they all work, and as always, for the best reasons. Biometrics is used for aviation security—in the wake of September 11, 2001, the United States demanded biometric passports, and all other countries are following suit, including the English who have so long boasted of English freedoms—British citizens were previously not even required to have an ID card. Biometrics again for industrial plant security, recognizing individuals authorized to use a computer terminal. Electronic bracelets to track sex offenders after their release. Genetic fingerprinting, initially used for sex offenders, has been extended to all offenders, i.e. all convicted offenders, since the 2005 "internal security" law. All offenders? Well, not all: financial offences are not concerned, so let's not exaggerate! On the other hand, trade unionists convicted of union activities are not exempt. What's more, you don't need to be convicted to be subject to DNA sampling—a simple stop is enough. We can bet that this will soon apply to all suspects, and soon to all citizens. Similarly, electronic bracelets for sex offenders will become widespread in one form or another. In large automated cowsheds, cows are not only banded (a ring in the ear, usually indicating their vaccination number), but also carry a microchip that allows them to order the feed ration they need. Humans are reduced to a herd of cows, under the guidance of the good cowherd that is the State!

There's a paradox here that's worth thinking about. We denounce the State, the centralizing State, the sovereign State, described as "Jacobin", although this is not a very complimentary term. Yet all the texts of 1789 and 1793 are authentically republican in the sense that the State's primary function is to guarantee freedom against domination—even if this guarantee is often very formal. At the same time, the Hobbesian conception of the State was rehabilitated. To put security first is, in effect, to take up Thomas Hobbes' conception of the state as the sovereign power to which subjects transfer all their rights, so that it can protect them against the violence of a "state of nature" characterized by the "war of each against each". Without the security guaranteed by absolute power (unchallengeable power), life would be miserable and short. But unlike the modern ideologists of the security state, Hobbes is not bullshitting: if the primary function of the state is security, then it's impossible to talk about freedom. With his characteristic roborative frankness, he asserts: "Although the name of liberty is engraved on the towers and gates of cities in large letters, yet it does not concern individuals, but the body of the city; and no more belongs to a republican city than to such another which is in the heart of the kingdom."

Freedom is impossible, except to fall back into the state of nature and thus expose one's life. In reality, Hobbes adds, most men who want freedom also want others to remain in servitude: "If one wishes to be free while all others are enslaved, what is that but to claim dominion?" This is exactly the essence of dominant thought that Hobbes, brilliant as ever, brutally reveals before our very eyes. Man's natural reality is war, whose civilized form—if we can call it that—is economic warfare, a veritable war of each against each. But the possessing classes seek security to guarantee their ownership and enjoy the wealth they accumulate, while retaining for themselves the freedom to act as they see fit. It's all about the will to dominate, and nothing else. This is why, in the revised hierarchy of "rights", it is security that comes first: freedom is merely a particular modality of this categorical imperative.

And that's why any protest by the dominated is equated with unbearable violence. If the unions call one of those ritual twenty-four hour strikes in the transport sector, more or less well attended and without a tomorrow, we see the representatives of employers and their henchmen with pens or cameras denouncing users "taken hostage". The hyperbole says precisely what the obsession with insecurity means: the intolerable insecurity of the owners, who might be forced by the social movement to give up a few crumbs from the feast they feast on with provocative shamelessness. In the old days, the troops were called in against strikers. Troops who fired into the heap more often than not. Today, we've come up with something much more effective: "rioters", more or less manipulated, more or less bribed, whose job it is to make demonstrations degenerate and make headlines on the news: demonstrators = rioters = insecurity. In short, we need to get everyone used to the idea that security is threatened by the freedom granted to members of the dangerous classes to move around as they please and enjoy their constitutional rights.

Word of the Wise:
The Question of Government Remains Central

So the state, seen in its repressive functions as "bands of armed men in the service of capital", is far from withering away. From this angle, all governments are constantly striving to prove Proudhon right, when he wrote: "to be governed is to be kept in view, inspected, spied on, directed, legislated, regulated, parked, indoctrinated, preached to, controlled, esteemed, appreciated, censured, commanded, by beings who have neither title, science nor virtue…"

Yet the state is indeed withering away. It is withering away precisely in that which alone gives it legitimacy: as a common organization of citizens, living under a law they accept, and deliberating on the choice of rulers and the policies to be implemented. The strengthening of the "neoliberal state" is thus accompanied by the decline of the "political state". Governance takes government out of the debate and, in the Marxian perspective, represents the transition from the government of men to the administration of things, with its corollary, the progressive withering away of democracy—which is also part of the program of Marxist communism. Here again, the course of history is, at least in part, in line with Marx's predictions, but it is still in nightmarish form that the so-called radiant future is realized.

Chapter VIII. Social Democracy, or the Myth of the Workers' Party

The first major attempt to give substance to Marxist perspectives was the Workers' International. Officially founded at the Saint-Martin Hall meeting in London in 1864, it was not to survive the failure of the Paris Commune and the conflicts between anarchist, Marxist and radical-democrat tendencies. Indeed, AIT sections never had a mass following, even though the leaders of the Paris Commune of 1871 were mostly members of the International. The "IInd International" thus failed in the weighty task of embodying Marxist predictions and dreams. By the end of the 19th century, "workers' parties" were springing up all over Europe, forming a new international workers' association, officially founded in July 1889 at the Paris Congress as the *Socialist International*. After the First World War and the split of the Communist parties, it was renamed the *Workers' and Socialist International*, and survives to this day under its original name of *Socialist International*.

Social Democracy:
The Genesis of the Workers' Party

The history of the Second International is exemplary in every respect. At its best, it embodies the perspectives of Marxism as it was taught in the last years of Marx's life and in the two or three decades that followed. Politically, it went bankrupt in 1914, when the main member parties of the International each rallied to their own government and sent "their" respective working classes to kill each other between Belgium, Northern and Eastern France. And yet, despite having clearly betrayed its most sacred principles and trampled internationalist ideals in the mud and blood of the trenches, the Second International survived, almost as if nothing had happened. And even today, when the word "socialism" has lost its meaning for almost all its leaders and adherents, when socialist and social-democratic parties are virtually indistinguishable from ordinary "bourgeois" parties, this "International" continues to be ritually reunited.

Let's be precise. The parties of the Socialist International were not all Marxist. The only party to make Marxism its official doctrine on the eve of the 1914 war was the SPD. Even so, Lassalle's followers retained a certain influence in the thinking of the "deep party", despite their official rallying to Marxism. In France, the Guesdists had to deal with all varieties of French socialism. In Great Britain and the Nordic countries, Marxism was very much in the minority, and the parties of the Socialist International were openly reformist. But all these parties wanted to be workers' parties, i.e. parties committed exclusively to asserting the "class interests" of the proletariat throughout society. In this sense, irrespective of the explicit ideas and motivations of their leaders, they were expressions of the real movement to abolish the existing order. With the development of large-scale industry, workers became more and more numerous, more and more concentrated, and more and more educated as a result of common struggles to defend their immediate material interests (wages, working conditions). They were led to organize themselves into a party independent of all other parties, and this very organization practically began the overthrow of the existing order, an overthrow that the seizure of political power was to crown, paving the way for the construction of socialism and organizing the transition to a classless society.

The uninterrupted growth of socialist parties seemed to prove this view of history right. Electoral progress was combined with the development of a whole network of trade unions, cooperatives, mutual aid societies and social works, making socialist and social democratic parties the organizers of a veritable counter-society within bourgeois society. We could cite here the numerous texts by Engels and the main leaders of the Second International, who argued that final victory was inevitable, that it was close at hand, and that we need only fear the provocations of the ruling classes, who would seek violent confrontation precisely to prevent this guaranteed victory for social democracy.

Theoretically, Kautsky in Germany and Plekhanov in Russia, with the help and under the patronage of Engels, developed the body of doctrine that would "ideologically" cement the movement, "orthodox Marxism". This doctrine rested on three pillars:

- a philosophy, "dialectical materialism", invented by Engels to transform the Marxian critique of idealist philosophy into a new philosophical system that would synthesize the materialism attributed to scientists and the Hegelian dialectic[77];
- a "scientific" conception of history, "historical materialism", most often summarized in terms of the five stages through which universal history is supposed to pass: Asian despotism, ancient slavery, feudalism, capitalism and communism[78]. This conception assures believers that they are on the speeding train to communism;
- a political strategy: the conquest of state power by the working class organized into a party. Tactical differences—on the question of alliance with radical "bourgeois" parties in defense of democracy, and correlatively the thorny issue of ministerial

---

77. We have already criticized this "dialectical materialism" on several occasions (see *Marx's Theory of Knowledge* and *Understanding Marx*).

78. In fact, there are several versions of the "five stages". In his introduction to the *Critique of Political Economy*, published in 1857, Marx places what he calls "primitive communism" at the top of the list. In 1859, the Asian mode of production opened the ball. This theoretical "nonchalance" simply demonstrates that these five stages are only vague indications, not a scientifically founded historical theory.

participation—did not call this premise into question, at least until the Second World War and the Cold War, and this explains the convoluted rhetoric of a Léon Blum distinguishing between the occupation of power and the exercise of power.

But this coherent discourse, delivered in the name of the author who had laid bare the mechanisms of ideology, was an entirely ideological discourse, i.e. it functioned as an inverted representation of reality.

Social Democracy: Organization for the Defense of Wage Earners

The reality of international social democracy is that it was never the organization of the proletariat for the abolition of wage-labour and employers, but rather the organization of the integration of the wage-earning class into the functioning of the capitalist mode of production. Far from stimulating workers' self-organization and autonomous activity, it was above all an instrument for framing workers' protest. Let's insist: it was that from the outset, even if the company's initiators were unaware of it and delivered rhetorical revolutionary speeches at banquets and meetings. As a workers' organization, social democracy linked its destiny to the maintenance of a strong, disciplined working class, and thus, whether we like it or not, to the maintenance and development of the capitalist mode of production, as we shall see shortly. Leninists and Trotskyists date the transformation of the parties of the Second International from revolutionary parties to parties that "definitively went over to the side of the bourgeois order" to 1914. This is a joke. These gigantic organizations, backed by a base of millions of men, workers and intellectuals forged by bitter struggles, could not have been so radically transformed in a matter of weeks or even years. The Leninist and Trotskyist assertion has an unspoken function: if social democracy suddenly changes its nature in 1914 with the vote on war credits, this abrupt change of nature preserves the purity of the doctrine that presided over the organization's development from 1889 to 1913, and Leninists and Trotskyists alike can act as if nothing had happened, taking up the good old orthodox Marxism recycled for the needs of the new historical period. And yet, we could already sense that this Marxism was no more than the spiritual aroma enveloping the rise of a new bourgeois or petty-bourgeois elite, asserting its rights through its ability to move workers' battalions like an army in the field. Rosa Luxemburg perceived very early on what was in fact this German social democracy that Lenin took as a model to be imitated[79]. Georges Sorel, who had close ties with French anarcho-syndicalism and was a theorist of the general strike and workers' violence, immediately understood the profoundly conservative nature of social democracy, and announced "the decomposition of Marxism" in a 1908 work of the same name[80]. Sorel lashed out fiercely at Marx's "disciples", who had made a name for themselves with "so many fantasies", notably Paul Lafargue. German socialism, notably the "pope of Marxism" Karl Kautsky, is also severely criticized. But the interest of Sorel's reflection lies in his search for the roots of conservatism in the socialism of the Second International. A review of social reformers, utopians and first-generation socialists leads him to the conclusion that all these revolutionaries feared revolution and ultimately had no other goal than the "aggregation of the proletariat to the bourgeoisie". The evolution of socialism in Germany offers a kind of concentrate. The polemic against Bernstein and "revisionism", and Bebelet Kautsky's defense of Marxist "orthodoxy", appear to be a trompe-l'oeil. As early as 1899, notes Sorel, the SPD was committed to defending a program of "purest state socialism", taking up measures explicitly condemned by Marx in the *Critique of the Gotha Program*. In the

---

79. Lenin's pamphlet *What to do? which* is the founding text of Bolshevism, curiously (and seemingly) takes the SPD and Karl Kautsky's thinking as the model from which the Russians should draw inspiration, adapting it, of course, to Russian conditions.
80. Éditions Marcel Rivière, reproduced on the "Les classiques des sciences sociales" website, http://classiques.uqac.ca

Chapter VIII. Social Democracy, or the Myth of the Workers' Party

end, Sorel shows how the great workers' organizations distance themselves from the class struggle to act as intermediaries in the service of pacifying class relations. Against the logic of the "party", which he characterizes as the attempt by an army of intellectuals to turn workers into cannon fodder for the political struggle, Sorel defends the logic of "class" and the action of revolutionary syndicalism based on the French example.

Robert Michels, a sociologist with close ties to anarcho-syndicalism for a time, describes the socialist parties of the Second International as the archetypal bureaucratic party responsible for recruiting and promoting a new governing elite. In *Les Partis politiques*[81], he makes an uncompromising diagnosis of these socialist parties. The problem is clear from the outset: there can be no political struggle without mass organization. And this is why organization has become "the vital principle of the working class", but, adds Michels, "organization constitutes precisely the source from which conservative currents pour onto the plain of democracy and cause devastating floods that render that plain unrecognizable." (p. 26) But while Sorel still places his hopes in the vitality of class action, Michels sees the process of bureaucratization as an inevitable phenomenon that relies on the masses' propensity for obedience and veneration of leaders, which explains why leaders can radically change their position, betraying all the most sacred resolutions without really having to pay the price. "The history of workers' parties offers us daily examples of cases where leaders have placed themselves in flagrant contradiction with the fundamental principles of the movement, and militants have not decided to draw all the consequences that logically follow." (p. 79) A premonition by the penetrating sociologist! A few years after the publication of Michels's book, the Socialist and Social Democratic parties "flagrantly contradicted fundamental principles" by joining the war on behalf of their respective governments. And indeed, the militants failed to draw the logical conclusions, since it was only

---

81. Robert Michels, *Les Partis politiques, op. cit.*

the Russian Revolution of 1917 that led to the split of the socialist parties and the creation of the communist parties.

Against those who, like Sorel, see the penetration of "bourgeois" and "petty-bourgeois" elements as one of the explanations for the reformist tendencies of the labor movement, Michels remarks that "it is, moreover, the most exclusivist labor movements that everywhere and always are the most penetrated by a reformist spirit[82]." Here again, nothing could be further from the truth: from the outset, the socialist parties of Northern Europe and the British *Labour Party* had a very working-class social composition, much more so than the parties of the South or even the SPD. But the revolutionary spirit hardly ever touched these parties. The example of Swedish social democracy, which effortlessly accommodated Sweden's cohabitation with the Nazi regime, is worth studying as a textbook case. If we look at the sociological cleavages at the time of the 1920 Tours Congress split between the old SFIO and the new SFIC, the Communist Party, we can see that the working-class strongholds of the Nord and Pas-de-Calais remained loyal to the old house, while the peasant regions around the Massif Central, on the other hand, switched to the new Communist Party in the majority.

Has Social Democracy Betrayed Us?

So there is no before and after 1914. If we stick to the surface of things, we can be astonished and observe, as Fernand Braudel does, that in 1914, social democracy missed a historic opportunity and lost all possibility of overthrowing the capitalist order. Drawing on the impressive progress of socialist and social-democratic organizations, he writes: "Under these conditions, without exaggerating the power of the Second International from 1901 onwards, we have the right to assert that the West, in 1914, as much as on the brink of war, is on the brink of socialism. Socialism is on the verge of seizing

---

82. Robert Michels, *Les Partis politiques, p. 232.*

power, of creating a Europe that is as modern, and perhaps more so, than it is today. In a few days, in a few hours, the war will have ruined these hopes. It was a huge mistake for European socialism at the time not to have been able to block the conflict. This is clearly felt by the most pro-socialist historians, who would like to know who exactly is responsible for this "reversal" of workers' politics. On July 27, 1914, in Brussels, Jouhaux and Dumoulin, secretaries of the French CGT, met with K. Legien, secretary of the German Central Trade Union. Did they meet by chance, in a café, or for no other purpose than to share their despair? We don't know, nor do we know the meaning to be attributed to Jean Jaurès' last words, on the very day he was assassinated (July 31, 1914)[83]. If European socialism was unable to block the conflict, and indeed made no real attempt to do so, the "fault" of which Braudel speaks is only a fault (and even a betrayal) in the eyes of those who believe that the socialist discourse of the Second International should be taken literally, whereas it is not a programmatic discourse, but a quasi-religious discourse, a discourse that makes it possible to accept a reality that is contrary to expectations.

In this process of adaptation of the major workers' parties to the social order they were supposed to fight against, the corruption of leaders, the prebends offered by elective positions in representative democracy, the all-too-human mechanisms of mass submission to those who know or think they know, speak well and have time to play politics—the general phenomena inherent in any organization and the very contradictions of democracy themselves obviously play an important role. But, from a Marxist point of view, the sharpening of class contradictions pushing workers into struggle should have stopped the mechanisms of bureaucratization and prompted regular reactions within workers' organizations to return to the fundamental principles of the movement. But we have seen virtually nothing like this, and, once again, the only major crisis to shake the Second International came not from a revolt at the base,

---

83. Fernand BRAUDEL, *Grammaire des civilisations*, Arthaud-Flammarion, 1987, p. 428.

but from the external impetus given by the October Revolution and the determined action of the Communist Party of the USSR to create a new international workers' organization.

Social democracy was never revolutionary, not because it was not a "workers' party", or because it had become a "bourgeois workers' party" or a party of "workers' lieutenants of the bourgeois class" (to use the classic Leninist and Trotskyite expressions), but precisely because it was a pure workers' party, a party founded first and foremost on the defense of the living conditions of the working class. To defend the working class condition is to defend the condition of the working class in capitalist society, and nothing else. And the idea that such a party is naturally, in some way, the focus of a movement for the revolutionary transformation of society is an illusion, the constitutive illusion of real Marxism, of that orthodox Marxism which has largely dominated political and intellectual life for a century. Let's try to shed some light on this question.

The working class that Marx saw, the one that rose up noisily and sometimes violently, the one that set up barricades in Paris in 1830 and 1848, the one that led the Commune in 1871, was a young working class, just emerging from the decomposition of the old modes of production. They included disaffected craftsmen—such as the canuts of Lyon, whose powerful revolt in 1831 has remained justly famous—and the homeless, who moved from town to town. Workers live in their own world, almost on the bangs of bourgeois society, whose moral laws they often ignore. This is a class that rarely marries and often lives "à la colle". In an ultrapuritan society, births out of wedlock are common and a certain freedom of morals reigns. It's a class of men and women who suffer terrible slavery, but who can still dream of a lost freedom that's not so far away. Indeed, utopian socialism is often marked by this nostalgia for lost freedom. This class seemed revolutionary because it believed it could still turn back the clock ("restore the individual property of the worker", as *Capital puts it*). Marx and Engels' incredible blindness to Blanqui as a proletarian hero deserves to be analyzed and explained. Blanqui was an advocate of action by avant-garde minorities, of a centralized party organized to carry out coups de main that would topple the old dominant order; he was a patriot, and in many respects, Blanquism is point by point opposed to "Marxism", this time both Marx's and that of his epigones: Marxism rejects the action of minorities, but relies on the mobilization and awareness of the masses (the emancipation of the workers will be the work of the workers themselves, said Marx). The aim is not political action, but social transformation. And finally, Marxism is internationalism. And yet, Marx maintains that the Blanquist party is the prototype of the proletarian revolutionary party. There's only one explanation for this contradiction: Blanqui embodies the revolutionary working class of Marx's dreams.

From the moment when capitalism is no longer built in the interstices of the old society, when hopes of a return to the past fade, when the real domination[84] of capital disciplines and intellectually trains workers to make them truly members of a "collective producer", workers organize themselves, not in hopeless revolts on fanciful slogans, but to protect their very existence within the capitalist mode of production and to obtain a better share in the "distribution" of income. This is the role of laws limiting the working day, restricting child labor and prohibiting night work for women, laws which Marx sees as the true meaning of the political struggle of the working class (see chapter X of Book I of *Capital*). It's also the struggle for collective wage bargaining, for the recognition of qualifications, for the establishment of social protection, etc. But all these struggles, however important, however heroic, remain within the boundaries of the capitalist mode of production. There is indeed a conflict between workers' interests and capitalist

---

84. Marx distinguishes between real and formal domination. As soon as a man sells his labor power to another, he is subject to that other's domination. But as long as the old modes of production remain, this domination is only formal - as is still the case in the factory, which simply brings together traditional trades under the same roof and under the same command. In the modern factory—with the development of machinismo —domination becomes real, as the capital/labour relationship is now inscribed in the work process itself.

interests, but this conflict finds its solution on the very terrain of capitalism, which has moreover often been able to use the concessions it has had to make as a spur to its own development.

In short, where Marx saw the dynamics of a struggle to overthrow capitalist domination, we have witnessed conflicts, often harsh and even deadly, that have been part of the very dynamics of the development of capitalism. And at its best and most positive, social democracy has always been just that. But the story doesn't end there. For Marx, the development of the capitalist mode of production was to simplify the structure of the social formations dominated by the capitalist mode of production. The petty bourgeoisie was doomed to proletarianization, while the concentration and centralization of capital would reduce the bourgeois class to a handful of parasites that should be easy enough to get rid of - which is why Marx, towards the end of his life, envisaged a peaceful transition to communism by parliamentary means in the advanced countries, where the proletariat, now the overwhelming majority of society, would judiciously use the instruments of political democracy to achieve its ends. But the development of capitalism, while effectively ruining independent producer-exchangers (peasants and craftsmen paid the price), also made the social structure more complex, at both poles. On the one hand, the proletariat is far from being a homogeneous class: living conditions, working conditions and qualifications differ widely between the upper strata of what Marxists would call the "labor aristocracy" (technicians, supervisors, highly-skilled workers, but also intellectual employees of all kinds) and precarious workers, living meagerly and constantly under the threat of falling even further. These differences within each country are compounded by differences between countries. At the other pole, the capitalist class is also highly differentiated, depending on the production sector, of course, but also between large firms and SMEs, between a "state bourgeoisie" and an entrepreneurial bourgeoisie, between financiers and industrial managers, and so on. This situation has several important consequences. Contradictions within the salaried workforce are far from secondary and, especially when the economic outlook darkens, each group tends to assert its interests to the detriment of the others. It's almost certain that the abusively liberal policies would never have taken hold without the consent to inequality increasingly clearly accepted by the privileged layers of the workforce. What's more, the management of social policies (the *welfare state*) has created a fairly large bureaucracy which claims to be at the service of wage earners, but whose real position is that of a fraction of the capitalist class: managers of mutual health and insurance companies or of all forms of "social economy", permanent officials of trade unions, largely financed by public funds, etc.

As a workers' party, founded to safeguard the interests of workers in capitalist society, social democracy naturally relied on the most integrated strata, on state officials, skilled workers, technicians, supervisors and managers, and on that bureaucracy which is the product of social-democratic influence itself. The parties of the Second International depend on the existence of a social state, basic political freedoms and a minimum of workers' rights, but they also depend on the existence of a capitalism strong enough to accept these general conditions. So the reasons why these socialist and social-democratic parties are workers' parties are also the reasons why they can champion their own capitalist class, or even the capitalist class of the dominant capitalist country—as is the case with European social-democratic parties, which are often far more Americanophile than the various European capitalist classes. And, once again, this does not date back to the betrayal of 1914! In Engels, we even find the beginnings of the justifications that would lead the German Social Democrats to vote for war credits. In a letter to Bebel, which deserves to be widely quoted, Engels writes about the position to be taken in the event of conflict between Germany and Russia:

> "the German Socialist Party, thanks to the uninterrupted efforts and sacrifices of thirty years, has conquered a position which none of the other socialist parties occupies, a position which assures it of the imminent attainment of

political power. Socialist Germany occupies the most advanced, honorable and responsible position in the international labor movement, and it is her duty to maintain this position against all odds. Now, if Russian victory over Germany means the crushing of socialism in that country, what will be the duty of German socialists in this eventuality? Should they passively submit to the events that threaten them with extinction, abandoning without resistance the position they have conquered, for which they answer to the proletariat of the whole world? Obviously not. In the interests of the European revolution, they are obliged to defend all the positions they have acquired, and not to capitulate, either to the enemy without or to the enemy within; and this they can only achieve by fighting Russia and its allies, whoever they may be, to the bitter end. If the French Republic were to place itself at the service of His Majesty the Czar and Autocrat of all the Russias, the German socialists would fight it with regret, but they would fight it all the same. To the German Empire, the French Republic could represent the bourgeois revolution. But vis-à-vis the republic of the Constans, the Rouviers and even the Clemenceaus, especially the republic that works for the Russian czar, German socialism represents proletarian revolution. A war in which the Russians and French invade Germany would be a war to the death, in which Germany would have to resort to the most revolutionary means to ensure its national existence. The present government would certainly not unleash revolution, unless forced to do so. But there is a strong party that would force it to do so, or, if need be, replace it: the Socialist Party. We have not forgotten the great example set by France in 1793. The centenary of ninety-three is approaching. If the Czar's thirst for conquest and the chauvinistic impatience of the French bourgeoisie stop the victorious but peaceful march of the German socialists, the latter are ready, rest assured, to prove that the German proletarians of today are not unworthy of the French sans-culottes of a hundred years ago, and that 1893 will be worth 1793. And then Constans' soldiers, as they set foot on German soil, will be greeted with the chant of: "What, these foreign cohorts would lay down the law in our homes[85]?"

---

85. See ENGELS, "Socialism in Germany", 1892, reproduced in Roger DANGEVILLE's *Le Parti de classe*, tome IV, pp. 88-89, Maspero, 1973.

Chapter VIII. Social Democracy, or the Myth of the Workers' Party

This text is not by some "social-chauvinist", but by Engels, Marx's companion and the true father of Marxism, and it contains all the reasoning that would lead to the catastrophe of 1914. At the same time, the entire history of social democracy could be explained here. Engels speaks of "socialist Germany" to designate German socialism: it is impossible to identify more clearly socialism and nation, and the interests of socialism with the interests of the nation that shelters it.

If we accept, then, that social democracy did not betray, but simply implemented, the very premises of orthodox Marxism, the successive evolutions of the Socialist International and its various component parties are easy to understand. Reconstituted after the conflict, social democracy maintained its dogma (class struggle, dictatorship of the proletariat, etc.), but settled into long-term collaboration with the "democratic" capitalists and, above all, American capitalism. The October Revolution is rightly analyzed as an aberration from official Marxist doctrine, which predicted that only the most advanced capitalist countries were sufficiently mature to make the transition to socialism and communism. That's why social-democracy was so radically hostile to revolutionary Russia, shamelessly supporting Allied intervention alongside the White armies during the civil war that followed the October Revolution. In the vocabulary of the old SFIO or the Force Ouvrière apparatus, communists remained "the Cossacks" for a very long time, and for the more benevolent, Soviet communism was "communism with Tartar sauce". Naturally, during the Cold War, social democracy sided with the United States and the Atlantic Alliance against the "communist peril". Here again, the police conception of history which sees in all this the hand of the CIA is of no help. It is true that the United States, via its agencies or through the intermediary of the AFL-CIO workers' confederation, played a role in helping the European social democracies and trade unions that rejected Communist control and grouped together in the ICFTU, opposed to the WFTU dominated by Eastern European and Soviet unions. Irving Brown, the

AFL-CIO's European delegate, played an important role, particularly in France, in the creation of Force Ouvrière, which made it possible to use approximate homophonies to make the CIA the instigator of the CGT split in 1947. No doubt Brown was not acting independently of the U.S. government, but the split was primarily due to the fears of many sectors of the labor movement about a rather worrying Stalinist stranglehold that many currents (socialists, anarchists, Trotskyists) saw as contradictory to the idea of an autonomous labor movement. And, in fact, the justifications for the Americanophilia of this faction of the labor movement were not fundamentally different from those used by Engels to prepare his comrades for war against the Russian Empire.

From the outset, European integration was conceived as a means of blocking the (supposed) advance of the Communists in Europe, even if it was based in large sections of public opinion on disgust at the wars that had ravaged Europe and the desire to build a lasting peace on the continent. Both the ideal justification and the strategic orientation were perfectly in line with the middle ideology of social democracy and, alongside the Christian Democrats, these parties were the main architects of what is now the European Union. There was some reluctance: in the Socialist Party of the early 1970s, the currents least linked to the social-democratic tradition showed at least some reservations about European construction. This was the case of certain former members of the Convention des Institutions Républicaines, such as Pierre Joxe, and another pillar of the Mitterrandist majority at the Épinay congress, the CERES led by Jean-Pierre Chevènement. But Mitterrand forced them to capitulate, and when the European question came up as a decisive issue for French Socialist policy, during the famous "austerity turn" of 1983, it was the fervent Europeanists (Christian Democrat Delors and SFIO leader Mauroy) who prevailed, relegating to the dustbin of history the musings on "French-style socialism". But the die was partly cast before 1983. In 1982, the G7 summit in Versailles had been the occasion for a spectacular reaffirmation of Franco-American friendship, with President Reagan's pompous reception.

Chapter VIII. Social Democracy, or the Myth of the Workers' Party

On January 20, 1983, in a famous speech to the Bundestag in Bonn, Mitterrand supported the deployment of American Pershing missiles on German soil in response to the installation of Soviet SS20 missiles.

It's neither its "social-patriotism", nor its Americanophilia, nor its support for imperialism and colonialism that discredits social democracy as a workers' party. Every socialist party defends "its" workers, "its" working class, the one it more or less fully supports, in the face of competition. Better living conditions and social benefits can only be negotiated with a capitalism powerful and wealthy enough to concede them. And so class struggle within a national capitalist formation is reconcilable with the support of workers' parties and unions for their capitalism in the face of other capitalisms, just as the workers of a company always prefer their company to be healthy in the face of competition. Not only is this "national" policy reconcilable with the class struggle, but even if Marx hadn't foreseen that the development of the workers' movement would follow this path, it's a fact that finds a perfectly "Marxian" explanation, i.e., without appealing to the wickedness or goodness of individuals or suspecting malicious plots, by sticking to the terrain of the dynamics of the social relations of production and exchange.

To this first determination of social democracy as the party of the wage-earners, we must now add a second one, the existence of which we have already emphasized, that of internal differentiations within the wage-earners. Since social democracy is the party that defends the place of wage earners in capitalist society, it naturally tends to defend the place of the best-placed wage earners. They are in a better position because capitalism needs them more, and they have used this to impose their demands on employers.

This "labor aristocracy", these intellectual wage earners, these bureaucrats of workers' organizations are well aware that their own advantages cannot be generalized to all wage earners. They are therefore the most fervent defenders of "meritocracy", and find in this the ideal link with the liberal bourgeois parties who also consider that the distribution of positions and wealth corresponds (or should correspond) to a natural distribution and that, if inequalities are natural, there is no injustice. Added to this is the fact that these relatively privileged strata prefer order, and fear that overly radical social movements could upset the fragile equilibrium on which they have based their position. The conservatism of the apparatuses already strongly analyzed by Michels is rooted in the very social situation of the social-democratic base. But these two traits lead social democracy to progressively lose its hold on the poorest and most exploited salaried strata, while the upper strata of the political and trade union apparatuses tend to integrate with the ruling class.

Social Democracy in its Death Throes

This is why, in the long term, the very existence of social democracy is threatened, not for external reasons (threats to basic democratic freedoms, competition from revolutionary currents), but by the very dynamics of this type of organization. Italy's evolution is symptomatic in this respect. The PSI disappeared body and soul in the storm of operation *mani pulite* in the early 1990s, and the PCI, which had gradually taken the place of a genuine mass social-democratic party, itself dissolved into a "center-left" formation of indeterminate contours, the PD. In England, *New Labour* now bears little resemblance to the old *Labour*, not least because it has completely emancipated itself from the trade-unions' control over the party. The fate of other European social-democratic parties is uncertain. Outside Europe, the social-democratic label and membership of the SI are often used as a cover for right-wing formations—as is the case in Venezuela and Brazil. The beginnings of a new international encompassing socialist parties and parties such as the Democratic Party in the USA are undoubtedly the harbinger of the demise of social democracy as an organization rooted in the working class and the labor movement.

We can ironize about the "end of reign" atmosphere of the socialist and social-democrat parties, led more often than not by mediocre politicians or marketing products worn out at an ever-increasing rate. But the important thing is elsewhere. The pitiful fate of social democracy marks the end of a certain conception of class struggle and the socialist or communist perspectives that could be deduced from it. Leaving aside the question of historical communism (that of the 20th century), to which we'll return in the next chapter, Veltroni's PD, Blair and Gordon Brown's *New Labour*, and France's PS (from who knows who) are the unmistakable sign that a certain Marxist dream has been transformed into a nightmare, and this is not just true of Social Democrats in perdition. It's not the Berlin Wall that's to blame—even if the collapse of the Soviet bloc accelerated the process. It's the logic of social relations.

This trajectory does not invalidate Marx's analysis, but it does show it to be partial and incomplete. Some Marxists (mainly Lenin and Gramsci) were aware of this gap between Marxism and the historical reality before their eyes. To cut a long story short, the first reason for this divorce is to be found in Marx's own text. There's a contradiction here, one too often overlooked by Marx's readers and most Marxists. In *Capital,* the overthrow of the capitalist mode of production and the transition to a production based on "associated producers" is by no means a task for the working class alone, but on the contrary a task that concerns, as we have already emphasized, all those who play an effective role in the production process—from the worker to the factory manager. From this point of view, Marx's comparison between the salaried manager of a capitalist company and the manager of a workers' production cooperative should be illuminating[86]. But when Marx speaks of political struggle, he proposes the working class, not the association of producers, as the "subject" of history.

---

86. See our *Comprendre Marx*, Armand Colin, 2006.

The second reason lies not in an internal contradiction in Marx's work, but in its incompleteness. *Capital* provides a masterly analysis of the functioning of the capitalist mode of production and the mechanisms of exploitation and alienation of workers. This part of his work is imperishable, and has never been seriously refuted, except by ignoramuses who are all the more adept at refuting Marx because they have never read him. But a society, or rather a social formation, cannot be reduced to the dominant mode of production. Generally speaking, alongside a dominant mode of production, there are other modes of production that play a more or less important role in the process by which people produce their material life, and thus produce themselves in a certain way. Moreover, the capitalist mode of production analyzed by Marx is a purified core that leaves aside the concrete class structure and the interplay of relations between all strata and classes of society. Finally, the political question itself is scarcely addressed, i.e., there is no real coherent theory of the state in Marx, even though Marxists have often engaged in laborious reconstructions. The original plan for *Capital* called for one book devoted to social classes and another to the state. However, not only did Marx never have the time to write these two books, but he never got beyond Book I of *Capital*, Books II and III being reduced to masses of manuscripts, of which Engels tried, as best he could, to produce a usable edition. But instead of taking this incompleteness as a starting point, Marxists after Marx considered that Marx had said what was essential, and that all that remained was to popularize or illustrate Marxist theory through current events. By the late nineteenth and early twentieth centuries, the cult of authority ("Marx dixit") and the cult of the great ancestor's personality had begun to stifle all real thought in socialist and social democratic parties. Georges Sorel, in his essay on *The Decomposition of Marxism*, notes these "feelings of religious humility" that "seem to have existed among a very large number of Marxists". As an illustration, he quotes Paul Lafargue: "It is bold, even to put it beyond dispute, to touch the work [of Marx and Engels] of these two giants of thought, whose economic and historical theories the socialists of both worlds will perhaps only have to *popularize* until the transformation of capitalist society[87]."

Social democracy is orthodox Marxism, an atrophied, impoverished, sterilized Marxism that ends up in the sorry spectacle we see every day.

87. *Devenir social*, April 1897, p. 290.

Chapter IX. The Collapse of Historical Communism in the 20th Century

What we have just said about social democracy has no pretensions to originality. We have merely synthesized and extended long-standing reflections. In fact, the 20th century, Eric Hobsbawm's "short 20th century" (1914-1989), also witnessed a heroic and particularly tragic attempt to provide Marxism with an alternative to the social democracy that was thought to have died in the trenches of the First World War. The basic facts are well known. Bolshevism was to give way to the Stalinist system of terror, but not before the entire Bolshevik old guard had been exterminated, notably in the sinister Moscow trials.

If we are to understand the historical impasse in the countries of "real socialism", we need to look beyond the specific historical circumstances to their theoretical roots. The Russian catastrophe and the Chinese turnaround express:

1) the impossibility of socializing misery without resurrecting the whole old mess;
2) the impossibility of "socialism in a single country";
3) the impossibility of voluntarily liquidating the division of society into classes through political action.

Lenin versus Marxism?

First of all, let's rule out explanations based on individual subjectivity or conspiracy. Analyses of the Stalinist system are too often reduced to explanations such as the dormant virtue of opium, so dear to Molière's physicians. Let's start with the political questions as they were posed to the players in this story. As early as 1903, Lenin conceived what was to become Bolshevism as a practical response to the question of Russia's political emancipation. In *What's to be done? there are* many proposals that arise quite simply from Russia's particular situation. How to organize the struggle against autocratic rule and a political police force without an underground apparatus? How to preserve an underground apparatus without discipline and centralization? And so on. Lenin challenged, but did not theorize, the fundamental dogma of Marxism, arguing that the working class could not achieve revolutionary consciousness by its own efforts, and remained trapped within the narrow confines of "trade-unionism", i.e. trade unionism calling for a better distribution of wealth in capitalist society, but not "the abolition of wage-labor and employers". Consequently, the working class can only be revolutionary if there is a party that is separate from the rest of society, but recruits from all classes and has a clear vision of the tasks required for social transformation. Lenin also stresses the importance of bourgeois intellectuals as the bearers of a global view of society. For a Marxist, Lenin's pamphlet is pure heresy, in spite of his hat tip to Kautsky and the German Socialist Party, a model centralized party led by "professional revolutionaries". But heretic or not, Lenin puts his finger on the number 1 problem facing the Russian revolution: can the working class seize and exercise power?

For, before considering the nature of the political regimes that emerged from the communist movements of the 20th century, we must first ask this question. The Russian Revolution is presented as the model of a proletarian revolution establishing the dictatorship of the proletariat, but the reality is quite different. The February

Revolution was a popular revolution, involving all strata of society, from the petty bourgeoisie to the peasantry and the working class. Although the workers of the large enterprises (the Vyborg "rayon" and the giant Poutilov factories in Petrograd[88]) naturally played an active role, it does not follow that the workers "led" the revolution. Moreover, Marxist theory had not foreseen that the workers could lead the revolution in a backward and still largely feudal country, where, according to the five-stage theory of historical materialism, the time was ripe for the accomplishment of bourgeois democratic and anti-feudal tasks, not for socialism. Faced with the weakness of the so-called national bourgeoisie, however, the Bolsheviks had to correct their theory, and argued that a "democratic dictatorship of the proletariat and peasantry" was the only way to lift the country out of its backwardness. But events were to sweep all formulas aside. In his "April Theses", Lenin largely endorsed Trotsky's long-held position that the democratic revolution should "grow out of" the socialist revolution, and that backward countries like Russia could not go through the same process as the countries of Western Europe. It was on the basis of the April theses that the Bolsheviks began to prepare for the proletariat's seizure of power, albeit with many obstacles and hesitations. Indeed, wary of popular spontaneity, which they might not have taken for granted (the class "per se" surely remained largely trade-unionist), the Bolsheviks staged a genuine coup d'état on October 25 (old calendar), but this coup had been prepared under cover of the military committee of the Petrograd soviet headed by Trotsky, and the capture of the Winter Palace with the fall of the Kerensky government was ratified by the Congress of Soviets. But beyond the legend, it was indeed the party that seized power, with the working class—in reality, some of its revolutionary bastions—there only to provide support and an auxiliary force.

---

88. See Leon TROTSKY, *History of the Russian Revolution*, Seuil, "Points" collection, 1967.

This is not to say that Lenin and his companions were wrong. The situation of a Russia unable to continue the war and unable to make peace, ruled by pusillanimous governments, faced with the threat of military coups—for example, the threat of insurrection led by General Kornilov—and the peasant revolt, all demanded energetic intervention and drastic measures that could only be revolutionary. Lenin was a true "statesman", a true Machiavellian prince, of remarkable *virtù*, i.e. political courage and constancy. His dreams were that the Russian revolution would be the first step towards European and world revolution. But his immediate goal, and all his actions from 1917 to 1924, were to build a national state worthy of the name, often wisely taking into account the enormous difficulties of the multinational empire he inherited—for example, on the question of nationalities, Lenin had a flexible, realistic approach that we'd like to see again today in the resolution of crises in the Caucasus.

It is therefore pointless to look for the origins of Stalinist tyranny in some kind of original sin of Bolshevism. Lenin's political acumen soon made him realize that communism could not be built on a forced march in a country ravaged by foreign and civil war, and the move towards NEP, combining state intervention with the development of the market and private initiative, could lead to anything but the Stalinist system that was truly established in a war to the death against NEP. The "totalitarian" Stalinist regime only came into being in the years 1929-1934, when Stalin, who had supported the NEP, abruptly spun out of control, introducing the plan, "full-steam ahead" industrialization and forced collectivization, which claimed millions of victims. At the end of this period, the first major trials set in motion the systematic destruction of whatever remained of Lenin's party. In 1934, the "victors' congress" consecrated Stalin's absolute domination, and Kirov's murder provided the pretext for purges within the dominant group.

Tragedy and its Characters

An incision is in order here. Trotsky and the "Left Opposition" (defeated in 1927 and expelled from the party) criticized Stalin and his early allies (Bukharin) for encouraging rich peasants and neglecting industrialization. Prisoners of the "permanent revolution" schema, they felt that the NEP gave capitalism pride of place and represented a kind of backward step, when Russian Marxists believed that Russia, before envisaging socialism, had to pass through a phase of capitalist development. Characterizing Stalin as a "Bonapartist", they portrayed him as preparing for the restoration (of capitalism in this case) because, as a "centrist", he constantly oscillated between the right-wingers (the supporters of Bukharin and the NEP) and the left-wing opposition. But if Stalin was the "Bonaparte" of the Russian revolution, to continue the analogy, he must also have been the one who would give the new property relations resulting from the revolution their stable foundation. In fact, the NEP did not provide the new ruling caste with a stable foundation. So, united behind Stalin, it took up the program of the Left Opposition, not to pursue the revolution dreamed of by the Trotskyists, but to bury it once and for all. And it was because of this twofold misunderstanding, both of the nature of the NEP and of the characterization of Stalinist power, that the Left Opposition was disoriented and dislocated by the turning point of 1929-1934. Much later, but too late, Trotsky was to recognize that the "right-wing" Bukharin represented a left-wing opposition to Stalin, in other words, that Stalin's liquidation of the NEP was not a communist policy implemented by the wrong means, but the construction of a new political and social regime.

The history of the Russian Revolution is an immense tragedy in which we find all the elements of tragedy. Victor Serge's *Memoirs of a Revolutionary* is perhaps the most vivid and poignant testimony to this. One of the hallmarks of tragedy is that the heroes fulfill a destiny that they have not chosen, and which is imposed on them no matter how hard they try to escape it. What's more, these very efforts turn against the intentions of their authors and contribute to the fulfillment of destiny: it was in his desire to escape the curse that Oedipus accomplished what the oracle had foretold. The Bolsheviks are tragic heroes of this kind. Fully committed to building a classless society, they rebuild a class society. Devoted to the cause of the working class, they are the ones who bring its political expropriation to its ultimate conclusion. In truth, the working class has never really been a candidate for the exercise of political power. The workers made the revolution, but never led it. In February 1917, the revolutionary uprising saddled the coalition of social democrats and bourgeois liberal parties. Socialist-revolutionaries, Mensheviks and independents like Kerensky imposed their rule. The "dual power" situation between the provisional government and the soviets was a temporary one, which could only be resolved by the crushing of the soviets or the seizure of power by the Bolsheviks, who now had a majority in the soviets. When the question arose directly, there were three positions in the Bolshevik party: those who were against revolutionary insurrection, those who thought that the decision on insurrection against the provisional government should come from the soviets, and finally those who, like Lenin, thought that it was up to the party to decide and lead this insurrection without relying on a decision by the soviets. Finally, on the initiative of Trotsky, then chairman of the Petrograd soviet, the soviet congress voted for armed insurrection, even though the process had already been set in motion by the Bolshevik party leadership. In this case, Trotsky's action preserved the fiction of the seizure of power in October 1917 (November according to the Catholic calendar) by the working class organized in its soviets. The political content, however, conforms to Lenin's line. It was the party that acted in the name and place of the working class, which he had said in 1903 was incapable of going beyond the "trade-unionist" point of view on its own. The Bolsheviks see the working class as an army whose officers they "naturally" are. The civil war only served to accentuate this phenomenon: the soviets were bloodless, representing only the revolutionary parties—Lenin's party and its allies, the left-wing

190

SRs and the anarchists—and soon the only revolutionary party left to speak, the ruling party, after the elimination of the left-wing SRs and the anarchists.

The mistake—the one made by anarchists and leftists alike—is to consider that the Bolsheviks had a conscious desire to dominate the working class. The truth is much simpler: that the few million Russian workers could be the ruling class was quite simply an absolute impossibility—unless we were to sink into the most disheveled idealism. In *The State and Revolution*, the basic textbook for the "revolutionary Marxist", Lenin had defined the dictatorship of the proletariat as the regime in which the cook would look after the affairs of state. What he meant was that she would take care of state affairs under the guidance of the party, that collective intellectual who was supposed to embody "class consciousness". For, in truth, the cook does the cooking and has no time to read the reports of the bureaucrats trying to run the economy, let alone carry out the tasks of command and direction that the effective exercise of power requires.

A Premature Revolution?

One might believe (and this is ultimately the ultimate explanation provided by Trotskyism and a section of left-wing communists) that in backward Russia, disorganized by civil war, the exercise of workers' democracy (i.e., power directly ruled by the workers) is rendered almost impossible by the specific reasons of place and time, but that in other circumstances, the predictions of Marxism could be fully realized. The Trotskyist theory of permanent revolution demands the extension of revolution to the main advanced capitalist countries as the only way to guarantee the possibility of a genuine transition to socialism. That the particularly tragic conditions of the revolution in Russia played an important role in the growing apathy of the popular masses and the concomitant extension of the role of the party apparatus as the backbone of the state is not in doubt. But all this reasoning—which aims to save revolutionary Marxist theory—falls short in one essential respect: it lacks a genuine Marxist explanation of these particular conditions in Russia. Why, contrary to what the theory implies, did the socialist or communist revolution take place in a country where objective conditions were the most unfavorable imaginable, and why, conversely, did the countries where the working class should have taken power—the United States, Great Britain, France, Germany—ultimately remain deaf to the calls of the Russian revolution? Was the Russian Revolution premature—just as Marx thought the Paris Commune of 1871 was premature, so that the working-class solo turned into a funeral dirge?

A second group of questions immediately follows. Is the final failure of the October Revolution linked to conjunctural reasons, or does it not rather express a fundamental question linked to the very project of a social revolution bringing power to the working class? And if the latter, then, as good Marxists, we should consider that everything that, in the last century, presented itself under the name of socialist or communist revolution was, in reality, no more than a mask for the accession to power of a new ruling caste, a new class society, quite profoundly different from capitalism, but just as exploitative of the working class.

The answers to these two groups of questions will undoubtedly help us understand why 20th-century communism was a tragic and colossal abortion. Let's start with the first group. On December 24, 1917, a few days after the Bolsheviks seized power, Gramsci published an article in the newspaper *Avanti!* entitled "Revolution against *Capital*". Gramsci pointed out that, in Russia, *Capital* was more the book of the bourgeoisie than that of the proletariat, since it demonstrated the need for the formation of a bourgeoisie in Russia and the opening of a capitalist era[89]. In

---

89. In truth, *Capital* demonstrated no such thing. Marx never supported the thesis that history had to pass through the five obligatory stages of historical materialism, and that we must necessarily pass through the "capitalism" stage to get to communism. On the

action, the Bolsheviks "disavowed Karl Marx" and showed that the laws of historical materialism were not the iron laws that had been thought. Gramsci's conclusion is not that Marx should be consigned to the dustbin of history, but that orthodox Marxism is merely a fossilized doctrine to be replaced by the action that brings Marx's thought to life. Almost the first of a long literary series in Marxism: the defense of Marx's living thought against its fossilization by the Second International[90]. But it was true that the Russian Revolution did not fit into the Marxist schema. The explanation of the Russian Revolution lies in a phrase coined by Lenin: the imperialist chain broke at its weakest link. But this link was the weakest simply because capitalism was weaker, less developed and less secure than elsewhere. And, consequently, because it was the least "ready" for "socialist transition", at least according to the canons of historical materialism.

Petty Bourgeois National Revolutions

The history of the following decades confirmed what the Russian revolution had shown: "socialist" (or similar) revolutions led by communist parties took place exclusively in "capitalist countries with backward development", to use Trotsky's expression (China, Cuba, Vietnam), in countries ruined by war (Eastern Europe in 1945), but not once did we see a genuine revolution arising from the autonomous action of the working class fighting for its demands. What's more, while the October Revolution was still an "old-style" revolution, in which the workers played a very active role, often in the vanguard and initially pushing the leadership to the left, the "revolutions" (although we hesitate to use this term) in

---

contrary, it was precisely with regard to the Russian case that Marx clearly distanced himself from this "Marxism", notably in his correspondence with Vera Zassoulitch.
90. On the same theme, there are brilliant works by subtle thinkers such as Lukacs, Korsch and Pannekoek, to name but a few. There's a whole critical Marxism here, unfortunately all too often swallowed up under the rubble of "real socialism".

Eastern Europe, China, Vietnam or Cuba never involved the organization of the working class fighting for its own goals. The Cuban revolution was a classic popular revolution based on peasants and petty-bourgeois intellectuals[91]—neither Castro nor Guevara knew anything about workers' militancy, class struggle or trade union action for demands. Whatever one's political judgement on their subsequent actions, they were the spokesmen of a national democratic revolution[92], like those that had taken place in Europe in the first half of the 19th century. The Chinese case is just as telling, and perhaps even more so. After the crushing of the Shanghai Commune in 1927, the workers played no further part in the revolutionary process. From the outset, a police regime was established that left no room for workers' action. Peng Shu-tse, leader and founder of the Chinese CP, who turned Trotskyite, recounts:

"After the defeat of the revolution in 1927, the Chinese Communist Party began to organize a secret police force. Its main purpose was to protect party cells from destruction by Kuomintang agents. Then, when Mao Tse-tung established the 'Government of Soviet China' in Kiangsu, this secret police organization was set up there and became the local secret police. After Mao and company retreated to Yenan in 1935, this secret police system continued to exist and develop, with the participation of the Soviet Union's GPU. As soon as the People's Government was established in Beijing in 1949, the secret police net immediately spread across the country, along with the official organization of public security. Russian experts from the GPU were invited as advisors to help draw up plans and train new officers to complete this public security police system[93]."

---

91. Let's repeat it for the distracted reader, for us these qualifications are in no way infamous: in a country dominated and in the hands of a few large families between mafia and feudalism, a petty-bourgeois democratic national revolution is a historical advance that deserves to be supported.

92. The subsequent evolution of the Castro regime cannot make us forget that the Cuban revolution was a revolution against the dictatorship of Batista, the man whose U.S. leaders said, "He's a son of a bitch, but he's our son of a bitch".

93. Peng SHU-TSE and Peng PI-LAN, *The Chinese Revolution*, notebooks published by the US Socialist Workers Party.

In cities where the Communist Party remained very weak, its first concern was to suppress in advance any possibility of an autonomous working-class movement. The small Trotskyist organization was decimated, and the luckiest of its militants went into exile.

The Maoist Communist Party was able to seize power not because it was a workers' party, but because it had been the great organizer of resistance to the Japanese invaders and because it had a military force backed by the poor peasantry. *Mutatis mutandis*, the same can be said of the Vietnamese Communist Party. Hô Chi Minh and Giap's strength lay not in a virtually non-existent working class, but in a patriotic popular insurrection. In Saigon, an embryonic revolutionary communist movement had fallen victim to repression by the French colonial power. Thus, in 1939, the Trotskyist deputies Tha-Thu-Tau and Tran-Van-Trach, triumphantly elected with 80% of the vote (in the indigenous college) against 15% for the government, were arrested and deported! Incarcerated in Poulo Condore during the war, Tha-Thu-Tau was assassinated in 1945 by the Stalinists. As in China, the enemy is the workers' movement!

The Cambodian case deserves a specific analysis. Between 2 and 3 million dead, depending on the source, roughly a third of the population: this is the generally accepted death toll from the mass massacres perpetrated by Angkar, the Khmer Rouge organization. Although this group was originally very close to Maoism (which supported it to the very end, followed by the United States...), its phobia of the city and of anything resembling culture radically distinguishes it from the various variants of "twentieth-century communism". By emptying Phnom Penh in one night (April 17 to 18, 1975), and organizing a hunt for anything that might appear intellectual (wearing glasses is a distinctive sign), the Khmer Rouge massacres foreshadowed the genocide in Rwanda perpetrated by some Hutus against Tutsis and Hutus opposed to genocide. We're still amazed at the extraordinary leniency shown to the Khmer Rouge by some of the Western left and far left, including the highly media-friendly and trendy LCR of Alain Krivine, the mentor of the gentle Besancenot. Be that as it may, Angkar, which seems to have sprung straight from Orwell's imagination in *1984,* is probably the only party in this monster-rich century to have set itself the goal of destroying urban civilization and the working class attached to it. To refresh our memories, it was the Vietnamese armies that liberated Cambodia from the Khmer Rouge terror (1979). For several years, the Khmer Rouge, driven out of Phnom Penh, waged a guerrilla war supported by Thailand (which generously sheltered them), China and the USA.

In Eastern Europe, the revolution was led by the Red Army and the Communist party apparatus, organically linked to the Soviet party and state apparatus. Neither in Germany, Hungary nor Czechoslovakia did the autonomous organizations of the workers' movement play a significant role. When workers awoke in these countries, they were accused of being "agents of imperialism" and met with ruthless repression from the Stalinist regime. This was the case in 1953, when construction workers in East Berlin's Stalinallee walked out and called for a general strike across Germany. Brecht commented on the event with bitter irony:

> *After the June 17 uprising*
> *Secretary of the Writers' Union*
> *Distributed leaflets in Stalin Valley.*
> *The people, it read, have through their own fault*
> *Lost the government's confidence*
> *And it's only by redoubling our efforts*
> *That he can win her back. Wouldn't it be*
> *Easier for the government*
> *To dissolve the people*
> *And to elect another*[94]*?*

In Hungary, Poland (1956) and then Czechoslovakia in 1968, the question once again arose of whether the regime of the "people's democracies" should "dissolve the people and elect another".

---

94. B. BRECHT, *The Solution*, translated from the German by Jean-Pierre Lefebvre.

The Historical Weakness of the Working Class

So, wherever capitalism was overthrown during the 20th century, the working class was either rapidly expelled from the leadership of political affairs (in the case of Russia) or played no real role at all (in all other cases). This brief historical observation seems hardly debatable, unless you want to get into the theological distinctions that some Marxists (particularly Trotskyists) are so fond of. In defense of the Bolsheviks, at least Lenin and his companions in the early years of the revolution, it must be acknowledged that they were fully aware of this reality, but felt authorized to act in the name of a bloodless working class in the brief interval, they believed, when the Western working class was to set itself in motion to take over from this "premature" revolution "against capital". But—and this is the second group of questions we've raised—nothing of the sort happened. The German revolution of 1919 was crushed by the social democrats, who covered up and sometimes directed the dirty work of the "corps francs", the junkers and the whole reaction that would soon pave the way to power for Hitler, who would crush the skulls of the social democrats, as well as anything reminiscent of the Weimar Republic or even the Second Reich. The Second German Revolution, scheduled for autumn 1923, was cancelled at the last minute by the *Comintern*. Trotskyists saw this as the great betrayal of the Zinoviev-Stalin clique. Perhaps they were partly right, but one wonders what the chances of success were for a social revolution that a whistle from Moscow was enough to bring to a screeching halt!

Elsewhere, the workers' movement has manifested itself, often vigorously, but nowhere has it really challenged the capitalist mode of production. Between the wars, the French and Spanish Popular Fronts are two classic examples of the emergence of the workers' movement independently of Moscow's orders and scheming. The French Popular Front was imposed by working-class reaction to the factional leagues' attempted coup de force on February 6, 1934: on February 12, workers marching in two separate processions—

197

that of the CGT and the CGTU—forced the leaders to unite. This "united front", CGT/CGTU and soon PCF/SFIO, was to be transformed into a coalition with Herriot and Daladier's Radical Party to form a Popular Front whose objectives were above all anti-fascist, with workers' demands reduced to the bare minimum (the 40-hour week and paid vacations were won by the general strike of June 1936, even though they were not included in the Popular Front program). In short, the autonomous working-class movement was put in tow of a coalition in which, *de facto,* it was the "democratic bourgeoisie" that provided the political direction of operations, and in which the function of the socialist, communist and syndicalist leaders was to enforce order and discipline in the working class in the name of anti-fascist unity. In infinitely more dramatic circumstances, the same process is taking place in Spain, but there the fate of the Popular Front coalition will be decided by civil war.

The final example of interest for our purposes is Portuguese. After the fall of the dictatorship of Caetano, Salazar's heir, provoked and organized by MFA officers and non-commissioned officers, Portugal experienced a revolutionary-type situation not unlike that of Russia in 1917. However, the battle was soon confined to the various factions in the army, from the most moderate (linked to the old regime) to the most "leftist" (such as Otelo de Carvalho's group), and the classic parties, the "bourgeois" party, for a time renamed the "social-democratic" party, and Mario Soares' socialist party. The only serious attempts to break away from a democratized capitalist system were launched by the military, firstly the MFA's plan to create an "apartite" constitution based on councils centralized by the MFA and excluding classical parliamentarianism, and above all Carvalho's revolutionary coup attempt. But none of this won the support of the workers, who aspired to an improvement in the social situation, to trade unions defending their interests not only against the bosses, but also against the state, even if "revolutionary", and to democratic political institutions. After April 25, 1974, all revolutionary groups saw Portugal as the testing ground for the new socialist revolution in Europe. It was the last great messianic illusion of the 20th century. Two years after April 25, Portugal, under the leadership of Mario Soares's Socialist Party (PS), began its normalization and joined the European construction process.

If we ask the "revolutionary Marxists" (e.g., the various Trotskyist factions) what explanation can be given for this overall development, which so radically contradicts the predictions on which their strategy is based, they give a generic answer: the betrayal of the ruling apparatuses of the major workers' parties, i.e., the social-democratic and communist parties. In the previous chapter, we explained the process by which the socialist and social-democratic parties of the Second International became the parties of the wage-earner, i.e., parties for the preservation of capitalism in forms acceptable to wage-earners, without the need for betrayal to intervene in this process. The betrayal of leaders could be a good explanation if it weren't so regularly repeated. What's more, it's hard to understand why proletarians are so easily fooled by these treacherous leaders, and don't put their trust in the true revolutionaries who constantly warn them of the betrayal of traitors… For people who claim to be Marxists, all these purely subjectivist explanations are totally extravagant. To treat in this way the experience of over a century of history, of grandiose movements, countless crimes, buried hopes and heroic sacrifices, is even rather undignified.

Everywhere, the communism of the 20th century has given way to capitalist regimes, whether frankly capitalist, as in Russia, or officially still communist, as in China and Vietnam, where the capitalist mode of production finds the shelter of the "communist" police state very favorable conditions for development. And we can bet that Raoul Castro will take the same path in Cuba. Elsewhere, communism exists only in a residual state. Europe's two main mass communist parties, the French and the Italian, are in their death throes. Surviving on the municipal remnants of its former glory, the PCF is no more than a marginal force, still attracting a little media attention once a year at the traditional "Fête de l'Huma". Deeply divided into factions with nothing in between, the PCF seems incapable of reacting, paralyzed as it is by a leadership whose only watchword is "don't touch it, it's broken". In Italy, the PCI has given way to a shapeless thing calling itself the "Democratic Party", modelled on the eponymous American party. The last heirs of the historic PCI, the PRC and PDCI, are paralyzed between a suicidal leftist syndrome and the regret of their electoral positions lost during their last adventures alongside the "center-left" coalition. One day, perhaps, we'll be able to make a precise history of the destruction of the PCI, i.e., a history of the relations between the young heir leaders of the old PCI and the representatives of the United States and the European Union, explaining how the Occhetto, d'Alema, Veltroni and *tutti quanti*, like spoiled children, squandered with impunity the assets of the historic organization of the Italian workers' movement. But we must also try to understand why the workers of the North have so often abandoned "their" historic party to rally behind Berlusconi or the thurifers of so-called "Padania". Just as we need to explain the break between the PCF and the French working class.

You can't get away with pirouetting. Those who say it wasn't communism that collapsed, but Stalinism, are hiding behind their little fingers. The Berlin Wall also fell on the heads of those who had fought the Stalinist system from the outset. A terrible injustice! But history is neither just nor unjust.

Chapter X. Looking Back to the USSR

To shed some light on the findings of the previous chapter, it's necessary to say a little more than a few words about this previously unknown social formation, "Soviet socialism", and the reasons behind its seemingly sudden collapse. In the 1970s, anti-Soviet propaganda was keen to stress the stability of the regime: it was necessary to frighten people and present the Moscow ogre in the most terrifying guise. But history was to confirm what even the most informed observers knew: this stability had always been the result of an unstable equilibrium, of the iron corset of the Guepeu holding together all political and social contradictions.

Studying the Moscow trials, Trotsky wrote that, in their own way, they expressed the absolute incompatibility between Soviet society and the Stalinist dictatorship. The camps, the omnipotence of the police and absolute monolithism were not gratuitous perversions for this regime, but rather the essential condition for its survival, since it could not benefit from any lasting consensus—only the "Great Patriotic War" had made such a consensus possible. While the Parisian champions of "anti-totalitarianism" denounced the omnipotence of ideology, it should be noted that the USSR was one of the states that relied least on consensus-building ideology and most on coercion, to borrow a distinction from Gramsci (thematized by Louis Althusser). Awareness of the separation of society between the ruling class and the people was massive; between "them" and "us", everyone knew the irremediable antagonism and drew the practical consequences (in particular, the use of doublespeak, cunning, etc.).

This observation is not in line with the idle rhetoric of "totalitarian" theorists, who give ideology the decisive role, but it is obvious to anyone with a little knowledge of real history, rather than history rewritten for the needs of war propaganda.

The Demise of "Historical Communism"

The Stalinist system proper was established after collectivization and the launch of the Five-Year Plan, and symbolically, what had been a fairly ordinary tyranny (alas!) became one of the worst regimes known to mankind, starting with the trials triggered by the murder (no doubt ordered by Stalin) of Kirov. Before that date, deportation camps already existed: they were an old tradition of Tsarism, shamelessly taken up by the Bolsheviks. Under the Stalinist regime, they took on a new dimension, sometimes even turning into mass extermination camps. The 1930s also saw the theorization of the need for periodic purges (mass arrests of party and economic cadres), show trials and the liquidation of all suspects by outright assassination in the cellars of the sinister Lubyanka, headquarters of the KGB (and today headquarters of the FSB). Just on the eve of the Second World War, one of these purges decimated the Red Army, which partly explains Russia's unpreparedness at the time of the German invasion… The Stalinist regime, which resembled the Nazi regime in every way, was above all a regime of terror and permanent civil war.

Talleyrand, or perhaps the Prince of Schwarzenberg, used to say that you could do anything with bayonets, except sit on them… As early as 1953, Moscow's hierarchs realized that the unleashing of the political police was getting out of hand. After the trial of the "white dung", new purges were in the pipeline, threatening to hit the top echelons of the Party and State even more brutally. The national mourning ceremonies were barely over, and "de-Stalinization" began.

Under the leadership of Nikita Khrushchev, the bureaucracy sought to loosen its grip, regain the support of part of the population and reassure bureaucrats at all levels. The fall of the sinister

Beria in 1953 was the first step in an evolution that would lead to the "secret report" ("attributed to Comrade Khrushchev", as we say in the PCF) of the XXth Congress and the report of the XXIInd Congress. For those who had bet on the regime's self-reform at the time, the Kremlin's masters took it upon themselves to provide the necessary denials: in August 1953, there was the merciless suppression of the workers' uprising in eastern Germany. In 1956, Russian tanks entered Budapest. The repression left at least 3,000 dead. The leaders of the Hungarian revolution, including former Communist leader Imre Nagy, were executed.

Under Khrushchev's leadership, the Kremlin bureaucracy constantly vacillated between the desire to limit the most blatant abuses of the repressive system, the denunciation of Stalinism—renamed the "personality cult period"—and the repression of popular movements that were shaking the glacis countries and beginning to affect the USSR with the development of a new opposition. But these swerves to the right and left could not be tolerated for long, especially as attempts at economic reform were failing. The publication of Solzhenitsyn's *A Day in the Life of Ivan Denisovich* in 1962 symbolized not only a "thaw" in the cultural sphere, but also a direct and public challenge to the repressive labor camp system that continued to operate under Khrushchev. From then on, Khrushchev's fate was sealed. Yet his downfall and replacement by Brezhnev did not put an end to the ongoing process.

Opposition demonstrations multiplied despite the repression. In 1967, the trial of Daniel and Siniavsky (who seems to have been denounced to the KGB by the CIA...) revealed to the West the extent of this opposition, whose clandestine publications, the "Samizdat", multiplied. Alongside the writers, the Medvedev brothers, General Grigorenko and Andrei Sakharov joined the fight against the regime. It was also the mathematician Leonid Plyushch who was freed after a long international campaign. While Brezhnev sought to commit himself to the official rehabilitation of Stalin, the opposition's struggle, weak as it seemed, put the brakes on this process. With the denunciation of the repressive regime, demands

Chapter X. Looking Back to the USSR

for nationality rights began to emerge. General Grigorenko, who had made a name for himself with a remarkable book denouncing Stalin's catastrophic role as a strategist during the Second World War, undertook a campaign in defense of the Crimean Tatars deported by the regime.

In the face of growing opposition and revolutionary crises in Czechoslovakia and Poland, the ruling caste saw its only salvation in repression and immobilism. In 1972, the defendants in the Yakir-Krassin trial "confessed" to their imaginary crimes, in the sinister tradition of Stalinist trials. While Leonid Plyushch was released from the psychiatric hospital where the regime had confined him, and deported to France, hundreds of other opponents took to the Gulag. A headlong rush that further isolated the regime, sweeping away all the hopes raised by the de-Stalinization undertaken after the 20th Congress.

On the economic front, the situation is not brilliant. The knout is a stimulant of dubious productivity. The old empire of the tsars had experienced this. The empire of the bureaucrats is testing this law once again. To justify their power, the ruling caste must constantly demonstrate the prodigious progress of the "planned economy". Unfortunately, Soviet planning, which expels producers and replaces them with commissars, appears to be the very opposite of what genuine socialist planning should be, in line with the ideas of the founding fathers. During the first decades, results (often grossly inflated by official statistics) could be achieved, at the cost of untold waste and suffering: "primitive socialist accumulation", like its capitalist counterpart, took place in mud and blood. But the system soon ran out of steam. The endemic agricultural stagnation revealed the state of society as a whole. What's more, since the regime had ruthlessly atomized all forms of employee organization and broken up all independent trade unions, workers were forced to revert to the most archaic forms of class struggle: sabotage, casting, absenteeism and so on. The result is hopelessly low labour productivity, mediocre production quality and an ever-widening technological gap with Western countries—despite some spectacular successes in areas directly controlled by the military, such as the conquest of space.

The Beginning of the End

This sluggish economy, threatened by growing anarchy, was under pressure from the military and its industries, which absorbed a considerable share of the gross national product. And, from 1980 onwards, the war in Afghanistan on the one hand, and the revival of the arms race on the other[95], gradually dislocated the entire Soviet economic machine, making reforms urgent and at the same time preventing them from succeeding: Gorbachev's tragedy was to be caught in this pincer movement.

The crisis of Soviet society is developing at every level and on every terrain. The ravages of alcoholism are not an epiphenomenon, but a tragic expression of this crisis, as are the widespread corruption and influence peddling, the multiplication of privileges and the considerable increase in social differences. Today's Russia—first Yeltsin's, then Putin's and Medvedev's—is the heir to all this, and we can't pass judgement on today's Russia by forgetting this history. As long as the country resembled a drunken boat under the leadership of a president imbibed to the last degree, and where the powers of the world could plunder everything without risking anything, Western leaders could only congratulate themselves on Russia's profound "democratic" transformation. Since Putin tried to put the country back on its feet and restore a little order to it, using methods he learned at the KGB, Russia has once again become a rival and even an enemy… A calmer judgment would no doubt be in order—except, of course, for those who always need a war threat to justify their power and direction.

---

95. US President Reagan's "Star Wars" initiative played a key role in this period. To this we can add the policy of French President Mitterrand, who supported the installation of US missiles in Germany.

The Soviet regime has been compared to the "Asian despotism" once studied by Marx and taken up by Wittfogel in his work on *Oriental Despotism*[96], a term which, according to this author, applies not only to "hydraulic societies" (all societies whose agriculture is based on the mastery of irrigation), but also to the USSR. From the 1970s onwards, this regime was profoundly destabilized. Attempts at economic reform under both Khrushchev and Brezhnev (see the Liebermann and Trapeznikov projects of 1965) had failed. The desire to restore flexibility to the economic machine by stimulating individual initiative constantly came up against the bureaucratic monopoly of power. Yet this monopoly is under severe strain. The bureaucratic caste is not homogeneous. The most diverse tendencies run through it. Aspirations, privileges and ideas vary greatly between the small local party leaders[97] and the heads of large companies, between those who are oriented towards foreign relations (managers, heads of financial or commercial institutions) and those who live solely from their position in an immutable yet unstable hierarchy, the famous "Nomenklatura". All this is reflected in fundamental differences of political orientation. As far back as the 1930s, when he defected to Mussolini's regime, Soviet diplomat Boutenko explained that many of Moscow's leaders were moving towards openly fascist positions. The signing of the German-Soviet Pact was therefore motivated not only by tactical reasons, but also by the fascination that Hitler and his regime exerted over a whole section of Kremlin leaders, starting with Stalin! Vassili Grossmann's magnificent book *Vie et Destin (Life and Destiny)* sheds light on this (often reciprocal) fascination between the two totalitarian regimes. Trotsky rightly described Stalin and Hitler as twin stars. Hitler left the scene first, Stalin

---

96. Karl August WITTFOGEL, *Le Despotisme oriental. Étude comparative du pouvoir total*, translated into French by Editions de Minuit, 1964.

97. Soviet republics tend to produce more or less autonomous bureaucracies. The "Uzbek mafia" that made the headlines was the mafia of the Uzbek Communist Party… State institutions also competed with each other. The KGB alone is a power that clashes with other powers.

barely ten years later, but the resemblance between the two tyrants owed nothing to chance or to some imaginary essence called totalitarianism. Just as Hitlerism expressed, in a paroxysmal but obvious way, the essence of capitalism, so Stalin's terror expressed, in an equally paroxysmal way, the essence of the "Soviet" system as a system of domination.

Behind an impenetrable façade, in the decades following the death of the "Little Father of the Peoples", practical links were forged between certain members of the Kremlin hierarchy and the leading spheres of North American and European capitalism. In the sixties and seventies, certain Soviet companies played a key role in the global capitalist economy. Such was the case of BCEN (Commercial Bank for Northern Europe), better known as Euro-Bank, which played a decisive role in setting up the Eurodollar market and deregulating the international monetary system. At the same time, the Soviets also played a key role in the grain and foodstuffs trade, both as the biggest buyers, but also as transporters and indirectly as traders through the Doumeng trust[98] or through other "emperors of hunger" such as the Italian Ferruzi group, which owed much of its fortune to fruitful trade with Moscow... The fact that these groups have disappeared does not change the essence of the matter: the Soviet economy played a significant role in the concentration of world trade and in the advent of the so-called liberal or neo-liberal phase of the capitalist mode of production. Reagan and Thatcher didn't do it all themselves...

At the other pole of society, new aspirations were emerging. By the 1970s, ideological support for the regime had all but disappeared. And if the leadership occasionally met with a degree of consensus, it was not on the grounds of so-called socialism, but on those of patriotism and the "struggle for peace"—for while there may be legitimate doubts about the peaceful intentions of the

---

98. A smallholder from Haute-Garonne, Jean-Baptiste Doumeng joined the PCF at the age of 16 and went on to become the head of the *Interagra* group, nicknamed "the red billionaire".

hierarchs, we must not forget the heavy price paid by the peoples of the Soviet Union in the last world war. And it is this legacy of adherence to the Soviet regime through the "Great Patriotic War" that Vladimir Putin has skilfully recuperated.

In the "post-Stalinist" Soviet regime, workers occupy some strong positions—not least because of the particular structure of the labor market, which allows them to leave their jobs at any time to take up employment elsewhere on better terms—but the real situation of the working class in the Soviet Union is far from reaching the level of advanced industrial countries, especially in Europe. Access to higher education obeys the same laws of reproduction as in capitalist countries, and the opposition between the "real freedoms" of Soviet workers and the "formal freedoms" of workers in capitalist countries, a classic theme of Communist party propaganda, is virtually meaningless. Just as in capitalist countries, rights written on paper[99] always end up giving way to the ruthless logic of power relations, and all the more so as the working class has no means of struggle or collective representation in the form of workers' unions or parties independent of the authorities. Significantly, the beginning of the process of collapse of the Stalinist system can be dated back to the Polish workers' movement of the late 1970s, with the creation of the Solidarnosc trade union, as an independent trade union[100]. This is a proletarian regime that shakes on its foundations and collapses as soon as the proletariat seeks to act on its own.

Among young people, too, the status quo became increasingly burdensome in the 1970s, and prevailing conformism increasingly intolerable. The success of rock and, more generally, of all the "decadent" fashions coming out of the West, bears witness to this.

---

99. Stalin presented the Soviet constitution of 1936 as "the most democratic in the world".

100. We'd have to tell the story of how the workers had their union confiscated, how the first shipyard activists were pushed aside by Walesa and the Catholic Church apparatus, which, incidentally, only had a free hand in this operation thanks to the benevolence of part of the Stalinist apparatus.

People often talk about the depoliticization of Russian youth, who are only interested in earning money and enjoying the benefits of a "consumer society". As always, this is certainly a one-sided view. But insofar as it is true, it's a phenomenon that goes back at least to the last two decades of the Soviet Union.

In short, the upheavals leading to the final downfall of Soviet society are neither the fruit of the action of an "enlightened despot", nor the by-product of the "will of the masses", but the result of a dialectic between bottom and top. When a revolution is brewing, all classes of society conspire to bring it about. It was in the salons of the aristocracy that the theories of the Enlightenment philosophers were propagated, it was the monarchy that ruined the power of the aristocracy, it was the enlightened bourgeoisie that launched the movement, and it was finally the popular irruption that transformed it into revolution. Such a combined process took place in the USSR: it was within the ruling bureaucracy that the process of disintegration was set in motion, and the movements of intellectual dissidence can largely be traced back to it. What is striking, however, is the extraordinary passivity of the Russian people, and of the workers in particular, whereas in the other countries of "real socialism" a movement from below also manifested itself, to varying degrees and with varying consequences. In the fall of the Soviet regime, Russian workers didn't go on strike, didn't demonstrate in the streets, didn't raise barricades. They simply slowly undermined the regime by working as little as possible in state enterprises, practicing a kind of beaded sabotage that was arguably the only possible form of opposition in the Brezhnev years. And, scalded by long experience, they never believed Gorbachev's self-management promises at the time of perestroika.

The "reformers" initially sought to energize the economy by injecting a measure of individual initiative into the system of centralized planning, but to achieve this they had to strike blows at the bureaucratic monopoly and, in so doing, unwittingly contributed to the dislocation of the system as a whole. Two men in particular illustrate this story: Gorbachev and Yeltsin, both pure products of the apparatus, both backed by powerful barons of the ruling caste. Gorbachev unwillingly, Yeltsin knowingly—played a risky game with the bureaucracy with great political skill, particularly during the "perestroika" period, and was not always the wreck he had become in the final years of his presidency.

In any case, the process that led to the collapse of "real socialism" was first and foremost an internal one, and there's no point in racking our brains trying to uncover CIA plots or obscure maneuvers by "class enemies". Western intelligence services obviously played a part in all this, and no doubt had contacts at the highest levels of the Soviet apparatus. But here, as elsewhere, the police conception of history does nothing to help us understand reality. We have also focused too much on the monstrous nature of the regime. Counting the dead according to the rather silly problematic of the *Black Book of Communism* leads nowhere. It's easy enough to count the deaths of capitalism over the course of the 20th century to arrive at such a terrifying result: add up the deaths of colonialism with real genocides of no interest to anyone, because then you'd have to incriminate England, Germany, Belgium, the deaths from the two world wars, the deaths from colonial wars, and the figure of 100 million deaths attributed to communism is far exceeded. And when we've finished with this macabre accounting, we'll realize that human history is just one long series of massacres, with the victors massacring the vanquished, which isn't exactly a mind-blowing discovery!

The USSR: Neither State Capitalism, nor Socialism, nor Communism

So it's best to try and understand the socio-economic structure that was put in place in the USSR, and the relationship between this base and the tyrannical government of Stalin and his successors.

A preliminary remark: the Soviet economic system was not born of the October Revolution, and while Lenin may have been somewhat at fault in the eyes of history, it would be unfair to hold him responsible for an economic organization he had always opposed. The theory of "war communism" was the work of the leftist tendency in the Bolshevik Party, represented by Bukharin[101]. By making a virtue of necessity, they were only trying to make the harsh laws of the state of siege acceptable to Marxist consciousness. But Lenin and Trotsky soon realized that it was impossible to proclaim communism in a backward country, with only 3 million workers for 100 million peasants. And so it was that the NEP, the New Political Economy, advocated the coexistence of a private economy, operating both according to the laws of the market and those of a "socialist" state-run economy. Lenin even went so far as to say that the future of socialism would depend on the ability of state-run trusts to beat private capitalism on the field of competition…

The Stalinist and post-Stalinist Soviet economic system was therefore unimaginable until the years 1927-1928. It was Stalin who led the implementation of this system at the turn of the 1930s, with the first five-year plans for forced industrialization and collectivization of the peasantry. We know that the peoples of the Soviet Union paid a terrible price for this turning point. Millions of peasants were arrested, deported to labor camps and exterminated by starvation in what appears today as the first Operation *Nacht und Nebel*. The Bolshevik revolution had won by giving the peasant the land; the Stalinist counter-revolution took it away, ruining Soviet agriculture for a long time to come. Estimates put the number of victims of collectivization at around 22 million, including those who were executed, those who died in the camps or on the road to deportation, and those who starved to death as a result of the

---

101. Bukharin had to make amends and became one of the defenders of the NEP, but the man who was "the Party's darling" ended up in 1938 under the bullets of Stalin's executioners.

dislocation of agricultural production. A catastrophe of this magnitude would be repeated in China at the time of the "Great Leap Forward" and a little later with the "Cultural Revolution". At the same time, workers were subjected to a new labor discipline that placed them entirely under the thumb of the state bureaucracy, with no means of defense. The "Stakhanovist" movement took up one of the worst methods of capitalist exploitation (as we say today, "work more to earn more!"). A considerable proportion of ordinary workers' labor was supplemented by the forced labor of deportees. As Engels said, without ancient slavery, there can be no modern socialism! In a striking historical shortcut, Stalin combined theory and practice. The party itself was "purified" from top to bottom. After the elimination of the Trotskyite "left" came the elimination of the Bukharinite "right"—these labels of "right" and "left" are meaningless in this case, as Stalin was neither to the left nor to the right of Trotsky, but represented a different social class, a different political regime.

The trauma caused by the introduction of the new economic regime based on the omnipotence of the central bureaucracy is enormous. Famine returned, reminiscent of the civil war years. Soviet society was on the brink of explosion, which is why, in 1934, the day after the first real Stalinist congress, dubbed "the congress of the victors", the assassination—on Stalin's orders—of Kirov ushered in the era of the Moscow trials.

At the end of the 1930s, the USSR was undergoing a social and political regime radically different from that established by the 1917 revolution. Even if there were elements of continuity—as there were between pre-1789 monarchical France and republican France—the ideology, principles and hopes common to the entire international socialist movement until after 1920 were liquidated throughout the Soviet Union. A new caste—partly heir to the Tsarist bureaucracy, partly an expression of 20th-century trends in monopoly capitalism—ran a particular economic system, equally far removed from capitalism and socialism as conceived by the "founding fathers", including Lenin. This regime is based

212

on the total interweaving of the repressive state apparatus and the economic apparatus, centralized planning by the bureaucracy and the transformation of the peasantry into a new serving class. When Nazi troops invaded the USSR in 1942, the October Revolution had been dead for several years. It had been destroyed by the deportations as well as by the forced collectivization that now formed the economic basis of the bureaucracy's political power.

The keystone of the new economic system is centralized planning, and the genuine "dictatorship over needs" that flows from it. A detailed analysis of planning is indispensable, for it is in the name of the so-called "logic of planning" that Trotskyists and most non-Stalinist Communists will continue to see the USSR's social regime as progressive, despite the horrors of political power. Basically, in their view, the economic basis was sound or almost so, and it was only the political superstructure that was wrong—the Trotskyite theory of the "degenerate workers' state". It was therefore necessary to defend planning and state ownership, and to concentrate fire against the repugnant methods of the Stalinist bureaucracy. The masters of historical materialism had just discovered a political superstructure opposed to the socio-economic infrastructure... But this so-called "logic of planning", "progressive" in itself, was a mystification of the same nature as Adam Smith's "invisible hand of the market". In reality, planning was nothing other than the organization of economic and political power for the bureaucratic caste at the head of the Soviet Union.

There was a time when Stalinist victory communiqués claimed to provide definitive proof of the superiority of the Soviet system over capitalism. From dithyrambic hymns to the Five-Year Plan, "Sputnik" and Gagarin, it was in the language of industrial production and technology that Soviet socialism was supposed to assert its superiority. But from the 1960s onwards, the tone began to change, as difficulties mounted.

Impossible Planning

In his book *L'Économie soviétique*[102], Alec Nove, an author not particularly hostile to the USSR, dismantled the mechanisms of the system, how and according to what criteria resources were allocated between the various sectors of production. Nove tries to break free from the formal categories used in the West, on both the right and the left, to analyze the Soviet economic system. While state ownership is obviously an important criterion, it is not sufficient, for the essential point is that "the Soviet system is based on administrative orders, not commercial ones" (p. 9). While there is an underground economy—which Gorbachev will seek to use by formalizing it—the economy as a whole nevertheless remains ordered and supervised, and "central regulation continues to extend to such details as the use of wire for baled hay" (p. 32). This system produced an enormous mess, which even the Soviet press had to denounce, in order to incriminate "saboteurs" and "bourgeois elements" unfit for proletarian discipline ("transparency" existed in this respect long before Gorbachev).

In truth, the problem is not the collapse of the USSR. Rather, one wonders by what miracle the USSR did not descend into indescribable chaos earlier. But as Nove again says (p. 33): "chaos is avoided by the fact that every year most companies produce more or less the same things as the previous year". Thus, planning, which was intended to be a voluntarist system of development and forecasting of the future—opposed in this respect to capitalist anarchy—becomes the basis of routine, and its operation constitutes a considerable brake on innovation as well as long-term calculations. It achieves the opposite of its proclaimed objectives. This lack of real long-term planning was particularly marked in certain fields, such as agriculture and industrial pollution. Like the race to maximize profit in capitalism, the success of the bureaucratic plan proved disastrous

---

102. Éditions Economica, Paris, 1981.

in establishing a fair proportion between the various branches of production, and excluded future generations from its calculations.

There are various reasons for this situation. The greed of the bureaucratic caste and the mentality it conveys all play a part. But the ruling caste has hardly changed since the end of the Soviet Union, and the effects are very different. So, rather than the psychology of those in power, it's the very nature of state planning that needs to be called into question. The spontaneous ideology of bureaucrats (and this doesn't just apply to the USSR) is that "managers decide everything"; their competence or their calculations must be able to put the whole real course of society into equations subject to administrative decree. Unfortunately, this ideology runs up against a more complex reality: "Mathematicians in Kiev have calculated that, in order to draw up a precise and completely integrated material and technical supply plan for the Republic of Ukraine alone and for one year, it would require the work of the entire population of the globe for millions of years." (Nove, p. 43). Obviously, as the economy becomes more international, needs increase (and this is the *sine qua non* of civilization) and the number of these calculations increases! In other words, there's no point in blaming the problems of Soviet planning on the backwardness inherited from Tsarist Russia. The poorer the country, the more efficient was Soviet planning, which proved to be an (equally costly) means of achieving in a backward country the primitive accumulation that had been achieved a century or two earlier in the advanced countries through far-flung trade, the plundering of colonies and the over-exploitation of workers. But the more the Soviet economy developed, the more its inhabitants became men "rich in need", to borrow a phrase from Marx, and the more Soviet planning asphyxiated itself. The USSR was able to "catch up and overtake" the West in coal and steel, but in the last decades of its existence, it fell behind in the field of advanced technologies, obviously more decisive than steel.

For these reasons, all attempts at reform from Khrushchev to Gorbachev, via the various attempts made by Brezhnev

Chapter X. Looking Back to the USSR

(Liebermann-Trapeznikov reforms in 1965, introduction of the brigade system in the 1970s), have sought to answer this question: how to maintain central planning in the "macroeconomic" sphere, while decentralizing "microeconomic" decisions. However, this new form of "mixed" economy, theoretically conceivable (see the writings of the Czech Ota Sik or the economic policy of a country like Hungary), clashes with reality. As Nove further explains, "in practical terms, it is not possible to delegate micro-decisions and maintain control only over the major headings" (p. 62). This practical impossibility has led to the failure of all attempts at reform.

State planning also comes up against another problem: since Adam Smith, it has been believed that productive forces grow with economies of scale and mass production. The USSR—like many capitalist trusts—has provided examples of "diseconomies" of scale and counter-productive technical progress. According to classical Marxist doctrine, the concentration and centralization of capital prepared the way for the transition to socialism. So, naturally, in a "socialist" society, there would eventually be only one company. But the degree of complexity of such an organization increases, from a certain point onwards, much faster than gains in scale: the size of the bureaucracy required for this mega-company is therefore clearly more than proportional to the size of the organization itself.

Finally, the way planning is calculated leads to aberrations. Stalin had sent land rent and the law of value to the devil. But the law of value imposed itself as the only means of accounting for the labor time socially spent in a given activity. The Soviet plan expresses its objectives in terms of physical quantities of production—when expressed in rubles, this is simply a presentation device, the figure being simply the product of the quantity produced multiplied by an authoritatively fixed profit coefficient. This leads to well-known perverse effects: "An electricity company was reprimanded for not fulfilling the plan. This was due, however, to an unusually mild winter, so that the demand for heating had been much lower." (Nove, p. 105) The whole logic of the system therefore led company managers to underestimate their production capacities and overestimate their input requirements and costs. This explains the frantic search over many years for new, more reliable economic indicators, as well as for a system of profit-sharing for managers. For "the essence of the problem is that the center strives to set up a system of incentives designed to promote greater efficiency, but because it does not and cannot know the specific circumstances, its instructions can frequently conflict with what people in the field know to be the sensible thing to do." (Nove p. 115)

All these contradictions are concentrated in the general absence (or near absence) of conformity between the supply plan and the production plan. After all, if production doesn't care about consumption, this is true not only for the buyer of shoes, but also for the buyer of machine tools or raw materials. Managers should be able to set their own production schedules in the light of consumer demands, but this would somehow mean a return to the market and the destruction of state planning. But since planning is both the justification and the economic foundation of the political power of the bureaucratic caste, a return to the market would mean the overthrow of the political regime instituted in the USSR since the First Five-Year Plan of 1928-1929 and the forced collectivization of agriculture. Gorbachev was also caught in a vicious circle, until the 1991 crisis and the near collapse of the "socialist economy" edifice. When perestroika sought to restore initiative to companies (including by proposing systems of worker election of management), the miracle didn't happen, because it couldn't happen. Gorbachev's measures even aggravated the chaos, while the advocates of liberal reforms inspired by capitalist countries gave free rein to their voices. The stiffening of the "old Stalinists" provided the pretext for the 1991 provocation that signed the USSR's death certificate.

The glorious (and largely falsified) balance sheets of the 1950s and '60s were an attempt to excuse the reality of the political regime on the grounds of economic success, which was supposed to give the people "real freedoms" to contrast with the "formal freedoms" of "bourgeois democracy". Strictly in terms of economic dynamics, the Soviet system has proved its inferiority to capitalism, and the matter seems settled. The reasons for this failure must be understood. Soviet planning was introduced as a means of ensuring the stability of the political regime of bureaucratic dictatorship that Stalin was building on the rubble of the October Revolution and the corpses of its heroes. It was to justify the omnipotence of the apparatus and demonstrate the possibility of "building socialism in one country". But "socialism in one country", this "national socialism" whose first theorizations developed in the right wing of German social democracy around people like Volmar, is nothing but a reactionary utopia, an ideological cover for a system fundamentally opposed to Marx's ideas, which wouldn't be too serious, but above all to the aspirations of individuals as shaped and developed by modernity. According to Marx, socialism is only possible on the basis of the highest development of productive forces, science, technology and workers' consciousness, and must have an international dimension from the outset. By this yardstick, it is clear that nothing socialist could be achieved in the isolated, backward USSR. If the bureaucracy clung to "socialism in one country" and to state planning, it was because it found in them the foundations not only of its political power, but also of its considerable material privileges. The USSR, a monstrous product of 20th-century history, paradoxically confirms the general laws laid down by orthodox Marxism.

But this negative confirmation only confirms at the same time the purely ideological character of this orthodox Marxism. For the tragedy of the USSR was that there was no alternative. When, in 1924-1925, the Bolshevik bureaucracy in power backed Stalin on the strategic line of "socialism in one country", there was an excellent reason for this: the revolution in Western Europe was not on the cards, and there was no hope that it would be in the short term. If the USSR is condemned to isolation, what should we do? We can address the world proletariat (this will become a great Trotskyist specialty), urging it to fulfill its historic mission. But at the same time, we have to make a living. If we don't want to build "socialism in a single country", there's nothing left to do but return the keys to the house to its former owners! In the absence of a world revolution, should the Bolsheviks have addressed the White Russian capitalists, whether emigrant or inland, and told them: "It's all right, we can't go any further today, because of these cowardly workers subservient to German, French or British social democracy. Take back power and we'll fight you in opposition." You only have to read this speech to realize how extravagant it is. The Bolsheviks had power, and they had to keep it, all the more so as they were expressing social interests installed in positions of power, not the interests of the working class, but those of the intellectual petty bourgeoisie administering the "socialist" state (the tsarist state repainted red, as Lenin put it). But in so doing, they were heading down a blind alley, and at the same time beginning to nail down the planks of the coffin in which they would all, except Stalin, end up before the end of 1940.

As we said earlier, there is a real tragic dimension to this story. Trotsky's fate is emblematic of this. He is the victor of October. He led the insurrection, he organized the Red Army and he won. As George Steiner points out, he is the first Jew since Joshua to be a true strategist. Without Lenin, the October Revolution would not have taken place, but without Trotsky, it would certainly have been defeated, either on October 25, 1917 (old calendar) or a few months later. It was he who imposed the use of "bourgeois specialists" in the army: officers from the Tsar's army were recycled into the Red Army under the control of political commissars. All this earned Trotsky strong enmities and inexhaustible hatred among the Bolsheviks. Above all, it was Trotsky who helped forge the political system that would crush him. After giving up the fight for a NEP avant la lettre, which he rightly believed indispensable, he rallied to "war communism", and devoted his literary talent to justifying the militarization of trade unions, forced labor and other such abominations. When, far too late (from 1925), he stood up against the rise of Stalinism, he was soon isolated. The armed prophet of 1917 would become the unarmed prophet, in Isaac Deutscher's words.

The question of the "nature of the USSR" has given rise to countless discussions in the workers' and revolutionary movement. Let's leave aside the Stalinist parties who, with hallucinating blindness, made paradise of it until it collapsed in the rubble of the Berlin Wall in November 1989. Early on, anarchists and left-wing communists (Pannekoek, Görter, Mattick, Korsch) saw in it the birth of a new form of state capitalism. Trotskyists (at least those who had not been expelled from the puny Trotskyist movement) saw the USSR as a "bureaucratically degenerated workers' state", in other words, a state whose foundations in terms of social relations remained those established by the October Revolution, and which therefore remained "workers'" in this sense, since the capitalist bourgeoisie had been expropriated. But on the other hand, a counter-revolutionary bureaucratic caste had politically expropriated the working class from its victory. Trotsky, on the eve of the Second World War, could write that "the question of the nature of the USSR has not yet been decided by history". But the coming war would unravel the contradiction: either capitalism would be restored to the USSR through violent counter-revolution, or the proletariat of the Soviet Union, resuming its revolutionary movement, would sweep away the bureaucratic caste through a political revolution that would once again bring together the political superstructure and the economic base.

The brief overview we have of the country's socio-economic structure is enough to refute the thesis of state capitalism: this is capitalism without capital and without the quest to maximize surplus value. Putin's Russia, on the other hand, has a strong "state capitalism" dimension. Trotskyist theory, however, is no better: the expropriation of the former exploiting classes does not make the "workers' state", nor does the planning of production. In fact, it is at the very moment when the kulak (the rural protocapitalist, according to the Marxist vulgate) is exterminated "as a class", and planning imposes its law, that the bureaucratic caste asserts its power. Moreover, history proved Trotsky's prognosis wrong: the war led neither to the restoration of capitalism nor to an anti-bureaucratic political revolution, but on the contrary to the extension of this neither capitalist nor socialist social system right up to the end of the 1970s.

Soviet Marxism

It's probably more pleasant to believe that Stalinism was nothing but a monstrous betrayal, and that revolutionary Marxism can remain as the immaculate theory of the emancipation of proletarians the world over. But this soothing vision does not stand up to analysis. Stalinism did not exist as a direct consequence of "Marxist ideology", as frenzied anti-communists claim, but only because it was historically impossible for the promises of classical Marxism to be fulfilled. It's impossible to rewrite history in the past conditional tense, and therefore somewhat pointless to ask what would have happened if the October Revolution hadn't taken place—for example, if Lenin had died in April or July 1917. But one thing seems certain: the fate of the 20th century, the unprecedented outburst of cruelty we have witnessed, is not the consequence of Bolshevik action. On the contrary, it is the action of the Bolsheviks, even at its most inexcusable and terrible, that is a link in the history of the 20th century. Historical revisionists (e.g., Nolte and his French followers) see Nazism and the horrors of the 20th century in general as mere responses or reactions to the actions of communism. Historical revisionists don't bother with history. Bolshevism triumphed in Russia because Europe had been set on fire by imperialist barbarism. The almost 10 million deaths (including 1.7 million Russians) caused by this war are a direct and shattering entry into modern savagery. Nazism would have been politically and psychologically impossible without this training for the worst, for which liberal capitalism bears direct and total responsibility (imperial Germany falls into this category). For Nolte and his followers, these millions of dead and tens of millions of wounded do not exist historically. It's quite simple: it's all Lenin's fault! If the Bolsheviks came to power, it was because they were the only ones to demand immediate peace. They put this into practice with the Brest-Litovsk agreements. Let's not forget that one of the main reasons for French and English hatred of the Bolsheviks was precisely their refusal to prolong the Russian people's participation in the great slaughter. Clemenceau, one of the main architects of the diplomatic disaster that was the Treaty of Versailles, was also one of the most enraged to lead the war against Bolshevik Russia. This is the whole story, not the original sin of "totalitarian Marxism". The error of orthodox Marxism before 1914 was simply to have believed that none of this could happen!

However, the Russian revolution brought to fruition a process that could already be discerned in the evolution of social-democratic parties: the formation of Marxism not as a scientific theory, but as the ideology of a class of organizers and managers, committed to the existence of a national economy and taking the place of a failing bourgeois class. In capitalist countries, this bureaucracy is limited to the management of trade unions, mutual insurance companies and anything else that helps oil the wheels of the capitalist machine. Where the national bourgeoisie is either non-existent, or incapable of positing itself as the class that acts in the name of the common interest of the entire nation, Marxism, reworked with Leninist analysis of imperialism and the place of national struggles, is the ideology best suited to this petty bourgeoisie that substitutes itself for the capitalist class. Marxism has two features perfectly suited to this substitute social class. Avant-gardism and the role of organization legitimize the party's central role in political life, and the complete subjugation of the state. Progressivism legitimizes the methods of painful delivery of a modern society (elimination of feudalism, national unification, industrialization, creation of a state capable of ensuring the education and health of the population). None of this is, strictly speaking, socialist or communist. And that's why this political system is so unstable. Capitalism is based on private property and the rights of capital, and it says so: the "Marxist" bureaucracy does just about the opposite of what it claims to do. It claims to emancipate the workers, when in fact all it does is create a working class that is exploited and exploitable by the capitalists under the most profitable conditions, as the Chinese and Vietnamese examples amply demonstrate. The horrors of these supposedly communist regimes are nothing out of the ordinary:

compare the blood price paid by the Russian or Chinese people with the blood price paid by the peoples of Europe and the four corners of the globe to capitalist development.

Generalizations are always risky, and the history of each "socialist" country is unique. Chinese history is very different from Russian history, and Mao Tse-tung's CCP is undoubtedly radically different from the Communist Party of the USSR at the time of Lenin's death, because its links with the traditional workers' movement are much more tenuous, and because the working class played no role in the CCP's seizure of power. Cuba and Vietnam are different stories. That's why thinking of all this under the single label of "communism" is the best way to understand nothing about it, and to replace scientific history with pure ideology. But it's precisely because the Russian revolution was the closest thing to a workers' revolution we could have dreamed of, and because it aroused a unique enthusiasm throughout the world, that the study of its reality and ultimate failure remains of the utmost importance.

A Brief Review

The collapse of 20th-century communism seems to have left the ideology of the ruling class, the liberal bourgeois ideology in its various guises, unchallenged. Not only have parties claiming to be communist all but disappeared, not only have regimes that presented themselves as socialist regimes in transition to communism vanished, but communism itself, as a current of social and political thought, seems to be no more than the "past of an illusion", in Furet's words. Le *Grand Larousse de la philosophie* aside, recent dictionaries of philosophy and political philosophy ignore communism superbly, whether it's the *Dictionnaire de philosophie politique* published by PUF under the direction of Philippe Reynaud, which also eliminates Rosa Luxemburg, Lenin and Trotsky from the list of political thinkers—a fine example of scientific objectivity—or the otherwise excellent *Vocabulaire européen*

Chapter X. Looking Back to the USSR

des philosophies edited by Barbara Cassin. Equating communism with the USSR must be enough to justify such a radical elimination of communism as a current of thought. Yet none of the regimes that have recently disappeared or are in the process of profound transformation (China, Cuba tomorrow) presented themselves as communist. The ruling parties still call themselves "communist", by virtue of a very old habit, but to remain consistent with the framework of Marxist ideology, it should be remembered that communism officially meant the disappearance of the state. Since, according to the official terminology, the State had no intention of disappearing, it was only a question of socialist countries, countries engaged in the first phase of social transformation. Indeed, if the tyrannical nature of the Stalinist and post-Stalinist regimes could be set aside, they could represent a more or less successful implementation of the pre-1914 ideal of socialism: the central role of nationalization and economic planning, the importance of the state as organizer of economic and social life, and the role of the party. But historically, communism was something quite different. To this we should add that some so-called "communist" countries have even officially repudiated Marxism or Marxism-Leninism. This is the case in North Korea, where the state officially defends a new ideology that has "surpassed Marxism-Leninism", under the inspiration of guru Kim Il-Sung and his son and successor Kim Jong-Il.

In other words, strictly speaking, the 20th century marks the failure of communism, because nowhere was it possible to take a single serious step towards communism. In fact, what radically failed was socialism:

- In its traditional form, that of Kautsky and the Second International, it was embodied in Stalinism, whose two watchwords are summed up as follows: "the class is but an amorphous mass, only organization can reign" (Kautsky, *The Dictatorship of the Proletariat*) and "the cadres decide everything" (Stalin, speech of May 4, 1935);

- in its anti-communist, anti-internationalist, statist form, it became fascism. Fascism, in fact, is not a reactionary movement, but a revolutionary national or racial movement incorporating many elements drawn from the socialist tradition, from its statism to the role of planning and partisan framing. Mussolini began as a socialist, as did Déat;
- In its "revisionist" form, in the tradition of Bernstein, it has purely and simply dissolved into liberal capitalism, and the transformation of socialist parties into democratic parties paves the way for social regression unprecedented in all advanced capitalist countries.

If we look at the organizations that still claim to be communist, we find only a few surviving groups of the old communist parties (as in Italy and France), not to mention the strange forms in which the Russian Communist Party continues to exist. There are still a myriad of Trotskyist organizations, generally reduced to a groupuscular state, or with, at best, only a few thousand militants with little influence on the political course of their country. A typical example is France, where Trotskyism has finally gained a certain electoral influence (between 5% and 10%): it is divided into three different groups, all very hostile to each other and of roughly equivalent size (a few thousand militants). But none of these groups appears under its own Communist name. The Internationalist Communist Union is known to the general public only as "Lutte ouvrière"; the Internationalist Communist Organization exists only through its "broad organization", the "Independent Workers' Party", a party which does not include communism in its programmatic objectives; finally, the Ligue communiste révolutionnaire has decided to dissolve into a party which, at the time of writing, will be called the "New Anti-Capitalist Party", whose acronym NPA is that of a "trendy" Canal + program… One can be a workers' party or a defender of workers' struggles without being a communist; as for anti-capitalism, it's an even vaguer term that can function as a catch-all but doesn't define a positive perspective, like anything that's content to be "anti".

Whichever way you look at it, communism appears to be "the past of an illusion", to use François Furet's expression. Yet, at a time when the illusions of the unlimited development of capitalism and a society self-organized by the market are dissipating, perhaps we should rather admit that it is only one historical form of communism that is dead and well dead, and that a new communism remains to be invented, or rather reinvented.

THIRD PART

**Out of the Nightmare:
Communism With and Without Marx**

Chapter XI.
Communism has a History and a Rationale

In 1989, we witnessed the collapse of the "historic communism" of the 20th century. But it wasn't communism that collapsed, only what Soviet bureaucrats and their lieutenants called "real socialism" or "actually existing socialism". But the following years, which were supposed to usher in a new liberal, peaceful and democratic world order, based on the benefits of the market and deregulation, disappointed the expectations of all those naïve prophets who dominate the major public and private media. Whatever the outcome of the economic crisis underway as these lines are written, it will not be the final crisis, and in the absence of a serious, widely shared alternative, capitalism will find the means to emerge, however costly those means may be. This is why the communist ideal can be given a new lease of life as a long-term horizon for action.

Communism is not Marx's Invention

Communism is as old as the great human civilizations, even if it has presented itself in singular forms, from Platonic communism and primitive Christianity to modern communism. But understanding the long history of communism requires us to clarify the very meaning we give to the term.

Communism can be identified neither with egalitarianism—there is a liberal egalitarianism, from Rousseau to Rawls or Dworkin, which is radically non-communist—nor with statism, which is rather the hallmark of socialism, even if for a long time, during the "great era" of social democracy between 1880 and 1914, the two terms were relatively confused. Communism can be defined quite simply by its etymology: it is the doctrine of the common. For the first communists, the Babouvists, it was an egalitarian system based on the community of goods. But to confine ourselves to Babouvist communism is to restrict the history of communism considerably.

Gérard Raulet[103] traces the origins of communism back to the Bible and the communities created by the prophet Samuel, and before coming to communism according to Marx, he devotes a few developments to discussions on egalitarianism and communism in Greek antiquity. Costanzo Preve[104] provides an overview of pre-capitalist communism, to which he contrasts Marx as the inventor not of communism, but of the communism of modernity.

For Preve, as for Raulet, the first pre-capitalist communism can be traced back to the biblical tradition. But for Preve, it is above all Christianity that is the bearer of this communism, conceived as the realization of God's will as revealed by his prophets. The injustice of a society where wealth is in the hands of a minority of exploiters and the masses are condemned to misery is never perceived as the product of a specific mode of production (which is Marx's discovery), but as the fruit of sin. To rediscover the straight path of the divine order is to rediscover the sense of a fraternal community, founded on the sharing of work and a frugal, luxury-free life.

> "In the case of Jesus of Nazareth, the communist content of his preaching emerges unequivocally if we endeavor to correlate the semantic content of

---

103. See the entry "Communisme" in the *Grand Dictionnaire Larousse de la philosophie,* edited by Michel Blay.
104. See Costanzo Preve, *La fine di una teoria. Il collasso del marxismo storico del novecento,* Edizioni Unicopli, 1996.

his messianic proclamation with the historical context in which his activity develops. Jesus' promise of social emancipation and debt relief for the poor is neither generic nor purely "moral", but has as its material and political presupposition the "cleansing" of the Temple of Jerusalem and the proclamation of a "year of the Lord's mercy" by a messianic authority, his own, which is both just and powerful because it has the backing of the heavenly Father. For Jesus of Nazareth, the communist distribution of goods is the realization of a very precise divine will, which intends to "revolutionize" the state of general injustice and oppression into which we had fallen because of the sins of men[105]."

This communism of egalitarian distribution runs throughout the history of Christianity, and expresses the "hope principle" of Ernst Bloch's philosophical thought[106]. It is not limited to Christianity, and expressions of it can be found in most of the world's major religions. The absence of private property and the often religious organization (around the Temple, for example) of production form the ancient historical basis of this egalitarian communism.

Preve isolates another, very different form of communism, born in the nomadic, warlike societies of the Indo-European peoples. Taking up Dumézil's thesis on the tripartition of functions (religious sovereignty, physical strength, fertility), the communism born in such a cultural soil will be an elitist, aristocratic communism, of which Plato's philosophy is the most accomplished expression. Inegalitarian, this communism is "the earthly and contingent manifestation of an eternal Being exempt from corruption and death", a Being revealed not by the words of the prophets, but by the use of human reason through the activity of philosophy. It might seem that the term "communism" is unsuitable for Plato's philosophy, which is a highly hierarchical form of thought: the tripartition of the ideal republic is reminiscent of Dumézil's tripartition. The guardian class in Plato's *Republic* is organized on a radically communist principle:

---

105. PREVE, *op. cit.* p. 26-27.
106. Ernst BLOCH, *Le Principe Espérance*, 3 volumes written between 1954 and 1959. French translation by Gallimard.

absence of private property, suppression of the family, community of children, possibility for women to join the guardians. The guardians work entirely for the common good. Plato takes it for granted that the mass of human beings cannot rise to the moral and intellectual level of the guardians and, consequently, the mass of these lower classes must occupy themselves with what suits them best, the activities that provide wealth for personal satisfaction. In other words, the accumulation of wealth, the preoccupation with property and commerce, are the hallmarks of vile men, and property, far from being a mark of social superiority, is on the contrary a mark of inferiority. Platonic social hierarchy, based on the stigmatization of property and the pursuit of money, is therefore strictly antinomic to that of modern capitalist society, in which the principle of utility and rational egoism are the sacred principles, but also to that of the class societies existing in his time (slavery) or even to that of the feudal world, since in these hierarchical societies property and power go hand in hand, and the absence of property is the mark of decay. In *The Laws*, a more complex and perhaps more "realistic" portrayal of the ideal republic, Plato maintains his opposition to money and the pursuit of wealth accumulation. It is for this reason, moreover, that he situates the well-constituted republic inland, the proximity of the sea favoring trade and the love of lucre.

Anachronistic analyses pitting the "conservative" Plato against the "progressive" Sophists are obviously misplaced, as are Karl Popper's rantings about Plato as the putative father of totalitarianism[107]. This is not the place to discuss Platonic philosophy, whose elitism has often made it suitable for a certain kind of "right-wing" thinking (whereas Christian communism was more spontaneously "left-wing"). The fact remains, however, that since these distinctions have lost almost all meaning, there's nothing to prevent the

---

107. Leaving aside a few interesting reflections on the philosophy of science, the "Popperism" fashionable in the years 1990-2000 is one of those philosophical impostures that owed their fame only to political and media manipulation. But the extinction of Popperism is underway.

figure of a revolutionary Plato from appearing on our ideological horizon.

Preve isolates a third form of pre-capitalist communism, that which manifests itself in the period immediately preceding the establishment of the capitalist mode of production. We also find it in Thomas Münzer's German Peasants' War—analyzed by Engels and Bloch. This communism is also expressed in the revolutionary currents of the first "bourgeois" revolutions, the *diggers* of the English revolution (the real one, in 1640, through the *glorious revolution* of the liberals) who, in 1649, proclaimed the right *to* dig common land and sought to restore the ancient community of enjoyment of the fruits of the earth under the authority of natural law, identified with the word of Christ.

Anthropology of Communism

Communism, in its many and varied forms, expresses a fundamental human aspiration, one that could be described as "eternal". For this simple reason, the collapse of historical communism in the 20th century cannot be seen as synonymous with the end of communism in general. If we want to understand the resonance of communism in the 20th century, again in a wide variety of forms—from pre-World War I social democracy to the various varieties of Third World communism—we can't confine ourselves to ordinary explanations. The strength of historical communism lay neither in the correspondence of Marx's ideas to political and social reality, nor in the propagandistic skill of the communists, nor in any of those explanations of "totalitarianism" that inevitably bring to mind the dormant virtue of opium in Molière's physicians. The quasi-religious dimension of 20th-century communism echoes this ancient tradition. It has been said that "Marxist" communism was the last of the great Christian heresies. Without wishing at all costs to fit reality into the seductive framework of a paradoxical formula, we have to agree that the communitarian ideal (equality and fraternity) and the expectation of a new "year of mercy" played a far more important role than the reading of *Capital*—an arduous and little-read text—or even that of the popularized versions of Marxism spread over millions of copies.

The causes of this anhistorical element of communism must be sought. At the risk of using a vocabulary that is decried today, it seems to us that these causes must be sought in human nature. And here we must sacrifice a moment to philosophical anthropology.

There's no doubt that man has a kind of natural aggression against social life, as ancient and modern authors (Hobbes, Freud) have said. On the basis of this observation, liberal authors make rational egoism the only possible foundation for social life: the calculating man will not love his fellow man, but will understand that respect for the law is, for him, the best way to satisfy his individual interests through his work or business activity. If this is so, the very existence of social life would be the result of a calculation, of an original pact, as all social contract theories explain. But logic, what we know about the origins of human history, and what experience teaches us, suggest that this conception is radically false, and reverses the order of factors. Man, *Homo sapiens sapiens*, is from the outset a social being, as were his ancestors and his "cousins" the great apes. The egoistic individual, or the individual separated from society, is not at the origin of society: on the contrary, he is only a late product of it.

There are many reasons to support this view.

When Aristotle says that man is a "political animal" (a *zoon politikon*), he is also distinguishing him from other "gregarious animals". Other animals communicate only to give each other pleasure and suffering," says Aristotle, "whereas humans, having language at their disposal, regulate their entire lives in this relationship to speech, which enables us to define what is useful and what is disadvantageous, as well as what is just and unjust, or good and evil. If language is the hallmark of the human race, it is only possible through the existence of human beings living in community. Human language, or speech, which Aristotle contrasts with the voice of animals, is both a product of human society and a condition of its existence. Aristotle's three definitions of man—a speaking animal, a logos-possessing animal and a political animal —are one and the same. The political community, in its diverse forms and variable "constitutions" (of which Aristotle provides a typology and assessment in his *Politics*), expresses *hic et nunc* this fundamental human reality, fundamental because it constitutes the foundation. We have no doubt not yet exhausted the full richness of Aristotle's thought, nor finished drawing lessons from it for understanding the present and thinking about the future.

The old Aristotelian thesis is reinforced by what we have learned from ethnology, ethology and psychology. The primary need of human beings is to "form society". Liberals make commercial exchange the model for all human exchanges, but it is rather the gift that is primary, as ethnology teaches us. There are enough studies on gift-giving that we don't need to elaborate much. Market exchange is aimed at the exchangers' own utility, whereas giving is aimed at nothing more than the establishment of bonds—even if these bonds may later prove to be very useful. As soon as the act of exchange is over (I have the merchandise I wanted and the seller has received my money), the exchangers revert to being isolated indi-viduals, indifferent to each other. On the contrary, once the ritual gifts have been exchanged, the two givers have become friends, allies or fiancés. We retain so many traces of these rites, which date back to the origins of mankind, that it's clear they constitute the deepest stratum of our social life.

And indeed, ethology also shows that our "cousins", the great anthropoid apes, have a developed and fairly precisely structured community social life. A complicated life in which conflicts are far from absent, but a social life that seems to have been selected by natural evolution as the only way to protect small hominids. Liberals often use a distorted and falsified Darwinism to justify that rivalry between individuals for scarce resources is the natural way for individuals to live. A basic understanding of evolutionary theory is enough to show, on the contrary, that humanity has only

235

been able to survive through its "communalization" and its propensity to help the weakest.

Psychology goes in the same direction. The "self" is only formed in relation to others. Henri Laborit puts it quite simply: "We are others, that is, we have become over time what others—our parents, family members, educators—have made of us, consciously or unconsciously. We are therefore always influenced, most often unwittingly, by the various systems of which we are a part[108]." Or, to use Marx's words again, the individual is nothing other than the totality of his social relations. And the more social relations he has, the more developed and "civilized" he is.

If man exists only through the political community (this term is more precise than society) that shelters him, allows him to grow and realize himself, if this is indeed his nature, through a historical evolution that is not ideal, and that gives its share to the accidents and contradictory effects of man's intellectual power, the memory of this ideal community cannot be lost. It is in this sense that we say that the aspiration to communism does indeed derive from human nature. This level of generalization, however unsatisfactory, enables us to understand why we value mutual aid over "every man for himself", why sharing and selflessness are held to be morally superior to selfishness and behavior guided solely by self-interest, and why this hierarchy of values is virtually universal. Only capitalist management schools teach contrary virtues, and only perfect cynics or sophists paid handsomely to do so defend the moral standards demanded by free and undistorted competition. Ancient philosophers, as well as more modern ones, hold friendship to be one of the highest moral values of social life. But if we are to believe Aristotle or Cicero, friends are spontaneously communists, since, as the saying goes, "between friends everything is common".

All the great political philosophies are founded on the idea of the common good: the political community is legitimized by the existence of a good common to all its members, who, in exchange for

---

108 Participation in Alain Resnais' film *Mon oncle d'Amérique*.

the right to enjoy this common good, must be prepared to sacrifice their possessions and even their lives for the good of all. Liberals cry foul when we talk of collectivizing this or that enterprise or land. But they find it perfectly normal to "collectivize" the lives of those who will die to save the fatherland. Since a man's life is infinitely more valuable than a piece of land or buildings and machinery, if the collectivization of an asset is good for the community, nothing should stand in its way. Besides, "liberal" constitutions always contain a clause limiting the right of ownership when the necessities of the public or common good so demand.

Of course, all this is not communism, but it does show that the egalitarian and communitarian principles of communism are far from alien to the most generally accepted moral principles, and even to the political principles recognized by modern democratic governments. It may be objected that to base communism on moral principles is to concede that it does not have a very solid foundation. Realists" and "strong minds" regard the moral ideas shared by the great mass of individuals as a flimsy cloak for human appetites and insatiable greed. This overlooks the fact that moral ideas encompass each individual's conception of his or her own worth, and can in certain circumstances have a far greater force than material needs, whatever the vulgar Marxist may think, for whom men only fight to earn more or work less[109]. Even strictly material demands are always mixed up with demands for human dignity. Although Marxists sovereignly despise moral considerations in favor of "economic infrastructures" and "material demands", Marxist communism itself makes abundant use of moral pathos. Why denounce the exploitation of workers if not for moral reasons? If we exclude morality, the exploitation of wage-earners or slavery become perfectly acceptable social relationships, provided they increase the overall wealth of society! Finally, historical socialism and communism were not simply the product of workers' protest

---

109. One might wonder about the depth of contempt for workers harbored in the workerist or syndicalist Marxism that forms the vulgate of much of the far left.

against capitalism, but also, and perhaps primarily, intellectual creations born of the moral or philosophical revolt of bourgeois or aristocratic intellectuals who found capitalism simply repugnant to a philosophical or simply cultivated mind.

In short, the argument that a purely moral foundation for communism is of no real significance is, in fact, a worthless argument. It can even be turned on its head: deprived of this moral foundation, communism is deprived of all political legitimacy. Let's be clear: it's not a question of replacing politics with a moralizing morality that would certainly be tyrannical. It's simply a question —and no politics can do without it—of defining a public conception of justice and the organization of common life in the city: the primacy of the common good over selfish interests, egalitarian sharing of wealth, solidarity—in short, all the principles that can be rooted in our best-founded moral intuitions.

Thinking a New Communism

Why is it necessary today to reaffirm such a public conception of human relations? Historical evolution itself calls for it. As Marx said, crises are the *memento mori* of capitalism: "Remember that you must die! On the scale of historical time, this injunction is not very far-reaching. All human social formations are mortal, and capitalism is no different. But, as Keynes said, "in the long run, we're dead". The problem is much more immediate. Capitalism can endure, but it can only do so by progressively undermining human civilization itself. What Nazism undertook with the provocative brutality that was its undoing, modern capitalism does quietly and gently. The triumph of "geneticism"—the ideology according to which man is nothing more than his genetic code —makes the fabrication of the human the object of an industry in the making. The triumph of the commodity enslaves inherited culture to *big business*, organizes the invasion of the public sphere by the worst kind of vulgarity, and destroys all moral sense and all

238

the values of common life. One only has to look at what European governments are doing to schools to understand what's at stake. All governments, right and left, are in agreement in reducing public education to its strict instrumental dimension and its function of shaping the "employability" of young people. Quite simply, it's about destroying the concept of culture as it was forged from Greek *paideia* to humanism and Enlightenment thinking.

The total triumph of capitalism, whatever its transitory forms, would mean the destruction of the human world. For the time being, our world is very far from being totally subject to the law of capital. Despite the serious setbacks of the last three decades, there are still a great many social institutions that are partially exempt from the capitalist mode of production. The family has not yet been totally destroyed. Forms of cooperation between neighbors, voluntary work and mutual aid still exist. Do-it-yourself and gardening activities are still very much alive, as forms of production focused on use value rather than exchange value. But all this is very fragile, and all non-capitalist social relations are tending more and more directly to be subjected to the logic of capital. Just think of what "humanitarian" associations have become, forms of *business* obeying the laws of marketing and the principle of profitability, even though officially they are not included in the circuit of surplus-value production.

This fragility of non-capitalist forms of social organization is such that we are seeing one barrier after another broken down, as those who dominate the economy and politics are the new Callicles[110] or Nietzschean "blond brutes" who stand "beyond good and evil". We

---

110. Certainly a fictional character in Plato's *Gorgias*, Callicles is the anti-Socrates. For him, Socratic morality is false because it is made by the multitude of the weak. The weak fear the strong and make laws to protect themselves. We're not far from Nietzsche, who denounces the resentment of the weak against the strong in both Socratic morality and democratic egalitarianism. Justice is a return to the law of nature, which dictates that the most capable must prevail. True virtue is nothing other than the ability to rise above the masses and dominate them, in short, to be the best.

face this eternal choice, and to surrender to the mediocre disciples of Callicles is to open wide the gates to barbarism.

A new communism is needed to counter this threat. A communism that makes no concessions to the "dictatorship of the proletariat" or to any other form of modern or ultramodern tyranny. But a communism that makes it possible once again to imagine a truly human society, a city or rather a plurality of cities in which the future can be thought of in a way other than the frightening perspectives offered by technoscience and capitalism.

CHAPTER XII. A NON-UTOPIAN COMMUNISM

What Marx means by communism is not an "ideal" that should be realized by the voluntarist action of a few "social engineers". It is, or should be, "the real movement" that is unfolding before our very eyes, abolishing the existing order.

We have already shown why the communist dream has become a nightmare. However, it is a realized utopia of the kind promised by the ideologues of capitalism. And it's paving the way for the same nightmare, but with infinitely more subtle and scientific means than the crude ones of communism "à la sauce tartare". Genuine communism can only be reborn by moving beyond utopia, by proposing a possible perspective based on our strongest moral and political intuitions. This means abandoning three utopias.

1) Renounce the utopia of a world without states and without conflict: on the foreseeable horizon, we can't think of eliminating social contradictions, and therefore we can't think of eliminating the state that expresses them;
2) Renounce the utopia of unlimited development of productive forces, which would exempt us from having to ask the question of the distribution of scarce resources;
3) Renounce communism as a return to the Garden of Eden. Work is an inescapable necessity, but we must try to keep it within reasonable bounds. But true freedom begins after work.

Let's examine these negative definitions one by one. In each case, this examination will enable us to determine what we mean by a non-utopian communism or a possible communism with a human horizon.

The Withering State, or the Republic?

Marxian and Marxist communism was based on the idea—also shared by anarchists—that the (gradual) disappearance of the state as an instrument of human government was a reasonable goal. Marx and Engels took up Saint-Simon's phrase, "passing from the government of men to the administration of things". This perspective derives from the "Marxist theory" of the State reduced to its sole function as an instrument of domination by one class over another: once classes disappear, the State loses all function. But this theory is both false and unrealistic. False, because the state is never reduced to its function as an instrument of oppression of one class over another, and unrealistic, because even if we assume the disappearance of class antagonisms pitting an exploiting class against an oppressed class, this does not mean that society would become homogeneous, or that the existence of social groups with different interests would disappear.

A state can only endure if it performs social functions that benefit society as a whole. The idea that the state embodies "the general will" and the "public good" is not, or not entirely, a deception from which exploiters benefit. For example, states are generally concerned with public health, education, security and protecting the country from the appetites of its neighbors. When citizens travel abroad, they enjoy the protection of their state. Of course, these functions also benefit the exploiting classes. It's good for capitalists to find educated labor, but it's just as good for workers to be educated. Sometimes, even, the state makes itself useful to the ruling class against its will. The first social laws (limiting the working day, regulating child labor) were imposed on capitalists even though they simply protected the physical existence of an exploitable working class... Even the police cannot be reduced to the CRS repressing demonstrations and strikes. Poor citizens as much as rich ones (who have gated communities and bodyguards) need protection from thuggery. As long as citizens do not all live under the guidance of reason, and as long as we cannot be sure that in all circumstances, morality will have the last word and will be able to overcome man's passions and natural aggressiveness, we will have to ensure the possibility of living together through fear and hope (or, more vulgarly, through carrots and sticks). In these circumstances, the only possible way to "wither away" the State is to turn every citizen into his neighbor's overseer. The separation between civil society and the State does disappear, but through the generalization of the State: if every citizen is a policeman, the State has infiltrated every corner of society, and this kind of "withering" State is that of the Stalinist USSR or other countries of "real socialism".

Moreover, in a society without antagonistic social classes, conflicts of interest remain inevitable. It is impossible to abolish the division of labor—unless we accept a considerable regression in the productive forces, given that cooperation (based on the division of labor) is the principal productive force, as Marx rightly maintained. No doubt the harmful effects of this division of labor can be mitigated, for example by the rotation of tasks in a workshop, by a non-Fordist/Taylorist organization of production, or by ever greater opportunities to change jobs in the course of one's life. But it's better for everyone if doctors specialize in medicine and aren't requisitioned for part of the year to work in the fields, as in the "good old days" of the Cultural Revolution, which was good for neither medicine nor agriculture. If a division of labor persists, then there are social groups, more or less organized, whose interests may seriously diverge and must therefore be submitted to arbitration representing the collective interest.

Finally, in a non-capitalist, possibly planned economy, there remains an antagonism between producers and consumers.

Producers must defend themselves as producers—defending their working conditions and their level of remuneration - while consumers always demand the cheapest products for the best quality. We'll say that producers and consumers are the same people, which is pretty much true: there's no producer who isn't a consumer, but the reverse isn't always true, and individual producers and consumers don't always coincide. Here again, there are conflicts that have nothing to do with this or that social structure, but with the very nature of a society that has gone beyond the level of mere subsistence.

The utopia of the decline of the state, the anarchist legacy of Marxism, is largely responsible for the inability of "Marxists" to understand, let *alone* combat, the transformation of their revolutionary aspirations into one of the worst tyrannies humanity has ever known. At the same time, statism (whether born out of the rubble of Marxist utopianism or as an extension of the liberal state) remains a danger to be guarded against. Indeed, one of the seemingly strange characteristics of 20th-century Marxism is its constant oscillation between a semi-anarchist vision of the state and an adulation of the "socialist" state. The problem that arises is this: is it possible to conceive of a state that is truly what it claims to be, i.e. the embodiment of the general will and not an instrument of domination by one part of society over another? There is something right in the anarchist or Marxist critique of the State that Rousseau had already laid bare with his customary clarity: the obedience of one man to another has no reasonable justification. It can only be based on fait accompli, not on legitimate reasons. A free man is one who obeys only the law he has given himself; any other obedience is servitude. The state, however, is founded on obedience, rarely on consenting, enlightened obedience, but rather on fear, and primarily fear for one's own life. The state is the organization that has a monopoly on legitimate violence," says Max Weber, perfectly aware that "legitimate violence" is a contradiction *in adjecto*. To these not merely theoretical difficulties of political philosophy, Rousseau gave an enigmatic answer: "To find a form of association which defends and protects with all the common force the person and property of each associate, and by which each one uniting with all nevertheless obeys only himself and remains as free as before." (*Contrat social*, I, VI, "Du pacte social"). This form of association, in which each individual remains free while uniting with all, is precisely what Marx's communism is after.

To find a solution to this question, the first thing to do is to write off the dictatorship of the proletariat. Orthodox Marxists criticized Western communist parties for abandoning this Marxist proposition—what became known as "Eurocommunism" in the 1970s included this rejection of the dictatorship of the proletariat. For these parties, it was undoubtedly a question of pledging to the ruling class that they could become loyal managers of capitalism, as the leaders of the PCI and the PCF proved time and again—the former going to the extreme of their approach by renouncing communism and ending up no longer even calling themselves "left-wing" but merely "democrats". But this historical reminder is no reason to piously preserve the relics of a formula that has proved historically either catastrophic or meaningless. When Marx spoke of the "dictatorship of the proletariat", he was essentially indicating that a brief transitional phase would be necessary for the "workers' party", during which it would have to employ exceptional means to break down the resistance of the old possessing classes—the historical reference was then to the dictatorship of the Committee of Public Safety during the French Revolution. But this strategic vision of the conquest of power doesn't fit in well with the historical perspective developed in *Capital*, where social revolution consists in replacing the domination of capital by "associated producers". Indeed, "associated producers" are all individuals who play a role in the productive process, not just proletarians. Marx believed, as we saw above, that these two terms would eventually coincide, since the class structure was to be simplified. But historical experience has shown this not to be the case, and consequently the association of producers can only be an alliance of classes and social groups, which deprives the idea of the "dictatorship of the proletariat" of its last legitimacy, even if we understand it in the acceptable sense of the Roman republican tradition, which carefully distinguishes dictatorship from tyranny, Cincinnatus from Julius Caesar.

So it's not just a question of getting rid of a cumbersome formula, given its historical fate. Above all, it's a question of considering a perspective for social change that takes account of reality and of what experience has taught us, namely that the working class cannot be a dominant class because it is not, as some Italian Marxist thinkers put it, an "intermodal class", i.e. a class capable of claiming to speak on behalf of all classes in society.

Rather than looking for some utopian perfect government, we should remember how Spinoza poses the question of the best government: all political formulas have already been invented. We must be content to see which would be the best, given the concrete situation, starting with men as they are and not as we would like them to be, in the knowledge that a government remains a government, and that the power conferred on the state is dangerous by nature. Strictly speaking, there is no such thing as a "communist government" (in this we remain faithful to Marx), but there are governments more or less favorable to the existence of a society where communist ideas can prevail.

By following this method, we can eliminate all forms of hierarchical government that are antinomic to the egalitarian requirements of communism. For a long time, and still today in certain groups stemming from "left-wing communism" or anarcho-communism, communism has been identified with "council democracy", i.e. a network of base councils (initially based on factory councils), base councils which must then be federated on the model of the Russian soviets of 1905 and 1917. Experience shows that such political organization quickly leads either to chaos or to the reconstruction of a pyramidal bureaucracy perfectly suited to passing off the dictatorship of a well-organized minority as the purest form of "direct democracy". The explanation of the Soviet Union's bureaucratization by the absence of direct democracy is therefore a weak one. On the contrary, it was the realization of the slogan "all power to the soviets" that gave rise to "all power to the Party" and then "all power to the Party apparatus", culminating in "all power to the General Secretary". Let's quickly explain why. In the classic anarchist vision, base committees or "communes" are loosely federated, but remain independent in any case, since the state has disappeared. But if we maintain a state, and even a state with a "dictatorship of the proletariat", the basic committees (e.g., the Russian soviets) must be coordinated and centralized. So factory or district councils coordinate by electing delegates to a city council and those to a provincial council, and so on up to the "central council of soviets", and so the so-called direct democracy has been transformed into a democracy with four or five degrees of suffrage—we find the election of the Senate by indirect suffrage undemocratic, so what are we to think of the system of councils or soviets? What's more, this system is easy to manipulate: only well-organized party activists will pass through all the levels of political power. And direct democracy is transformed into "partitocracy", i.e., the power of partisan apparatuses[111]. A good illustration of this phenomenon, fortunately in benign forms, can be found in the "coordinations" that spring up whenever there is a small-scale movement, mainly among students, where the unions are very weak, but also in certain guilds (nurses, railway workers).

If we eliminate hierarchical government and direct democracy —in truth, the impossible direct democracy—we are left with little choice but republican government, understood in the sense of the republicanist tradition[112], i.e. that tradition which makes the well-ordered political institution the guarantor of individual freedom, protecting them against domination.

---

111. As is often the case, Rousseau saw the problem clearly. Direct democracy requires that individuals cannot form factions or parties. Isolated individuals must deliberate in the silence of their passions.

112. See our *Revive la République*, Armand Colin, 2005.

Since the elimination of conflicts between social classes, between social groups and between individuals is not conceivable as a realistic prospect, we must first consider political institutions as means designed to protect the weakest individuals against the domination that could be imposed on them by the strongest. This includes the possibility for individuals to defend themselves even against a state that claims to be the embodiment of the common good, and whose magistrates have been appointed by popular suffrage. In a workers' production cooperative, workers as workers must be able to defend themselves against the company's elected management, through independent trade unions, just as in the most democratic state, the one most independent of the moneyed powers, citizens must still have the means to defend themselves against the tyranny of the majority.

Against the Marxist theory of workers' government as both legislative and executive, we must support and deepen the republican conception of the separation of powers, the only possible guarantee, however fragile, that power is limited by power. What is profoundly right in anarchist intuitions and distrust of the State can therefore be taken into account in the republican constitution of the State. We shall see in the final chapter that republicanism, understood in its radical sense, can be precisely the link between what is best in the tradition of philosophical and political modernity and the new communism we need to reinvent.

The Utopia of Unlimited Development of Productive Forces

If we want to think about a new communism, we have to break with the utopia of unlimited growth in productive forces and an affluent society. As long as we cannot distribute wealth according to the principle of "to each according to his needs", it is necessary, Marx said, to maintain "equal rights", i.e. the principle of "to each according to his work", a "bourgeois" principle in essence. This

248

is why, according to Marx[113], only a tremendous development of the productive forces, currently hampered by capitalist relations of production, can really enable the transition from phase I of communism (that of communism as it emerges from bourgeois society) to phase II, that of true communism on whose flag is written the motto: "From each according to his ability, to each according to his needs."

The problem is that the very notion of abundance, like that of need (and capacity), is almost indeterminate.

Abundance can be defined as the possibility for everyone to satisfy all their needs effortlessly. It's the land of milk and honey. Basically, in the capitalist socio-economic system, abundance is reserved for a privileged minority, and its counterpart is the misery of the many. What's more, since capitalism always produces more for a too-small market, it is condemned to periodic crisis and periodic destruction of social wealth, ranging from simple economic crisis to war. In short, it is the private appropriation of the social surplus that, in orthodox Marxism, explains why abundance for all is impossible. At the same time, by developing science and technology, the capitalist mode of production opens up the possibility of a free society, effortlessly meeting all human needs—the Internet, with its free consumption of information and goods, gives us a foretaste of this. In a society of unlimited development of the productive forces, the "man rich in needs" could develop fully through the enjoyment of all the goods that the productive power of science and technology would make possible. Alas or fortunately, such a perspective is utterly utopian. Utopian because natural resources are limited and must be managed economically (in the true sense of the word), as Marx

---

113. Finally, this is above all the Marx of the *Gloses marginales sur le programme de Gotha*, a Marx who indulges in an exercise in fussy radicalism to better delimit himself from Lassalle's supporters, but a Marx who seems rather aberrant in relation to the general course of his thought in those years when he sought to complete *Le Capital* while drawing the lessons of the Paris Commune to a close. On this point, see *Comprendre Marx, op. cit.* chapter V.

points out in the passage from *Capital* that Engels places at the end of Book III. Oil (for example) is not inexhaustible, and as yet unknown resources will require a considerable expenditure of labor, not to mention environmental costs. More generally, the objective limits to capitalist accumulation mentioned above also apply to a possible communist system. It is fundamentally foolish to think that all needs could be met without difficulty, precisely because there is no objective, universally valid definition of these needs. The reason for this is that the expression of human needs is not a biological phenomenon, but the manifestation of a desire ("appetite accompanied by consciousness", as Spinoza puts it) that fixes itself on its imaginary object. We therefore need to be able to distinguish between "healthy" desires, those that correspond to "real", objectively determined needs, and "vain desires", those that can never be truly satisfied, or whose satisfaction brings no additional happiness. And since such a departure is impossible, the motto "to each according to his needs" turns into a "dictatorship over needs" (to use Agnes Heller's expression).[114]

There is another definition of abundance. A poor society that works very little because it self-limits its needs is an abundant society in the sense defined by Marshall Sahlins (see his book *Âge de pierre, âge d'abondance. Économie des sociétés primitives*). We don't have to go back to the Stone Age! But following the theses of proponents of "degrowth" like Serge Latouche, we could very quickly achieve a certain form of abundance, while reducing the drain on natural resources. For those willing to look at things from a distance, it's pretty clear that a considerable part of the Earth's wealth, and that produced by human labor, is squandered in the most stupid way possible, in the accumulation of a production of objects that are made only to be worn out with increasing rapidity, in order to replenish demand and keep the (capitalist) economic machine running. We could therefore follow Latouche and his friends in

---

114. *La Théorie des besoins chez Marx*, UGE, 1978.

recognizing that degrowth would not be a catastrophe, but on the contrary an opportunity for a profound transformation of society.

Serge Latouche's theses often hit the nail on the head. The idea of development is very simple: all we have to do is make the cake bigger, so that everyone has enough to eat. As a result, there's no question of reducing some people's share! Yet this is how all variants of the left have posed the question of social justice for over half a century. Social democracy makes a point of implementing a genuine growth policy that will benefit everyone, including the richest. This is, in another form, the hard core of capitalist ideology: everyone pursuing their own selfish goals contributes to the greater good of all. Sustainable development (or sustainable development, or other similar nonsense) is simply a variation on this old antiphon. Latouche is at pains to point out the insoluble contradictions these pious intentions run up against. Growth is increasingly about waste. The unlimited accumulation of material goods is meaningless. If, in order to avoid one more unemployed person, we have to scrap cars and household appliances that work perfectly well, where is the social benefit? Above all, unlimited growth is impossible. When every Chinese person consumes as much oil and emits as much CO2 as the average American, oxygen will become a rare commodity and will be as hard to obtain as drinking water in Brittany… In short, for Latouche, a disciple of Jacques Ellul and Ivan Illitch, we need to put an end to the domination of the economic and move towards a "degrowth society". He proposes that we move towards a society that gives more room to conviviality (an old idea of Illitch's) and to consumption that is more reduced in quantity, but more attentive to quality, a society in which the fulfillment of individuals, their true wealth, would reside in social relations, a fulfillment that can be achieved "in a healthy world", and with "serenity in frugality, sobriety, even a certain austerity in material consumption". Latouche makes it clear that this is not a matter of asceticism, since, as he explains, "modern consumption is not sufficiently interested in the pleasures of the flesh, is not sufficiently concerned with sensory experience, is too obsessed with a whole series of products that filter sensory and erotic gratifications and distance us from them[115]."

It's tempting, if you've been educated in the Marxist tradition, to see Latouche's theses as a combination of utopian socialism and reactionary socialism, which Marx had already dealt with in the *Communist Manifesto*. But this is not the right way to approach the question, as these theses constitute elements of a radical critique of the capitalist mode of production, and therefore militate in favor of a radical transformation of the mode of production (and not just of legal property relations). If growth presupposes the growth of transport for the sake of mobility, delocalization and "just-in-time" flows, the multiplication of kilometers of freeways, the increase in pollution, this growth is only the growth of the waste of social labor. Starting from a truly global perspective, we could easily show that the overall balance sheet of growth is catastrophic. If agriculture in advanced countries survives only on subsidies, and subsidies are all the more massive the more "productive" the sector, it's because in reality industrial agriculture consumes more than it produces—ecological damage notwithstanding. Direct state subsidies keep most farms from going bankrupt, including subsidies for aberrant farming methods, such as systematic watering along France's Atlantic seaboard! Conversely, well-designed organic farming could be far more productive, i.e. far more economical in terms of social labor per unit produced. In other words, it's not a question of setting a moral utopia against economic calculation and the rationality of "science", but rather of showing that this so-called "science" disguises reality by means of financial artifice.

The growth indicators used today by political leaders are highly fanciful. No one can say exactly what 2% or 3% growth means. If it's a mild winter, electricity consumption will fall and so will energy costs. This will reduce growth, since the value added by energy suppliers will fall. It has been calculated that if, by any

---

115. *Revue du MAUSS* n° 20, 2nd semester 2002, Serge LATOUCHE, "D'autres mondes sont possibles, pas une autre mondialisation".

chance, road accidents were to be completely eliminated, this would lead to a decline of around 2% in GDP, due to lost earnings for bodybuilders, mechanics, car dealers, hospitals, clinics and other undertakers. Advertising expenditure is a typical parasitic expense generated by the capitalist mode of production: it aims to take market share from competitors and stimulate the appetite for consumption, even and especially when it is flagging. These expenses represent 8% of the sales of the agri-food industries, not to mention government advertising to advise consumers against the chocolate bars and other fatty sandwiches that the agri-food industries' advertising has just shown them. If we were to do away with advertising altogether, while maintaining the salaries of employees in this sector, we'd be neither richer nor less rich.

In reality, what Latouche is pointing out, without developing it properly from a theoretical point of view, is something that Marxists not completely intoxicated by the myths of progress and the indefinite growth of "productive forces" had already analyzed: namely, that the "growth of productive forces" in the age of senile capitalism is first and foremost the growth of parasitism and putrefaction. To fight for growth—even "other growth"—without raising the question of property relations, is simply to endorse the existing order as the "unsurpassable horizon of our time". It means embracing the spontaneous ideology of the capitalist, Marx's "fanatical agent of production for production's sake".

Secondly, the question of the meaning of growth cannot be ignored. The long-standing criticism of the "consumer society" may seem indecent when the vast majority of the planet's population lacks the bare minimum. But the spectacle of unbridled waste in the richest societies, the gradual reduction of life to consumption, omnipresent advertising, the growing role of "brands" in the minds and concerns of the young—and sometimes even the very young or not young at all: these are all features of our societies that prove Latouche and degrowth theorists right. Growth of 3% per annum —typically the figure announced by economists as the minimum likely to stem the rise in unemployment—enables

GDP to double every 24 years. Of course, with such growth, all other things being equal, the RMI recipient will end up with the income of a current minimum wage earner. But to achieve such a result, the wealthiest people have to be twice as rich and, above all, consume twice as much. In many families, not even capitalist nabobs, but simply the *upper middle class* in wealthy countries, every member of the family has his or her own television set, a car as soon as he or she is old enough to drive, and a not inconsiderable proportion of household expenditure is devoted to slimming down. Do we really need to be able to change cars every day of the week like we change ties or socks to beat unemployment and enable the poor to be a little less so?

The capitalist mode of production can only develop by destroying the two main sources of wealth: land and labor. Marx's assertion describes present-day reality as closely as possible. At the same time, capital never ceases to demand labor power for immediate consumption, and is on the offensive everywhere against all legislation limiting working hours—the question of pensions should be seen in this light[116]. At the same time, it is "fallowing" the workforce to an unprecedented extent. While "growth" means putting children to work in the poorest countries, tens of millions of young people in the richest countries are unable to find real employment before they reach an advanced age. At a time when legal working hours are being extended, workers over the age of 50 are less and less "employable" and must prepare to live in increasingly precarious conditions. At a time when resources are known to be finite and everyone is warned of the relatively short-term consequences of air and water pollution, waste is reaching unprecedented levels. The global division of labor is generating rapid growth in the transport and exchange of goods, far in excess of industrial growth—in other words, rapid growth in the incidental costs of the production process. Distribution methods are increasingly wasteful—one need

---

116. At a time when unemployment is set to rise at a rate unprecedented in decades, the French government has just raised the retirement age to 70…

only think of supermarkets or industrial food production to see the extent to which capitalism is wasting food resources[117]. As Marx put it, the "growth of productive forces" appears to be the growth of destructive forces.

That's why people like Serge Latouche are to be thanked for putting their foot down and attacking the mythology of growth, which has poisoned all the socialist and communist thinking of the last century, and led to the worst disasters. The so-called "communist" regimes made people pay a high price for economic growth and the "development of productive forces".

The difficulty with "sustainable degrowth" is that it presupposes a strong community *ethos*. Latouche himself has to concede that religion is a good way of getting individuals to accept the self-limitation of needs that degrowth implies. Although Latouche is personally an atheist, he maintains that degrowth is only possible by making a radical break with the legacy of the Renaissance and the Enlightenment, and by restoring a "new transcendence" to its rightful place[118]. Refounding communism with the help of Latouche and his theory of degrowth would therefore be tantamount to taking the path of a reactionary communism in the strict sense of the term. There's a paradox in this approach: on the one hand, we propose that people try to master their own future, instead of being subjected to the blind power of their exchanges (as Marx would say), and on the other hand, we ultimately demand that they renounce the ideal of the Enlightenment, the ideal of autonomy, of man's ability to get "out of the state of minority in which he keeps himself through his own fault[119]". The never-ending race for growth for consumption's sake and consumption for growth's sake is properly infantile, deriving from the fantasy of infantile omnipotence, and to become an adult is precisely to emerge from this state. Distrustful of democracy, Latouche considers that man

---

117. For more on this subject, see Agnès Varda's excellent film *Les glaneurs et la glaneuse*.
118. See *Décoloniser l'imaginaire*, Parangon, 2003.
119. KANT, What is *Enlightenment?*

Chapter XII. A Non-Utopian Communism

cannot become an adult—that is, master his own destiny through democratic deliberation—and must renounce the use of his own understanding. In this, he joins an ecological theorist like Hans Jonas, who makes no secret of his preference for authoritarian government as the only way to keep unlimited desire in check, since according to Jonas the right rule of conduct, in the face of the ecological disaster that threatens us, is to treat men like children[120].

This anthropological pessimism, however, has no basis other than the idea that human beings are fundamentally incapable of moral progress, even though numerous examples attest to the contrary. The question of "moral progress" could be debated for a long time and still not be resolved. And yet, while it's true that today's professional moralists are often no match for Socrates or Aristotle, it's also true that, on the whole, our societies are often more sensitive to discrimination, to the wrongs done to certain categories of individuals or to the rights of each individual than were ancient societies. Perhaps, one day, the organizers of so-called "reality shows" will reintroduce the circus games, but for the time being such an initiative would arouse almost unanimous revulsion. In short, we have reason to believe that people can and do educate themselves through political action, even if there are too many examples to suggest otherwise.

Secondly, abandoning the insane ideal of unlimited development of productive forces does not mean returning to the Stone Age. On the other hand, it means ruthlessly chasing away all waste, because waste is first and foremost the waste of social labor, the expenditure of human sweat and tears in pure waste, often with harmful consequences. This does not mean going back on the democratic advances of modernity, but rather giving them their full meaning. It's no longer a question of designating, for several years to come, who will conduct the same policy, always considered to be "the only possible policy", but of taking one's destiny

---

120. See our review of Hans Jonas at http://denis-collin.viabloga.com/news/hans-jonas-le-principe-responsabilite.

into one's own hands on all the issues that concern all individuals. Making the wisest choices, and at the same time those most in line with the aspirations of the greatest number of people, presupposes enlightened citizens, not ones who accept self-limitation only if they have been reduced to superstitious fears.

Thirdly, we should be wary of the term "degrowth", which merely inverts the myth of growth and therefore remains dependent on it. The decline in the production of junk to be renewed every year could be doubled by the growth in the production of durable goods in the true sense of the word, and not in the hackneyed sense in which it has been used. The decline in the production of print advertising, commercials and other such junk could be doubled by a major increase in the production of truly cultural works. The decline in mortifying industrial agriculture could go hand in hand with growth in research to turn organic farming into high-tech agriculture that contributes to the growth of biodiversity. And so on.

But, as we can see, in all cases, it is impossible to rely on the spontaneity of individuals who would receive from the community "to each according to his needs".

The Impossible Return to the Garden of Eden

The third utopia is that of a transparent world, free from the constraints of work. Marx himself was well aware of the utopian nature of this Edenic society. Work satisfies needs, but at the same time creates new needs. Hence the anhistorical character of the necessity of work, i.e. work that is not free activity, but constraint. Only beyond the sphere of work itself, of work dictated by nature, can true human freedom emerge. Consequently, the question of working hours remains, and will remain, an essential one. Even now, if production remains constant, a radical reduction in working hours is possible, on two conditions:

1) Distribute work among all those willing and able to work—in all industrialized countries, between 10% and 15% of the working population is "set aside" as the "industrial reserve army", i.e. the army of the unemployed that enables pressure to be exerted on wages and working conditions. In other words, if the accumulation of profits for a minority of plutocrats is not the ultimate goal of social organization, then it is immediately possible to reduce the working week from the current 41 hours to 35 hours in France and most other rich countries[121];

2) Put an end to the enormous amount of useless and purely parasitic work. All organizations, not just state administrations, are crumbling under insane bureaucracy. Many activities exist only because capital is thirsty for accumulation by any means necessary. Just think of the activities generated by financial speculation: the fact that polytechnicians are hired as traders in financial capitals instead of doing their job as top-level engineers should outrage any rational person[122].

These two conditions of simple common sense presuppose a radical change in social relations and, once again, an economy that truly deserves its name, i.e. an economy based on use value and no longer on exchange value for profit. In this case, further productivity gains would be made immediately; today's employees are putting the brakes on the rationalization of the productive process as much as they can, and are even hiding the good ideas they have for improving the efficiency of work[123] and for good reason: an employee knows perfectly well that any increase in productivity

---

121. We know that the actual working week is a long way from the official 35-hour week blamed for all the ills.

122. The financial crisis has highlighted the extravagant weight of speculation in economic activity. It is estimated that in London (the world's leading financial centre before the end of 2008), finance generated almost 30% of employment, directly or indirectly.

123. The 1980s saw the emergence of quality circles and other "participative" management tools for the work process, which simply aimed to expropriate workers' knowledge.

will be directly or indirectly detrimental to him or her, either by allowing the elimination of jobs or by speeding up the pace of work. As soon as workers take control of the economy, they will no longer have any such fears, and we will realize that there are enormous "deposits" of productivity, based on cooperation, which, by its very nature, capitalism must leave untapped.

Marx posits the prospect of a communist society as follows: "The associated producers—socialized man—rationally regulate their organic exchanges with nature and subject them to their common control instead of being dominated by the blind power of these exchanges; and they accomplish them with the least possible expenditure of energy, under the most dignified conditions, most in keeping with their human nature." But such a society is not a society free of the burden of labor. True freedom, says Marx, begins beyond work dictated by necessity, and lies in activities not subject to an "external end"—that is, in his mind, truly creative, artistic or intellectual activities.

As for the other miracles of old-style communist utopia, we can leave them to their sad fate, alongside the sea turned into lemonade that Charles Fourier imagined.

Association and Freedom

Having renounced utopia, it is necessary not to describe what a non-utopian communism should be—such a detailed description would be a new form of utopia, albeit a more modest one—but to lay down some general principles. Staying true to the core of Marx's thought, our starting point must be the aspiration to freedom that has been the driving force of revolutionary development, first in Europe and then elsewhere, for perhaps a thousand years, since the moment when, in the communes, merchants and artisans shook off the chains of feudalism and clerical domination. This vast emancipatory movement paved the way for the development of capitalism, which rebuilt a new form of subjection, that of wage-labor. Under normal conditions, we spend roughly a third of our lives working, and another third resting to go back to work the next day. For the most part, then, active man, when he manifests his human essence, does so in the condition of salaried worker, meaning that work is alienation for him.

"What does alienation from work consist in? Firstly, in the fact that work is external to the worker, that is to say, it does not belong to his essence, and that therefore, in his work, the worker does not assert himself but denies himself, does not feel at ease but unhappy, does not deploy free physical and intellectual activity but mortifies his body and ruins his mind. As a result, the worker only feels at home outside work, and in work he feels outside himself. He feels at home when he's not working, and when he is working, he doesn't feel at home. His work is therefore not voluntary, but forced. It is not, therefore, the satisfaction of a need, but merely a means of satisfying needs outside of work. The alien nature of work is clearly demonstrated by the fact that, as soon as there is no physical or other constraint, work is shunned like the plague. External work, work in which man alienates himself, is work of self-sacrifice, of mortification. Finally, the fact that work is not the worker's own property, but that of another, that it does not belong to him, that in work the worker does not belong to himself, but to another. Just as, in religion, the proper activity of the human imagination, the human brain and the human heart, acts on the individual independently of him, i.e. as a divine or diabolical foreign activity, so the worker's activity is not his own. It belongs to another; it is the loss of self.
The result is that man (the worker) no longer feels freely active other than in his animal functions—eating, drinking and procreating—and, at most, still in his dwelling, as an animal. The bestial becomes the human, and the human becomes the bestial". (Karl Marx, Manuscripts of 1844).

Being under the dependence/domination of another man at work is a situation totally contradictory to any idea of freedom. Like the dog in La Fontaine's fable, we've become so accustomed to the collar that we end up forgetting it, since the chain guarantees our sustenance, and we're usually content to negotiate the length of the chain and the quality of the kibble as best we can. But can we call this situation anything other than wage slavery, as Marx put it? If the vast majority of human beings spend most of their social life at work, they are treated simply as means to an end, and never as ends in themselves, to borrow a phrase from old Kant. In other words, they are deprived of their dignity, to use Kantian vocabulary again. Moreover, capitalists no longer even conceal the "reification" (transformation of men into things) implicit in wage-labour. They used to have personnel managers (a term that still includes the legal subject of the individual), but they've replaced them with "human resources" managers, an expression whose obscenity escapes only those who have lost all moral sense. This reification does not only concern hours worked, as the worker can escape domination in "free time". Indeed, it's the very life of the worker that depends on the capitalist: when the crisis throws millions of wage-earners out into the street, when pensioners see their pension funds melt away and have to start looking for work again, when young people have to work for free in pseudo-qualification internships in the hope of one day being hired elsewhere, where is the famous freedom the liberals keep harping on about?

In a word, the only prospect worthy of civilized man, the man who can walk on the Moon and harness (more or less) atomic energy, the man who can communicate instantaneously with any other man on the entire planet, is the "abolition of wage-labor and employers" that the old CGT inscribed on its flag at its Amiens congress in 1905. If we continue our reading of Marx, we find a more precise formulation in the penultimate (actually last) chapter of Book I of *Capital*:

"Capitalist appropriation, in line with the capitalist mode of production, constitutes the first negation of private property, which is merely the corollary of independent, individual labor. But capitalist production itself engenders its own negation with the fatality that presides over the metamorphoses of nature. It is the negation of negation. It re-establishes not the private property of the worker, but his individual property, founded on the acquests of the capitalist era, on cooperation and common possession of all the means of production, including the soil." (*Capital*, I, section VIII, chap. XXXII in Joseph Roy's translation)

The aim is to re-establish individual worker ownership, but not private ownership, which would mean destroying all the assets of the capitalist era. Individual ownership on a cooperative basis cannot mean anything other than associative ownership by workers, as exemplified by the workers' production cooperatives (SCOP). Nationalization, typical of the socialism of the last century, is not common ownership of the means of production. In a nationalized company, the worker remains subject, not to the individual capitalist, but to the government-appointed manager. A change in class domination, but by no means the abolition of wage-earners and employers. On the contrary, an organization based on the association of producers would presuppose the direct participation of workers in the management of companies and in economic life, exactly as happens when craftsmen or other self-employed workers associate either for all or part of their activities—for example, in the GAECs (Groupements agricoles d'exploitation en commun) which are a kind of kolkhoz minus the Soviet bureaucracy!

There's no doubt about the possibility of building companies owned by the producers' association. Where the questions get trickier is when we move from small-scale production to large integrated units. An example of this is Mondragon, a SCOP born in the Basque country which today groups together tens of thousands of cooperators in Spain and elsewhere. This SCOP operates in the industrial sector (tools, sports equipment, etc.), finance, food retailing, and so on. Mondragon has now been in existence for half a century and remains a capitalist enterprise insofar as it is subject to competition and must obey the management rules of capitalist companies, on pain of disappearing. Moreover, only half of the group's employees are cooperators, since Mondragon has acquired non-cooperative companies which remain normal capitalist companies, even though the capitalist this time is an association of producers. But the existence of a very large cooperative company is enough to show that the association of producers is not a pipe dream or an organization viable only in a few ecological niches.

More complex is the question of overall coordination, on the scale of a nation or group of nations. There are two known ways of allocating available resources between the various branches of production: the market and the plan. The central plan has not proved very brilliant in known experiments and, as pointed out above, the cause of failure lies not only in the particular character of the Soviet bureaucratic caste, but in more general and fundamental problems. However, pure "market socialism"—i.e., a competitive economic organization in which capitalist enterprises are simply replaced by workers' cooperatives—is a far from satisfactory type of society, since it merely reproduces on another scale the capitalist principle that men are naturally competitors or rivals. There is a whole literature which, under the general heading of "models of socialism", discusses various ways of articulating the social appropriation of the means of production and the market. We cannot go into detail here, and refer the reader in particular to the works of Tony Andréani[124].

It will be argued that this common organization of production is merely that of collective freedom, and not, strictly speaking, of individual freedom. However, we are merely taking up the approach already outlined by Rousseau in the *Social Contract*. Instead of the impossible and impoverished natural freedom of the individual separated from other men, the freedom of the few that is paid for by the subjection of the vast majority, known as liberalism, we are substituting a civil freedom that is infinitely richer, since it is founded on the involvement of all in the organization and definition of the goals of the production of the material and spiritual life

---

124. Particularly: *Socialism is coming. 2: Les possibles.* Syllepse, 2004, or the collective work *Le Socialisme de marché à la croisée des chemins,* edited by Tony Andréani, Le Temps des Cerises, 2003.

of all. The question remains of how to articulate what is proper to the individual and what belongs to the common good.

The individual is the sum of his social relations," asserted Marx. This is to be understood in two dialectically opposed yet indissociable ways. On the one hand, the individual only exists in and through the social relations that constitute him or her, and liberal individualism, which assumes a natural subject existing prior to society, is a conception that clearly bears no relation to reality. But on the other hand, the more social relations develop and become complex, the more the individual becomes an individual rich in social relations and, consequently, more apt to claim the autonomy of his existence. In other words, it is precisely because he is more social, more inserted in a complex network of links with other human beings, that contemporary man seeks to emancipate himself from traditional social determinations and claims the right to choose for himself in all areas, be it sexuality, professional activity or beliefs. The "historical communism" of the 20th century is definitively out of political use because it has always thought of the community of workers as a community into which individuals had to merge without return, denouncing the demand for individual freedom as "petty-bourgeois" individualism. Since they had probably never read Marx, these orthodox, uncompromising Marxists believed that, in communism, collective happiness was the condition for individual happiness, whereas, on the contrary, the happiness of each individual was the condition for the happiness of all. Lucien Sève[125], a former member of the PCF Central Committee, recalls the case of the GDR writer who defended "the well-known Marxist thesis" that "the free development of all is the condition of the free development of each individual", whereas the *Communist Manifesto* explicitly states: "In place of the old bourgeois society, with its classes and class antagonisms, there arises an association in which the free development of each individual is the condition of the free

---

125. Lucien Sève, *Penser avec Marx aujourd'hui. I Marx et nous, La Dispute*, 2004, p. 36.

264

development of all." The development of "free individuality" lies at the heart of Marx's thinking, and it is precisely for this reason that communism can never be conceived—in his view—as a regression to the old forms of society based on bonds of personal dependence. On the contrary, he praises capitalism for ruthlessly shattering these old ties, those of "holistic" or "organicist" societies.[126]

Is it possible to conceive of a social organization that is in every respect the manifestation of individual freedom? Or is it possible to overcome the contradiction between the individual and society? This is the question on which all revolutionary thought ultimately stumbles. Anarchism offers an impossible solution: the absolute affirmation of the individual, who would live with others without imposing any constraints and without imposing any constraints on himself. Collectivism—even if it's called "communism"—proposes a solution that is unacceptable and unbearable in the long term. The contradiction between the individual and society cannot be overcome. And the development of community institutions, of a freely chosen community life, is only possible if at the same time the individual can protect himself from collective tyranny, if he has his own legally inviolable sphere of intimacy. This sphere includes traditional individual freedoms (freedom of conscience, freedom of expression, freedom of movement, etc.) as well as the recognition of private property. A distinction must be drawn between private ownership of one's home and possessions, and private ownership of the means of production. The latter is not a property over things, but a social relationship that implies domination, whereas the former is simply the affirmation of the individual's right to inhabit the common world.

More generally, in a society dominated by communist principles, power should not be concentrated (even in the hands of a social

---

126. We have already shown how Marx's individualism is profoundly different from the methodological individualism of sociologists or liberal individualism: see *La Théorie de la connaissance chez Marx*, L'Harmattan, 1996. Relevant analyses can also be found in Costanzo Preve's *Marx inattuale*, chapter IV, "Marx e l'individualismo", Bollati Boringhieri, Torino, 2004.

republican state), and everyone should be allowed to live the life of their choice as far as possible. At the start of the Soviet revolution under Lenin, anarchists were for a time able to implement their own social concepts, as Victor Serge, who lived in an anarchist farming community, reports[127]. A social organization dominated by coercion should be replaced as far as possible by freely chosen community allegiances. For this reason, a communist society could also perfectly accept a sphere of small-scale independent production in the arts, crafts or "liberal professions". Anyone who wants to produce alone and not accept the discipline of the production cooperative should be able to do so without harm. It's up to cooperatives to show that they really are superior to individual initiative!

In the same vein, a non-utopian communism would be internationalist, but would recognize the inescapable existence of nations. Internationalism means the solidarity of peoples and their union in a treaty of perpetual peace, in the manner of Kant or Rawls[128], but it does not imply the idea of a universal republic, a world state—one of the most terrifying perspectives imaginable. Here again, the dispersal of power makes it possible to envisage the safeguarding of freedom, while the "world central committee of workers' councils" would merely reconstitute the "supreme soviet".

Everything we've just outlined has nothing to do with "integral communism" and the "new man" that goes with it, nothing to do with the now-defunct utopia of 20th-century historical communism. It's just the broad outlines of a possible social transformation that can be partially and progressively implemented right now.

---

127. See Victor SERGE, *Memoirs of a Revolutionary*: "Ever since Kronstadt, a few friends and I had been wondering what would become of us. We didn't have the slightest desire to join the ruling bureaucracy and become heads of offices or secretaries of institutions [...]. North of Petrograd, not far from Lake Ladoga, and there, together with French communists, Hungarian prisoners, a Tolstoyan doctor and my father-in-law, Roussakov, we founded the *French Commune of Novaya-Ladoga*." (Seuil, 1965, p. 162-165)
128. See John RAWLS, *The Law of Peoples and Public Reason*, La Découverte, 2003.

Chapter XIII. Forces and Strategy for a Radical Alternative

We won't be doing any more cooking in the pots of the future. Now that the broad outlines have been laid down, it's not very complicated to look for the immediate measures that would enable us to take a step forward in this direction. The real difficulty is that, for the time being, most of the organized forces still claiming to resist capitalism are content to propose immediate, more or less sophisticated programs, most often based on the expertise of economic specialists, without once asking themselves what all this might mean. An association like ATTAC was built on the idea that experts were needed to counter the official experts, and so it specialized in "scientific" expertise—ATTAC is best known for its "scientific council", a sort of republic to the left of the *think-tanks* of the liberal left and right. As soon as the first wind blew, however, i.e. as soon as the demands of political struggle became apparent, the association exploded, and we realized that political life is not a matter of expertise, but of strategies and groupings of real forces.

To avoid being condemned to impotent daydreaming, we need to answer three questions:

1) Are there sufficiently numerous social forces capable of taking action that might be interested in the prospect of a non-utopian communism?

2) Are there any premises in today's society that would turn this abstract possibility into a material one?

3) Is it possible to define a political strategy to make this rebuilding of communism effective?

The answer to all three questions is yes.

Communism Can be a Communitarian Ideal

We have explained why orthodox Marxism cannot be anything other than the ideology of a new ruling class working in place of a working class incapable, by its own efforts, of becoming a ruling class. The specific "material" interests of the working class as a wage-earning class do not lead beyond the demand for an improvement in the situation of the wage-earner as a wage-earner—we remain in the relationship of domination-submission of wage-earning while negotiating (not insignificantly) the length of the chain. But at the same time, we have noted that the communist ideal came from all classes of society, and not by chance.

The convulsions of the capitalist mode of production, if they do not produce a "final crisis", are an opportunity to awaken sleeping minds to the dangers this system poses to the whole of humanity. Not only will wage earners be in the front line of the victims, but also all the middle classes who live from their work, whether they be the traditional middle classes or the new salaried middle classes whose decline has been underway for many years already[129].

In this way, material motivations—poverty, unemployment, etc.—can come together with broader spiritual motivations. For capitalism not only destroys the foundations of the material wealth

---

129. The "no" vote in the 2005 referendum on the European Constitutional Treaty was largely due to white-collar workers, teachers and junior executives siding with those opposed to the European Union. This vote expressed the disarray of these "proletarianized" social strata, who joined the workers on the European electoral terrain.

of human societies (land and labor), it also irreparably sterilizes culture. Able to exploit and commodify the masterpieces of the past—a past reduced to theme parks—it is clearly running out of steam when it comes to producing artistic masterpieces itself. The immense technical resources available to artists are essentially used to produce junk for use as backdrops for advertising clips. And what's more: today, we continue to exploit a culture that has still been partially transmitted by schools and universities steeped in conformism and archaism. The radical transformation of schools and universities into machines for producing employees adapted to the needs of capitalism is eradicating the transmission of the past. Successive Italian governments have set out to shatter whatever remains of classical culture, and to subject schools to the imperative of the "three I's" (*Imprese, Inglese, Informatica*). French governments are following the same line. Of course, the catastrophic effects of these measures cannot be measured. For reasons that are easy to understand, it will take two generations. But it's the destruction of humanist culture that's on the horizon. And if we place ourselves on the broadest possible terrain, that of the defense of civilization, rebels can be recruited from all strata of society.

Finally, it's moral or ethical reasons that can ultimately reverse the present situation. Stupidly enough, Marxists made a point of not claiming communism for moral reasons, but only for "scientific" ones. "Scientifically", we'll never find a reason to fight for equality, justice, civic friendship and so on. It is moral reasons that are decisive in the fight for communism, because all the terms by which we have sought to define what a new communism can be are terms of a fundamentally moral nature: the common good, friendship between citizens, the protection of freedom against domination, all these are marked out by questions of morality. No one can watch the wars in the DRC for control of the country's mineral wealth without being deeply revolted by a system that is engendering what is becoming rampant genocide. Any man with a basic sense of justice will admit that the corporate bastards who finance these wars and supply them with weapons, these characters who haunt the major financial centers, are of the calibre of those Nazi leaders who had Beethoven's works performed in the courtyard of the Auschwitz camp.

Communism is quite simply the indisputable recognition of the ineradicable nature of this revolt, which was at the heart of the first Christian movements, and which is to be found in all the revolutions of the modern era, and which also gave rise to the workers' movement. Unless we sink into the misanthropy and depression that accompany self-hatred, we can reasonably assume that the vast majority of human beings will gradually come to accept that the capitalist system has had its day, and that we need to turn the page.

Numerous Forces of Resistance: Beyond the Right/Left Divide

We don't need to take a leap of faith to be convinced. Even as the decomposition of workers' organizations and the collapse of Marxism produce mass disarray and despair, the hotbeds of resistance remain important, sometimes reaching continental dimensions, as in Latin America. We can analyze the leaders of these movements as we wish, and be suspicious and even more suspicious of Chavez and the old Latin American tradition of the "caudillo". The fact remains that the popular movement supporting these governments is fundamentally a movement of resistance to the system, as is the Indian movement supporting Morales in Bolivia. On another scale, the formation or development of radical movements in Europe, France, Holland, Denmark and Germany, some of which have emerged from traditional reformist organizations, must be taken seriously, even if we remain critical of this or that "revolutionary" leader who has become a media darling. The sum of these movements does not make a revolution. Experience teaches that small revolutionary leaders are just as capable of leading their troops into the wall as old reformist crocodiles and elephants. What matters, however, is the state of mind of the people expressed by these movements.

Yet these directly political forms are only the surface of things. In the absence of a living, credible, non-utopian form of communist thought, resistance to capitalism, the desire to rediscover a sense of human community, takes on faces that are sometimes unsympathetic, but just as undeniable. The movements that the beautiful people disdainfully call "populist" are among them. For a time, the Front National in France was able to attract to itself a section of the "little people" whom the governmental left had abandoned. To understand the progress of radical Islamism in Lebanon (with Hezbollah) and Palestine (with Hamas), as well as in Egypt and Morocco, we must never forget that these movements rely on the underprivileged, to whom they offer what is dramatically lacking: a sense of solidarity, of sharing common values, and of transforming the other into a brother or sister. It is not our intention to extol Islamism as a new revolutionary movement *sui generis, as* some leftists do. It's simply a question of understanding the cause of these movements, and the cause is not the intoxication of the stupefied masses by the sermons of clerics, as the strong-minded "secularists" in Europe believe. Religion binds, while capitalism unbinds. So, of course, religion is an illusory bond for an illusory community. But it's not by attacking illusions that we undo them, but by attacking the causes of those illusions. Let's send back to Marx our rationalists and freethinkers who make the anti-religious struggle a substitute for the class struggle:

"The true happiness of the people demands that religion be abolished as the illusory happiness of the people. To demand the renunciation of illusions concerning our own situation is to demand the renunciation of a situation that needs illusions. The critique of religion is therefore, in essence, the critique of this vale of tears, of which religion is the halo.

Criticism has stripped away the imaginary flowers that cover the chain, not so that man can wear the prosaic, desolate chain, but so that he can shake off the chain and pick the living flower. The critique of religion disillusions man, so that he thinks, acts and shapes his reality as a disillusioned man who has become reasonable, so that he moves around himself and therefore around his true sun. Religion is but the illusory sun that moves around man, so long as he does not move around himself." (Marx, *Contribution to Hegel's Critique of the Philosophy of Right*, 1843)

A Long-Term Political Strategy

The last question, the strategic one, is naturally less obvious, as it lends itself less to generalizations. It presupposes that, within these "anti-systemic" forces, a broad debate is taking place on the nature of the objectives to be pursued, and this makes traditional right/left divides obsolete. A significant part of the so-called left in Europe—and in the United States—is indistinguishable from the liberal right, whose fundamental values and objectives it shares: "liberal" individualism, the defense of "free enterprise" and the market economy, European construction, and so on. Norberto Bobbio, in one of his most recent books, attempted to show that the question of equality was the real right/left divide[130]. Blairism in Great Britain, the evolution of the PS in France and the outright dissolution of the "reformist" left in Italy are all empirical proof of Bobbio's error. The "reformist" left is perfectly willing to accept inequalities, and indeed, the profiteers of inequalities are quite happy to oblige. In the 2007 French presidential election, the Socialist candidate won a clear majority among people who "get by very easily" (54%), whereas she obtained just 49% among blue-collar and white-collar workers.

Many left-wing activists disappointed by the social-democratic left are seeking to rebuild, refound or renovate the left. The idea

---

130. Norberto Bobbio, *Destra e sinistra. Ragioni e significati di una distinzione politica*, Donzelli Editore, Roma, 1994. To Bobbio, Perry Anderson, editor of the *New Left Review*, replied that the right/left distinction had lost all meaning and was maintained only by old habits whose origins everyone had forgotten. Ideological labels can endure even when they no longer cover any substance, like the conflicts between the "Blues" and the "Greens", factions of chariot drivers in ancient Rome that dominated political life in Byzantium for centuries.

is to return to mythical origins—like all origins—to rebuild a radical reformism (that of the Conseil National de la Résistance and the social Keynesianism of the PS in the 1970s), or to build an anti-capitalist party, or a new independent workers' party. However explicable these attempts may be, however attractive they may be, since they have all the sweet sadness of nostalgia, they are undoubtedly doomed to failure. The "trente glorieuses" version of reformism died in the 1970s, and it's easy to forget that it only worked because of the Cold War: capitalists only conceded broad social gains out of fear of Soviet "communism". The examples of left-wing socialist parties in Europe, such as *Die Linke* in Germany, are indicative of the real aspirations of a not inconsiderable proportion of the population, but at the same time they are very confused both theoretically and politically, and would require a profound transformation for them to become a genuine political alternative.

Being anti-capitalist can only be the trademark of a discontented front, but by no means a long-term political project. It is undoubtedly better to call oneself anti-capitalist than to affirm the eternity of capitalism, as socialist leaders almost openly do. But no lasting agreement can be reached on a simple refusal: two individuals can agree to dislike green, but one will like blue and the other red! Far-left anti-capitalism is thus forced to walk a fine line between "societal" demands (rather hastily dubbed anti-capitalist) and support for fundamentalist Islamic movements, between ultra-liberal watchwords and friendship with Fidel Castro, and so on. Nothing serious can be built, no communist movement can be reborn if we continue to let people believe that Cuba embodies communism. Nor can we take seriously as an expression of a new radicalism such a prominent philosopher who continues to claim Mao Tse-tung and the so-called "cultural revolution".

Finally, to rebuild an independent workers' party, as some Trotskyists propose, is to rebuild a political force based on workers' identity, even though all this has been irretrievably undone since the 20th century, with social democracy and Stalinism, demonstrated the theoretical and practical impasse of the old Marxism. To want to remake the socialist parties of the Second International one hundred and thirty years on, is to want to run the time machine.

On the contrary, it is necessary to start from the unifying political demands that arise from the present situation. First and foremost, the demand to give people back control over their own destiny. While Antonio Negri saw the *Empire as* the revolutionary transition, we must assert loud and clear that no social transformation is possible within the framework of the empires that dominate the world today, be it the vacillating American empire, the aborted "Fortress Europe" empire, or the new imperial wills of Russia and perhaps China.

People's sovereignty in turn requires political regimes that protect them against political expropriation by an oligarchy or a military-bureaucratic caste, and only the republican form reworked in a radical sense can guarantee this (as far as history can guarantee anything!). The demand for popular sovereignty necessarily goes hand in hand with the quest for perpetual peace, based not on the domination of uncontrollable supranational bodies, but on the free association of peoples[131].

Last but not least, egalitarian demands need to be re-emphasized in all areas. Egalitarianism does not demand absolute equality, but rather that no-one should become rich at the expense of others. It does not demand that everyone should have the right to live like a mogul, but that everyone should be able to enjoy a decent life. At the same time, it demands that all contribute to the common wealth, and that, as the strong words of the *Internationale put it,* "the idle shall take lodgings elsewhere".

These few guidelines (popular sovereignty, perpetual peace, political republicanism and social egalitarianism) can form the basis of a new political program that can be applied as soon as "ideas take hold of the masses, they become material forces". But ideas need to be produced and spread. This book is intended as a contribu-

---

131. We have had occasion to show how reworking the intuitions of Kant or Rawls on these questions could be fruitful.

tion to the necessary work of developing a new way of thinking about emancipation. Rosa Luxemburg ends her last article, "Order reigns in Berlin" (1919) with a quotation from the poet Ferdinand Freiligrath.

> Tomorrow the revolution "will rise again with a bang", proclaiming with a trumpet blast, to your great horror
>
> I was, I am, I will be!

Let's not fall back into messianism as we draw to a close. History is not responsible for honouring the treaties we so willingly draw. And the "science of history" offers no certainty for the times to come. But if we regard the struggle for communism as an almost Pascalian gamble, we can make sense of Freiligrath and Rosa's phrase. Even if no ideal society comes into being, even if we only have partial realizations of communist ideals, the struggle will not be in vain. And it is far better to set one's sights on the common good, concern for others, equality and the quest for a fraternal community than to proclaim egoism the supreme law of mankind, and to deploy all the efforts of human genius to satisfy the insatiable greed and wickedness so often displayed by men submissive to their passions. If communism is almost as old as written human history, there is no reason to think that the human aspirations it expresses will die out forever. At a time when certainties about the liberal end of history are being seriously shaken, it's not a bad thing for Karl Marx to come back to haunt the nights of the haves and have-nots.

BIBLIOGRAPHY

ANDRÉANI (Tony), *Le socialisme est à venir, tome II: Les modèles*, Syllepse, 2004.

ANDRÉANI (Tony), *Le socialisme de marché à la croisée des chemins*, Le Temps des Cerises, 2003.

ARIÈS (Paul), *Le Mésusage*, Parangon/Vs, Lyon, 2007.

ARONDEL (Madeleine ARONDEL-ROHAUT and Philippe ARONDEL), *Gouvernance, une démocratie sans le peuple?*, Ellipses, 2008.

BASSO (Pietro), *Temps modernes, horaires antiques*, Éditions Page Deux, Lausanne, 2005.

BEAUD (Stéphane), PIALOUX (Michel), *Retour sur la condition ouvrière. Enquête aux usines Peugeot de Sochaux-Montbéliard*, Fayard, 1999.

BIDET (Jacques), *Théorie générale*, PUF, "Actuel Marx" collection, 1999.

BOBBIO (Norberto), *Destra e sinistra. Ragioni e significati di una distinzione politica*, Donzelli Editore, Roma, 1994.

BRAUDEL (Fernand), *Civilisation matérielle, économie, capitalisme, XVe-XVIIIe siècle*, 3 volumes, Armand Colin, republished in "Le Livre de poche", 1993.

BRAUDEL (Fernand), *Grammaire des civilisations*, Arthaud-Flammarion, 1987.

CHESNAIS (François), *La Mondialisation financière*, Syros, 1997.

COLLIN (Denis), *La Théorie de la connaissance chez Marx*, L'Harmattan, 1996.

Collin (Denis), *La Fin du travail et la mondialisation. Idéologie et réalité sociale*, L'Harmattan, 1997.

Collin (Denis), *Revive la République*, Armand Colin, 2005.

Collin (Denis), *Comprendre Marx*, Armand Colin, 2006.

Collin (Denis), Cotta (Jacques), *L'Illusion plurielle. Pourquoi la gauche n'est plus la gauche*, JC Lattès 2001.

Cotta (Jacques), *7 million working poor*, Fayard, 2007.

Cusset (François), *La Décennie: le grand cauchemar des années 80*, La Découverte, new edition 2008.

Durkheim (Émile), *Les Formes élémentaires de la vie religieuse*, reprinted in CNRS Sociologie, 2008.

Filoche (Gérard), *Life, health and love are precarious. Why shouldn't work be?* Jean-Claude Gawsewitch, 2006.

Galbraith (John K.), *The Economic Crisis of 1929. Anatomy of a Financial Crisis, 1961*, Petite Bibliothèque Payot, 1981.

Heller (Agnes), *La Théorie des besoins chez Marx*, UGE, 1978.

Kant (Emmanuel), "Qu'est-ce que les Lumières?", in *Œuvres II*, La Pléiade, Gallimard, 1985.

La Grassa (Gianfranco), *Il capitalismo oggi*, Petite Plaisance, 2004.

La Grassa (Gianfranco), *Gli strateghi del capitale*, ManifestoLibri, 2005.

Lasch (Christopher), *La Révolte des élites*, translated from English by Christian Fournier, Climats, 1996.

Latouche (Serge), *Décoloniser l'imaginaire*, Parangon, 2003.

Legendre (Pierre), *Dominium mundi*. Text for the film by Gérald Caillat. Éditions Mille et une nuits, 2007.

Locke (John), *Treatise on Civil Government*, Flammarion, GF collection, 1999.

Losurdo (Domenico), *Heidegger et l'idéologie de la guerre*, PUF, 1998, "Actuel Marx Confrontation" collection.

Marcuse (Hebert), *L'Homme unidimensionnel*, éditions de Minuit, 1968, Seuil, 1970, "Points" collection.

Marx (Karl), *Capital*, Book 1: "The Development of Capitalist Production" (translation by Jean Roy), Éditions Sociales, 1971.

- Book Two: "Le procès de circulation du capital" (French translation by Julian Borchardt and Hippolyte Vanderrydt), Paris V, Giard et Brière, 1900, 592 pages.
- Book Three: "Le procès d'ensemble de la production capitaliste" (French translation by Julian Borchardt and Hippolyte Vanderrydt), Paris V, Giard et E. Brière, booksellers-publishers, 1901 and 1902.

MARX (Karl) and ENGELS (Frederich), *La Correspondance Marx-Engels*, Dangeville edition.

MATTICK (Paul), "La théorie des crises chez Marx", in *Crises et théories des crises*, translated from the German, Éditions Champ Libre, 1976.

MICHELS (Robert), *Les Partis politiques*, Flammarion, Collections "Champs".

NOVE (Alec), *L'Économie soviétique*, Éditions Economica, Paris, 1981.

PORCHNEV (Boris), Les Soulèvements populaires en France au XVIIe siècle, Flammarion, 1972.

Preve (Costanzo), La fine di una teoria. Il collasso del marxismo storico del novecento, Edizioni Unicopli, 1996.

PREVE (Costanzo), *Marx inattuale*, Bollati Boringhieri, Torino, 2004.

RAWLS (John), *The Law of Peoples and Public Reason*, La Découverte, 2003.

ROUSSEAU (Jean-Jacques), "Le contrat social", in *Œuvres III*, La Pléiade, Gallimard, 1964.

SÈVE (Lucien), *Penser avec Marx aujourd'hui. I Marx et nous*, La Dispute, 2004.

SERGE (Victor), *Mémoires d'un révolutionnaire*, Seuil, 1965.

TODD (Emmanuel), *La Chute finale*, Robert Laffont, 1976.

TROTSKY (Leon), *History of the Russian Revolution*, Seuil, "Points" collection, 1967.

WALLERSTEIN (Immanuel), *Le Capitalisme historique*, La Découverte, 1996.

WITTFOGEL (Karl August), *Le Despotisme oriental. Étude comparative du pouvoir total*, translated into French by Editions de Minuit, 1964.

Table of Contents

SECOND PART

*Socialism and Communism in the Last Century:
Deadly Illusions*

Best sellers Max Milo Editions

Hitler's banker, Jean-François Bouchard

Confessions of a forger, Éric Piedoie Le Tiec

The Koran and the flesh, Ludovic-Mohamed Zahed

Governing by fake news, Jacques Baud

Governing by chaos, Collectif

A political history of food, Paul Ariès

Mad in U.S.A.: The ravages of the "American model",
Michel Desmurget

Mondial soccer club geopolitics, Kévin Veyssière

Putin: Game master?, Jacques Braud

Treatise on the three impostors: Moses, Jesus, Muhammad,
The Spirit of Spinoza

TV Lobotomy, Michel Desmurget